Es

AS Chemistry
for OCR

Ted Lister
Janet Renshaw

Published in 2004 by:
Nelson Thornes Ltd
Delta Place
27 Bath Road
CHELTENHAM
GL53 7TH
United Kingdom

05 06 07 08 / 10 9 8 7 6 5 4 3

A catalogue record for this book is available from the British Library

ISBN 0 7487 8505 1

Illustrations by IFA Design

Page make-up by Tech-Set Ltd

Printed and bound in Croatia by Zrinski

Contents

Module 3   How far, how fast?

Appendix   Mathematics

For Joseph, Thomas, Georgia, Ella and Louis – chemists of the future?

Introduction

This book has been written to meet the Oxford, Cambridge and RSA (OCR) specification for Advanced Supplementary (AS) Chemistry. It matches the specification and has therefore been endorsed by OCR. The subject content is divided into three modules (**Foundation chemistry, Chains and rings** and **How Far? How Fast?**) that correspond to the three modules of the OCR specification) plus an appendix, **Mathematics in Chemistry**. Each module is subdivided into chapters that broadly correspond to the sub-divisions of these modules in the OCR specification. The layout is designed to be as clear as possible with each double-page spread covering a particular topic.

Its features include:

- **Double-page units** each covering a single topic and dividing the content into manageable portions.
- **Numbered sections** to further divide the content into bite-sized pieces and to allow easy cross referencing.
- **Extensive use of bullet points** to produce lists of information that make learning and revision easier.
- **Full colour diagrams** to aid understanding and improve clarity.
- **Colour photographs** for extra impact and realism.
- **Accessible language** to make understanding easier.

- **Bold type** to emphasise key words and ideas.
- **Purple type** to refer to explanations and definitions in the glossary.
- **Comprehensive glossary** of explanations and definitions.
- **Extensive cross referencing** to link different topics and allow an understanding of chemistry as a whole.
- **Quick questions** after each double page spread to test your understanding of each topic.
- **OCR exam questions** after each major section to test the skills expected at AS level including application of knowledge, understanding, analysis, synthesis and evaluation.

There is also a **CD ROM** of teacher support material and resources including extra support for students to be used alongside the book, answers to the OCR exam questions (with examiners' commentary), help with practical work, links to useful websites and much more.

We hope that you will enjoy using this book and that it will lead to success in your AS Chemistry examinations.

Ted Lister and Janet Renshaw

Acknowledgements

The authors would like to thank John Payne for helpful comments and discussions on the manuscript and for advice on syllabus matching.

The authors would also like to thank the team at Nelson Thornes for their help in producing this book – Beth Hutchins, commissioning editor; John Hepburn and Marilyn Grant, editors; and John Bailey and Stuart Sweatmore, picture research.

The authors and publishers are grateful to Oxford, Cambridge and RSA Examinations for kind permission to reproduce examination questions.

Photograph acknowledgements

Alamy: Science Photos 64; British Gas: 57T; Corel 54 (NT): 57M; Corel 219 (NT): 106; Corel 501 (NT): 38, 51B; Corel 677 (NT): 62, 114; Corel 681 (NT): 91; Corel 704 (NT): 119; Corel 779 (NT): 16; Corus: 57B; Digital Vision 1 (NT): 41; Digital Vision 4 (NT): 125B; IBM: 6; Image Source 28 (NT): 51TL; Last Resort Picture Library: 103; Martyn Chillmaid: 18B, 24L, R, 39, 63B, 82, 87T, B, 97, 125T, 130; Perkin Elmer: 112; Photodisc 22 (NT): 95R; Photodisc 31 (NT): 90; Photodisc 72 (NT): 51TR; Science Photolibrary: 11, Rosenfeld Images Ltd 10, TEV 18T, 77T, M, B, Martyn Chillmaid 58, 63T; Still Pictures: Andre Maslennikov 146; Stockbyte 28 (NT): 94; Stockbyte 29 (NT): 96; Stockbyte 36 (NT): 103; Topham Picturepoint: John Maier Jr, The Image Works 95L.

Every effort has been made to trace all the copyright holders but if any have been overlooked the publisher will be pleased to make the necessary arrangements at the first opportunity.

1

Atomic structure

1.1

Introduction

Chemical elements are made up of atoms. The atoms of each element are different from the atoms of every other element. For over a century, we have known that atoms themselves are made up of smaller particles – sub-atomic particles.

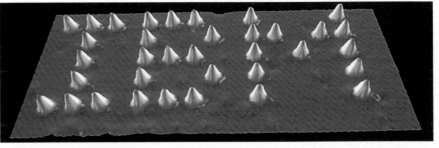

Atoms can only be seen indirectly. This photograph, in which the letters are made up of individual atoms, was taken by an instrument called a scanning tunnelling electron microscope

1.1.1 The sub-atomic particles

Atoms are made of three main particles – **protons, neutrons** and **electrons**.

- The protons and neutrons form the **nucleus**, in the centre of the atom.
- Protons and neutrons are sometimes called **nucleons**, because they are found in the nucleus.
- The electrons surround the nucleus (see Figure 1.1).

The properties of the sub-atomic particles are shown in Table 1.1.

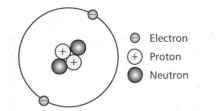

Fig 1.1 *The sub-atomic particles in a helium atom (not to scale)*

- ⊖ Electron
- ⊕ Proton
- ⬤ Neutron

Table 1.1 *The properties of the sub-atomic particles. Remember that charge is measured in coulombs, C*

Property	proton	neutron	electron
Mass/kg	1.673×10^{-27}	1.675×10^{-27}	0.911×10^{-30} (very nearly 0)
Charge/C	$+1.602 \times 10^{-19}$	0	-1.602×10^{-19}
Position	in the nucleus	in the nucleus	around the nucleus

These numbers are extremely small. In practice, we use the *relative* masses and charges.

1.1.2 Relative atomic mass, A_r

Hydrogen has one proton and one electron. It is the lightest element. It was originally given a *relative* **atomic mass, A_r,** of 1. Helium atoms are on average four times heavier than hydrogen atoms so on this scale the relative atomic mass, A_r, of helium is 4. Lithium atoms are on average seven times heavier than hydrogen atoms, so lithium has a relative atomic mass of 7 (to the nearest whole number).

The relative charge on a proton is taken to be $+1$, so that on an electron is -1, see Table 1.2.

1.1.3 The atomic number, Z

- The number of protons in an atom is called the **atomic number** or the **proton number** and has the abbreviation Z.
- Atoms are neutral, so the number of electrons in any atom is always equal to the number of protons.

Atomic number, Z = number of protons = number of electrons

1.1.4 The mass number, A

- Since electrons have (almost) no mass, the relative mass of an atom is the same as the total number of protons and neutrons. This is called the **mass number** (or **nucleon number**), A, of the atom.

Mass number, A = number of protons + number of neutrons

- Atoms are often written with the mass number above and to the left of the chemical symbol and the atomic number below and to the left, for example, lithium $^7_3$Li.
- From the mass number and the atomic number, you can find the number of protons, neutrons and electrons in an atom of any element.

Number of neutrons = mass number − atomic number

For example, in lithium, Li:

7 — mass number (= number of protons + neutrons)
 Li
3 — atomic number (= number of protons = number of electrons)

So in an atom of lithium, Li:

number of protons = 3
number of electrons = 3
number of neutrons = $(7 - 3) = 4$

In the same way, for fluorine $^{19}_9$F:

number of protons = 9
number of electrons = 9
number of neutrons = $(19 - 9) = 10$

1.1.5 Ions

Atoms that have lost or gained electrons, so that they are no longer neutral, are called **ions**. The number of electrons is no longer the same as the number of protons. For example a lithium atom loses an electron to form a positive lithium ion. A lithium ion has the following number of sub-atomic particles:

number of protons = 3
number of electrons = 2
number of neutrons = $(7 - 3) - 4$

A fluorine atom gains an electron to form a negative fluoride ion. A fluoride ion has the following number of sub-atomic particles:

number of protons = 9
number of electrons = 10
number of neutrons = $(19 - 9) = 10$

Table 1.2 *The relative masses and charges of the sub-atomic particles*

	Proton	Neutron	Electron
Relative mass	1	1	1/1840
Relative charge	+1	0	−1

HINT

Sometimes you may see the symbol for an atom written with the positions of the mass number and the atomic number reversed, e.g. $^{11}_{23}$Na. Just remember that the larger number is always the mass number.

QUICK QUESTIONS

1 Work out the number of sub-atomic particles in an atom of
  a beryllium,
  b phosphorus,
  c nitrogen,
  d potassium.

2 Potassium loses an electron to form an ion. What sub-atomic particles does the ion contain?

3 Nitrogen gains three electrons to form an ion. What sub-atomic particles does the ion contain?

4 What is
  a the atomic number,
  b the mass number and
  c the nucleon number of an atom of calcium?

5 Why do we take no account of the number of electrons when working out the relative mass of an atom?

1.2.1 Isotopes

Every single atom of any particular element has the same number of protons in its nucleus. But, it is possible for the number of neutrons to vary.

Atoms with the same number of protons but different numbers of neutrons, are called **isotopes**.

- It is the number of protons, the atomic number Z, which defines the element.
- Different isotopes of the same element will react chemically in exactly the same way.
- Different isotopes of the same element vary in mass because of their different numbers of neutrons.
- The nuclei of some isotopes are unstable; they are radioactive.
- Virtually all elements have isotopes, but in most elements there is one main isotope. For example, carbon-12 is the main carbon isotope (see Table 1.3).
- In some elements there is no single main isotope. This may make a big difference to the average mass of the atoms of the element and therefore to the relative atomic mass (see *Isotopes of chlorine*, below).

Isotopes of carbon

Carbon has three isotopes but the element consists mainly of carbon-12. The isotopes are shown in Table 1.3. The abundance gives the percentage of a given isotope in a sample of carbon.

Table 1.3 *Isotopes of carbon*

Name of isotope	Carbon-12	Carbon-13	Carbon-14
Symbol	$^{12}_{6}C$	$^{13}_{6}C$	$^{14}_{6}C$
Number of protons	6	6	6
Number of neutrons	6	7	8
Abundance	98.89%	1.11%	trace

Isotopes of chlorine

Chlorine has a relative atomic mass of 35.5 because it is made of two isotopes. They are $^{35}_{17}Cl$, with a mass number of 35, and $^{37}_{17}Cl$, with a mass number of 37. They occur in the ratio of almost exactly $3:1$:

$$^{35}Cl \quad ^{35}Cl \quad ^{35}Cl \qquad ^{37}Cl$$
three of these   to every one of this

The average mass of these is 35.5, as shown below.

Mass of four atoms $= 35 + 35 + 35 + 37 = 142$

Average mass $= \dfrac{142}{4} = 35.5$

This is the relative atomic mass.

To find the relative atomic mass, A_r, we have to take account of the relative abundance of different isotopes. A_r of chlorine is *not* the simple average $\dfrac{(35 + 37)}{2} = 36$. Chlorine has a relative atomic mass of 35.5 because there are more ^{35}Cl atoms than ^{37}Cl atoms.

1.2.2 The carbon-12 scale of atomic masses

Relative atomic mass, A_r

- The relative atomic mass, A_r, was originally based on a scale where the relative mass of a hydrogen atom was *defined* as exactly 1.

- Since 1961, relative atomic masses have been based on a scale where A_r of an atom of the carbon-12 isotope is *defined* as exactly 12 and other atoms are compared with this (instead of hydrogen).
- This means that the atoms of the carbon-12 isotope are the only ones with a relative atomic mass which is *exactly* a whole number.
- The formal definition of relative atomic mass, A_r of an element on the ^{12}C scale is given by:

$$A_r = \frac{\text{Average mass of an atom of the element (in g)}}{\frac{1}{12}\text{th mass of 1 atom of } ^{12}C \text{ (in g)}}$$

- For the element carbon, $A_r = 12.0111$. This is the average of the isotopes of carbon which have different relative atomic masses and abundances.

Example

10 000 carbon atoms consist of 9889 atoms of carbon-12 and 111 of carbon-13.

Relative mass of carbon-12 atoms =	$9889 \times 12 =$	118 668
Relative mass of carbon-13 atoms =	$111 \times 13 =$	1443
Total relative mass =		120 111
Average relative mass = 120 111/10 000 = 12.0111		

On the carbon-12 scale, neither the relative mass of the proton nor that of the neutron is exactly 1, see Table 1.4.

The difference between the H = 1 and the ^{12}C = 12 scales is so small that we can ignore it for most calculations.

Relative molecular mass and relative formula mass, M_r

- For compounds or elements made up of molecules, we use the term **relative molecular mass, M_r**.
- We call this the **relative formula mass**, M_r, when we are dealing with ionic compounds, because ionic compounds do not exist as molecules, but we use the same symbol, M_r.
- M_r is found from the formula, by adding together the relative atomic masses of the atoms in the simplest formula unit. The simplest formula unit is sometimes called an **entity**.
- The formal definition of relative molecular mass on the ^{12}C scale is given by:

$$M_r = \frac{\text{Average mass of an entity (in g)}}{\frac{1}{12}\text{th mass of 1 atom of } ^{12}C \text{ (in g)}}$$

- For most purposes, we can use relative atomic masses that have been rounded off to the nearest whole number. This is why, in practice, there is little difference between the scale based on hydrogen (H = 1) and the scale based on carbon-12 (^{12}C = 12).

Working out M_r

A molecule of carbon dioxide, CO_2, has:

one carbon atom, $A_r = 12.0$	1×12.0	= 12.0
two atoms of oxygen, $A_r = 16.0$	2×16.0	= 32.0
So its relative molecular mass is 12.0 + 32.0		= 44.0.

An entity of sodium carbonate, Na_2CO_3 has:

two sodium atoms, $A_r = 23.0$	2×23.0	= 46.0
one carbon atom, $A_r = 12.0$	1×12.0	= 12.0
three oxygen atoms, $A_r = 16.0$	3×16.0	= 48.0
So its relative formula mass is 46.0 + 12.0 + 48.0		= 106.0

Table 1.4 *Relative masses of sub-atomic particles*

Particle	A_r on the carbon-12 scale
Proton	1.0072
Neutron	1.0086
Electron	0.000 548

HINT

The mass number, A refers to a particular atom. The relative atomic mass, A_r, refers to the average mass of the atoms of an element.

QUICK QUESTIONS

1 Neon has two isotopes, $^{20}_{10}Ne$ and $^{22}_{10}Ne$, whose abundances are in the ratio 9 : 1. What is the relative atomic mass of neon?

2 $^{31}_{15}W$, $^{14}_{7}X$, $^{16}_{8}Y$, $^{15}_{7}Z$; which of these atoms (not their real symbols) is a pair of isotopes?

3 Work out the relative molecular mass of sulphuric acid, H_2SO_4.

4 Work out the relative formula mass of sodium sulphate, Na_2SO_4.

5 Why do we refer to the relative molecular mass of sulphuric acid but the relative formula mass of sodium sulphate?

The mass spectrometer

The mass spectrometer is one of the most useful instruments for the accurate measurement of relative atomic and relative molecular masses. In effect it weighs separate atoms or molecules. The layout of one type of mass spectrometer is shown in Figure 1.2.

A mass spectrometer

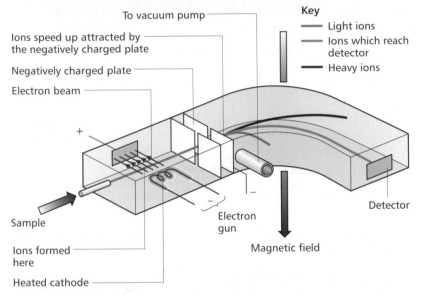

Fig 1.2 *The layout of a mass spectrometer*

1.3.1 What happens in a mass spectrometer?

There are four key stages which are:

- Ionisation
- Acceleration
- Deflection
- Detection

These are referred to below.

- The sample is investigated in the gaseous state. If the sample is a gas or a volatile liquid it is injected into the instrument directly. If the sample is a solid it is vaporised first by heating.
- Ionisation – a beam of electrons from an **electron gun** knocks out electrons from molecules or atoms of the sample so that they form positive ions. Nearly all the molecules or atoms lose just one electron and form ions with a 1^+ charge.
- Acceleration – these positive ions are attracted towards **negatively charged plates** which accelerate them to a high speed. (The instrument is kept under a high vacuum so that these ions do not collide with air molecules, which might stop them reaching the detector.)
- Some ions pass through a pair of slits in these plates. This forms the ions into a beam. The speed they reach depends on their mass – the lighter the ions the faster they go.
- Deflection – the beam then moves into a magnetic field at right angles to its direction of travel. The magnetic field bends the beam of ions into an arc of a circle. The deflection of a 1^+ ion depends on: **mass** – heavier ions are deflected less than lighter ones and the **magnetic field strength** – the stronger the field, the greater the deflection.

- Detection – the magnetic field is gradually increased so that ions of increasing mass enter the **detector** one after another. The detector produces a signal proportional to the number of ions reaching it.
- From the strength of the magnetic field at which a particular ion hits the detector, a computer works out the mass of the original ion. A read-out called a **mass spectrum** is produced (Figure 1.3).

1.3.2 Mass spectra of elements

The mass spectrometer can be used to identify the different isotopes that make up an element. It detects individual ions, so different isotopes are detected separately because they have different masses.

The output is normally presented as a graph of relative abundance of ions against mass number. (This axis is usually labelled 'mass/charge ratio', see Figure 1.3, but since nearly all the ions have one unit of charge, this is numerically the same as the mass number.)

For example, neon gives the mass spectrum shown in Figure 1.3. This shows that neon has *two* isotopes, of mass numbers 20 and 22, present in the approximate ratio 9:1. From this we can say that neon has an average relative atomic mass of:

$$\frac{[(9 \times 20) + (1 \times 22)]}{10} = 20.2$$

Note that:

- The peak height gives the relative *abundance* of each isotope and the horizontal scale gives the *mass number*.
- When calculating the relative atomic mass of an element, you must take account of the relative abundances of the isotopes. The relative atomic mass of neon is not 21, because there are far more atoms of the lighter isotope.

1.3.3 Identifying elements

All elements have a characteristic pattern which shows the relative abundances of their isotopes. This can be used to help identify any particular element.

More sophisticated mass spectrometers can measure the masses of atoms to several decimal places. This allows us to identify elements by the exact masses of their atoms.

Mass spectrometers have been incuded in space probes such as the Viking Martian lander and used to identify the elements in rock samples.

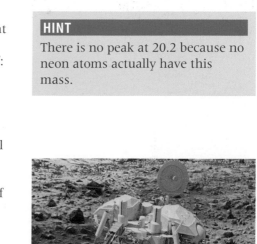

Fig 1.3 *The mass spectrum of neon*

HINT

There is no peak at 20.2 because no neon atoms actually have this mass.

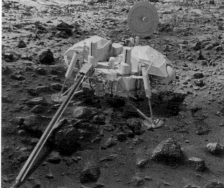

The Viking Martian lander carried a mass spectrometer

QUICK QUESTIONS

1 Explain why the ions formed in a mass spectrometer have a positive charge.

2 Explain what causes the ions to accelerate through the mass spectrometer.

3 What forms the ions into a beam?

4 What bends the ions into the arc of a circle?

5 Figure 1.4 shows the mass spectrum of copper. Work out the relative atomic mass of copper.

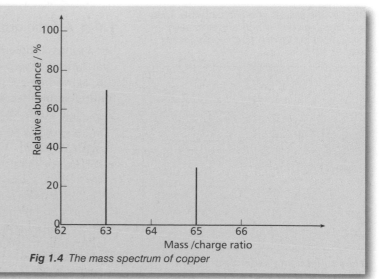

Fig 1.4 *The mass spectrum of copper*

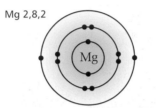

First shell holds 2 electrons

Second shell holds 8 electrons

Third shell holds 8 electrons (but has reserve space for 10 more

Fig 1.5 *The first three electron shells*

Mg 2,8,2

Fig 1.6 *The electron arrangement of magnesium*

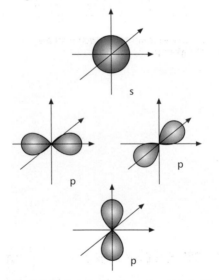

s

p

p

p

Fig 1.7 *The shapes of s- and p-orbitals. There are three p-orbitals at right angles to each other. (d- and f-orbitals have more complex shapes still.)*

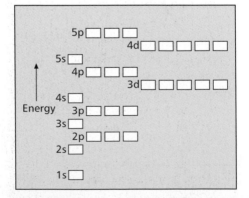

Fig 1.8 *The energy levels of the first few atomic orbitals*

The sub-atomic particles (protons, neutrons and electrons) are arranged in the atom as shown in Figure 1.1 in Topic 1.1.

- The protons and neutrons are in the centre of the atom, held together by a force, called the **strong nuclear force**. This is much stronger than the **electrostatic forces** that hold electrons and protons together in the atom, but it only acts over very short distances, i.e. within the nucleus.
- The nucleus is surrounded by electrons. Electrons are found in a series of orbits or shells which get further and further away from the nucleus.

1.4.1 The scale of the atom

A typical atom has a nucleus that is about 1×10^{-15} m across, while the atom itself is about 1×10^{-10} m across. This makes the nucleus about 10 000 times smaller than the atom itself. The shells of electrons are (relatively) a huge distance from the nucleus and an atom is mostly empty space.

1.4.2 The arrangement of the electrons

Figure 1.5 shows the first three shells.

The electron shells can hold different numbers of electrons. The first shell, which is closest to the nucleus, fills first, then the second and so on:

- The first shell holds up to 2 electrons.
- The second shell holds up to 8 electrons.
- The third shell holds up to 8 electrons with reserve space for 10 more.

1.4.3 Electron diagrams

If we know the atomic number of an atom, we know the number of electrons it has. We can therefore draw an electron diagram in the same style as Figure 1.5 for any element. For example, magnesium has 12 electrons, Figure 1.6.

We can write electron diagrams in shorthand:

- Write the number of electrons in each shell, starting with the inner shell and working outwards.
- Separate each number by a comma.
- For magnesium we would write 2,8,2.

1.4.4 Atomic orbitals

For a more complete description of the electrons in atoms we use a theory called quantum mechanics. This describes the atom mathematically by an equation (the Schrödinger equation). The solutions to this equation give the *probability* of finding an electron in a given *volume* of space.

- The electron is no longer considered to be a particle moving round a nucleus, but a cloud of negative charge. An electron fills a volume in space called its **orbital**.
- Different orbitals have different energy levels that correspond to the electron shells 1, 2, 3 etc.
- The orbitals have different shapes which are described by the letters s, p, d and f. The s and p shapes are shown in Figure 1.7.
- These shapes represent a volume of space in which there is a 95% probability of finding an electron.
- Any single orbital can hold a maximum of two electrons.
- s-orbitals can hold up to two electrons and come singly.

- p-orbitals can hold up to two electrons each, but always come in groups of three of the same energy, to give a total of up to six electrons.
- d-orbitals can hold up to two electrons each, but come in groups of five of the same energy to give a total of up to 10 electrons.

The energy level diagram in Figure 1.8 shows the orbitals for the first few elements of the Periodic Table. Notice that:

- Level 1 has only an s-orbital, level 2 has s- and p-, level 3 has s-, p- and d-, and so on.
- Each 'box' in Figure 1.8 represents an orbital of the appropriate shape that can hold up to two electrons.
- 4s is actually of slightly lower energy than 3d.

1.4.5 Spin

Electrons also have the property called spin:

- Two electrons in the same orbital must have opposite spins.
- The electrons are usually represented by arrows pointing up or down to show the different directions of spin.

1.4.6 Putting electrons into orbitals

There are two rules for allocating electrons to orbitals:

- Orbitals of lower energy are filled first.
- Orbitals of the same energy fill singly before pairing starts. This is because electrons repel each other.

The electron diagrams for the elements hydrogen to sodium are shown in Figure 1.9.

1.4.7 Writing electronic structures

A shorthand way of writing electronic structures is as follows. For example for sodium, which has 11 electrons:

$1s^2 \quad 2s^2 \quad 2p^6 \quad 3s^1$ Note how this matches the
  2   8   1   simpler 2, 8, 1.

Calcium, with 20 electrons would be:

$1s^2 \quad 2s^2 \quad 2p^6 \quad 3s^2 \quad 3p^6 \quad 4s^2$ which matches 2,8,8,2

Notice how the 4s orbital is filled before the 3d orbital because it is of lower energy. After calcium, electrons begin to fill the 3d orbitals, so vanadium with 23 electrons is:

$1s^2 \quad 2s^2 \quad 2p^6 \quad 3s^2 \quad 3p^6 \quad 3d^3 \quad 4s^2$

and krypton with 36 electrons would be:

$1s^2 \quad 2s^2 \quad 2p^6 \quad 3s^2 \quad 3p^6 \quad 3d^{10} \quad 4s^2 \quad 4p^6$

Sometimes it simplifies things to use to the previous noble gas symbol. So the electron arrangement of calcium, Ca, could be written [Ar]$4s^2$ as a shorthand for [$1s^2 2s^2 2p^6 3s^2 3p^6 4s^2$] because $1s^2 2s^2 2p^6 3s^2 3p^6$ is the electron arrangement of argon.

1.4.8 Molecular orbitals

When atoms approach one another closely, their atomic orbitals can merge to form new orbitals (called molecular orbitals) that spread over more than one atom, see Topic 7.8.

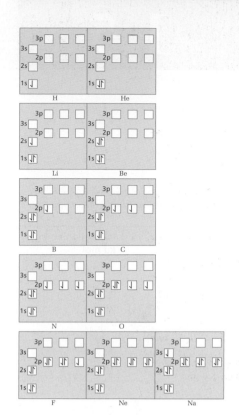

Fig 1.9 *The electron arrangements for the elements hydrogen to sodium*

QUICK QUESTIONS

1 Draw an electron diagram for phosphorus.

2 Write down the shorthand electron arrangement for phosphorus.

3 Write down the electron arrangement for phosphorus using $1s^2$ etc.

4 Write the electron arrangement for phosphorus using an inert gas symbol as shorthand.

5 Draw a diagram of the electron arrangement of phosphorus using boxes to represent orbitals as in Figure 1.9.

During chemical reactions, atoms may lose and gain electrons from their outer shells as part of the process of chemical bonding.

1.5.1 Ionisation energy

Electrons can also be removed from atoms by hitting the atoms with a beam of electrons from an 'electron gun'. This allows us to measure the energy it takes to remove the electrons. This is called **ionisation energy** because as the electrons are removed, the atoms become positive ions.

The energy required to remove a mole of electrons from a mole of atoms in the gaseous state is called the ionisation energy (strictly enthalpy of ionisation) and is measured in kJ mol^{-1}. Ionisation energy has the abbreviation IE.

1.5.2 Removing the electrons one by one

We can measure the energies required to remove the electrons one by one from an atom, starting from the outer electrons and working in.

- The first electron needs the least energy to remove it because it is being removed from a neutral atom. This is the first IE.
- The second electron needs more energy than the first because it is being removed from a 1^+ ion. This is the second IE.
- The third electron needs even more energy to remove, because it is being removed from a 2^+ ion. This is the third IE.
- The fourth needs yet more, and so on.
- We call these **successive ionisation energies**.

For example sodium:

$$Na(g) \rightarrow Na^+(g) + e^-$$ first IE $= +496$ kJ mol^{-1}
$$Na^+(g) \rightarrow Na^{2+}(g) + e^-$$ second IE $= +4563$ kJ mol^{-1}
$$Na^{2+}(g) \rightarrow Na^{3+}(g) + e^-$$ third IE $= +6913$ kJ mol^{-1}

and so on, see Table 1.5.

Notice that the second IE is *not* the energy change for:

$$Na(g) \rightarrow Na^{2+}(g) + 2e^-$$

The energy for this process would be (first IE + second IE).

If we plot a graph of the values in Table 1.5 we get Figure 1.11.

Notice that one electron is relatively easy to remove, then comes a group of eight that are more difficult to remove, and then two that are very difficult to remove.

This suggests that sodium has:

- *one* electron furthest away from the positive nucleus (easy to remove)
- *eight* nearer to the nucleus (harder to remove)
- *two* very close to the nucleus (very difficult to remove because they are nearest to the positive charge of the nucleus).

This tells us about the number of electrons in each shell or orbit – 2,8,1. The eight electrons are in fact sub-divided into two further groups that correspond to the $2s^2$, $2p^6$ electrons in the second shell, but this is not visible on the scale of Figure 1.11.

We can find the number of electrons in each shell of *any* element by looking at the jumps in successive ionisation energies, see Section 4.4.3.

Table 1.5 *Successive ionisation energies of sodium*

Electron removed	Ionisation energy/ kJ mol^{-1}
1st	496
2nd	4565
3rd	6913
4th	9544
5th	13 352
6th	16 611
7th	20 115
8th	25 491
9th	28 934
10th	141 367
11th	159 079

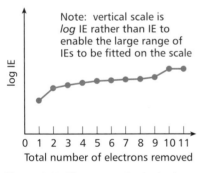

Note: vertical scale is *log* IE rather than IE to enable the large range of IEs to be fitted on the scale

Figure 1.10 *The successive ionisation energies of sodium*

HINT

The shape of the graph in Figure 1.11 can be confusing. The first electron removed is in the outer shell and the tenth and eleventh electrons removed are in the innermost shell.

1.5.3 Patterns in ionisation energies

The first ionisation energy of an element depends on three things:

- **The size of the charge on the nucleus** (the atomic number) – the more positive the nucleus is, the more difficult it is to remove an electron from the atom. So, as the atomic number, Z, goes up, the first ionisation energy goes up. For example, the first ionisation energy of sodium, $Z = 11$, is 496 kJ mol^{-1} and that of magnesium, $Z = 12$, is 738 kJ mol^{-1}.
- **The distance of the outer electron from the nucleus** – it is easier to remove an electron that is further away from the nucleus, because it is already some distance away from the positive charge of the nucleus. So, as the distance of the outer electron from the nucleus goes up, the first ionisation energy goes down. For example, the first ionisation energy of sodium, 496 kJ mol^{-1}, is smaller than that of lithium, 520 kJ mol^{-1}, although in each case the electron being removed 'feels' the same positive charge attracting it to the nucleus – see the next point.
- **Shielding by the inner electrons** – an electron in the outer shell of an atom (apart from hydrogen and helium) does not feel the attraction of the whole nuclear charge. This is because the negative charge of the inner electrons has the effect of cancelling out some of the positive charge on the nucleus. The charge actually felt by the outer electrons is called the **shielded nuclear charge** or the **effective nuclear charge**.

Shielded nuclear charge = atomic number (the number of protons) – number of electrons in the inner shells.

So for example, in sodium, electron arrangement 2,8,1, the outer electron feels a nuclear charge of 11, shielded by the ten inner electrons – in effect a nuclear charge of just +1. In potassium, electron arrangement 2,8,8,1, the outer electron feels a nuclear charge of 19, shielded by the 18 inner electrons – again, a nuclear charge of just +1.

All elements in the same group of the Periodic Table have the same shielded nuclear charge.

In fluorine, electron arrangement 2,7, the outer electrons feel a nuclear charge of 9, shielded by the two inner electrons – in effect a nuclear charge of +7.

For the three reasons above, the first ionisation energy generally gets bigger across a period and get smaller down a group of the Periodic Table, see Table 1.6.

Table 1.6 First ionisation energies of elements in Periods 2 to 4, in kJ mol^{-1}

IEs generally increase across a period (nuclear charge increasing, shielding remaining the same)

Li, 520	Be, 900	B, 801	C, 1086	N, 1402	O, 1314	F, 1681	Ne, 2081
Na, 496	Mg, 738	Al, 578	Si, 789	P, 1012	S, 1000	Cl, 1251	Ar, 1521
K, 419	Ca, 590	Ga, 579	Ge, 762	As, 947	Se, 941	Br, 1140	Kr, 1351

IEs decrease down a group (distance of outer electrons from nucleus increasing)

QUICK QUESTIONS

1 Why is the second ionisation energy of any atom larger than the first ionisation energy?

2 Sketch a graph similar to Fig 1.10 of the successive ionisation energies of aluminium.

3 Work out the shielded nuclear charge felt by the outer electrons in **a** fluorine, **b** sulphur, **c** calcium.

4 In Table 1.6, in which three elements do the outer electrons feel a shielded nuclear charge of 3$^+$?

5 Which of the noble gases in Table 1.6 is most likely to form positive ions?

2 Atoms, molecules and stoichiometry

2.1 Amounts of substance – the idea of the mole

A mole is the amount of any substance that contains a certain fixed number of particles. Using the mole, we can compare the *numbers* of different particles that take part in chemical reactions.

2.1.1 Counting atoms by weighing them

One atom of any element is too small to see with an optical microscope and impossible to weigh individually. So, to count atoms, chemists must weigh large numbers of them. This is how cashiers count money in a bank.

2.1.2 Relative atomic mass A_r, and relative molecular mass, M_r

The relative atomic mass, A_r is the average mass of an atom of an element relative to an atom of carbon-12 which has a relative atomic mass of 12 exactly, see Section 1.2.2.

$$A_r = \frac{\text{mass of one atom}}{\frac{1}{12}\text{th mass of an atom of } ^{12}\text{C}}$$

Examples (using whole numbers only) are:

Element	A_r
Hydrogen	1
Helium	4
Lithium	7

So, a helium atom is four times heavier than an atom of hydrogen. A lithium atom is seven times heavier than an atom of hydrogen. To get the same number of atoms in a sample of helium or lithium as there are atoms in 1 g of hydrogen, we must take 4 g of helium or 7 g of lithium.

In fact if we weigh out the relative atomic mass of *any* element, this amount will also contain this same number of atoms.

The relative molecular mass of a molecule is the mass of that molecule compared to an atom of carbon-12 which has a relative atomic mass of 12 exactly. In practice, this is virtually the same as the scale based on hydrogen = 1.

Examples (using whole numbers only):

Entity	Formula	A_r of atoms	M_r
Water	H_2O	$(2 \times 1) + 16$	18
Carbon dioxide	CO_2	$12 + (2 \times 16)$	44
Magnesium oxide	MgO	$24 + 16$	40

For example, water, H_2O, has a relative molecular mass, M_r, of 18. So, one molecule of water is 18 times heavier than one atom of hydrogen. Therefore, 18 g of water contains the same number of *molecules* as there are atoms in 1 g hydrogen.

A molecule of carbon dioxide is 44 times heavier than an atom of hydrogen, so 44 g of carbon dioxide contains this same number of molecules.

Large numbers of coins or bank notes are counted by weighing them

An entity of magnesium oxide (an ionic compound) is 40 times heavier than an atom of hydrogen, so 40 g of magnesium oxide contains this same number of entities.

If we weigh out the relative molecular mass (or formula mass) M_r, of a compound in grams we have *this same number* of entities.

> **NOTE**
>
> The word entity is a general word for a particle. It refers to the simplest formula unit of a giant structure, such as magnesium oxide, and also an atom, molecule, ion or even an electron.

2.1.3 The Avogadro constant

The actual number of atoms in 1 g of hydrogen is unimaginably huge:
602 200 000 000 000 000 000 000 usually written 6.022×10^{23}.

This number is called the **Avogadro constant**.

(Strictly the Avogadro constant is the number of atoms in 12 g of carbon-12, but the difference is negligible.)

2.1.4 The mole

The amount of substance that contains 6.022×10^{23} particles is called **a mole**.

- The relative atomic mass of an element in grams contains one mole of atoms.
- The relative molecular mass (or relative formula mass) of a substance in grams contains one mole of entities.
- We can also have a mole of ions or electrons.

> **NOTE**
>
> We can also use the term *molar mass,* which is the mass per mole of substance. It has units – kg mol^{-1} or g mol^{-1}. The molar mass in g mol^{-1} is the same numerically as M_r.

It is easy to confuse moles of *atoms* and moles of *molecules*, so always give the formula when working out the mass of a mole of entities.

Examples

Entities	Formula	Relative mass	Mass of a mole/g
Oxygen atoms	O	16.0	16.0
Oxygen molecules	O_2	32.0	32.0
Sodium ions	Na^+	23.0	23.0
Sodium chloride	NaCl	58.5	58.5

2.1.5 Number of moles

If we want to find out how many moles are present in a particular mass of a substance we need to know the substance's formula – from the formula we can work out the mass of one mole of the substance.

We use:

$$\text{Number of moles} = \frac{\text{mass in g}}{\text{mass of 1 mole in g}}$$

Example:

How many moles of atoms are there in 64.2 g of sulphur, S? (A_r S = 32.1, so 1 mole of sulphur has a mass of 32.1 g)

$$\text{Number of moles} = \frac{64.2}{32.1} = 2.00$$

Example:

How many moles of entities are there in 9.85 g of barium carbonate, $BaCO_3$? (A_r Ba = 137, A_r C = 12.0, A_r O = 16.0, so M_r of $BaCO_3$ = 137 + 12.0 + (3 × 16.0) = 197, so 1 mole of barium carbonate has a mass of 197 g).

$$\text{Number of moles} = \frac{9.85}{197} = 0.05$$

Example:

You have 3.94 g, of gold, Au, and 2.70 g of silver, Ag. Which contains the greater number of atoms? A_r Au = 197, A_r Ag = 108

$$\text{Number of moles of gold} = \frac{3.94}{197} = 0.02$$

$$\text{Number of moles of silver} = \frac{2.70}{108} = 0.025$$

There are more atoms of silver.

QUICK QUESTIONS

1 Use the Periodic Table to find the element for which the mass of a mole is

   a 79.0 g   b 9.0 g   c 45.0 g.

2 Work out M_r for

   a CH_4 b Na_2CO_3 c $Mg(OH)_2$ d $(NH_4)_2SO_4$.

3 How many moles are there in

   a 32 g CH_4 b 5.30 g Na_2CO_3 c 2.9 g $Mg(OH)_2$?

4 Which contains the least number of molecules – 0.5 g of hydrogen, 4 g of oxygen or 11 g of carbon dioxide?

5 Which of the quantities in 4 contains the greatest number of *atoms*?

2.2 Empirical formula (simplest formula)

The carbon dioxide molecule

The **empirical formula** is the simplest ratio of the atoms present in a compound. For example, the empirical formula of carbon dioxide, CO_2, tells us that for every carbon atom there two oxygen atoms.

To find an empirical formula:

1. Find the masses of each of the elements present in a compound.
2. Work out the number of moles of atoms of each element.

Use: Number of moles = $\dfrac{\text{mass of element (in grams)}}{\text{relative atomic mass of element}}$

3. Convert the number of moles of each element into a whole number ratio.

2.2.1 Examples

Example 1 Finding the empirical formula of copper oxide

0.795 g of black copper oxide are reduced to 0.635 g of copper when heated in a stream of hydrogen. What is the formula of copper oxide? A_r Cu = 63.5, A_r O = 16.0

1. Find the masses of each element:
   Mass of copper = 0.635 g
   We started with 0.795 g of copper oxide and 0.635 g of copper were left, so:
   Mass of oxygen = 0.795 − 0.635 = 0.160 g.

2. Find the number of moles of atoms of each element:
   A_r Cu = 63.5 Number of moles of copper = 0.635/63.5 = 0.01
   A_r O = 16.0 Number of moles of oxygen = 0.16/16 = 0.01

3 Find the simplest ratio
   So the ratio of moles of copper to moles of oxygen is:

       copper : oxygen
         0.01 : 0.01

And the simplest whole number ratio is 1 : 1
The simplest formula of copper oxide is therefore one Cu to one O, CuO.

Reducing copper oxide with hydrogen

	Copper, Cu	Oxygen, O
Mass of element	0.635 g	0.16 g
A_r of element	63.5	16.0
Number of moles = $\dfrac{\text{mass of element}}{A_r}$	$\dfrac{0.635}{63.5}$ = 0.01	$\dfrac{0.16}{16.0}$ = 0.01
Ratio of elements	1	1

Finding the empirical formula of copper oxide

Example 2

10.01 g of a white solid contains 4.01 g of calcium, 1.20 g of carbon and 4.80 g of oxygen. What is its empirical formula?

(A_r Ca = 40.1, A_r C = 12.0, A_r O = 16.0)

1. Find the masses of each element:
   Mass of calcium = 4.01 g
   Mass of carbon = 1.20 g
   Mass of oxygen = 4.80 g.

2. Find the number of moles of atoms of each element:
   A_r Ca = 40.1 Number of moles of calcium = 4.01/40.1 = 0.10

   A_r C = 12 Number of moles of carbon = 1.20/12 = 0.10

   A_r O = 16 Number of moles of oxygen = 4.80/16 = 0.30

3. Find the simplest ratio:
   Ratio in moles of   calcium : carbon : oxygen
                          0.10 : 0.10 : 0.30

   And the simplest
   whole number ratio is: 1   :   1   :   3

   The formula is therefore $CaCO_3$ (This is calcium carbonate.)

2.2.2 Finding the simplest ratio of elements

Sometimes you will end up with ratios of moles of elements that are not easy to convert to whole numbers. If you divide each number by the smallest number you will end up with whole numbers (or ratios you can recognise easily). Here is an example:

Compound X contains 50.2 g sulphur and 50.0 g oxygen. A_r S = 32.1, A_r O = 16.0. What is its empirical formula?

1. Find the mass of each element: Mass of sulphur = 50.2 g
   Mass of oxygen = 50.0 g.

2. Find the number of moles of atoms of each element:
   A_r S = 32.1 Number of moles of sulphur = 50.2/32.1 = 1.563

   A_r O = 16.0 Number of moles of oxygen = 50.0/16.0 = 3.125

3. Find the simplest ratio:

   Ratio of sulphur : oxygen
           1.563 : 3.125

Now divide each of the numbers by the smallest number.

Ratio of sulphur : oxygen
$$\frac{1.563}{1.563} : \frac{3.125}{1.563}$$
$$= \quad 1 \quad : \quad 2$$

The empirical formula is therefore SO_2. (This is sulphur dioxide.)

2.2.3 Finding the molecular formula

The **molecular formula** tells us how many of each type of atoms are present in one molecule of the substance. (It applies only to substances that exist as molecules).

The empirical formula is the simplest ratio of the elements present in the compound.

The empirical formula is not always the same as the molecular formula. There may be several units of the empirical formula in the molecular formula. For example ethane (C_2H_6) would have an empirical formula of CH_3.

To find the number of units of the empirical formula in the molecular formula, divide the relative molecular mass by the relative mass of the empirical formula.

For example, ethene has a relative molecular mass of 28.0, but its empirical formula, CH_2, has a relative mass of 14.0.

$$\frac{\text{Relative molecular mass of ethene}}{\text{Relative mass of empirical formula of ethene}} = \frac{28.0}{14.0} = 2$$

So there must be two units of the empirical formula in the molecule of ethene. So ethene is $(CH_2)_2$ or C_2H_4.

QUICK QUESTIONS

1 What is the empirical formula of the following compounds? (You could try and name them too.)

   a A liquid containing 2.0 g of hydrogen, 32.1 g sulphur and 64.0 g oxygen.

   b A white solid containing 0.9 g beryllium, 3.2 g oxygen and 0.2 g hydrogen.

   c A white solid containing 0.243 g magnesium and 0.710 g chlorine.

2 3.888 g magnesium ribbon was burnt completely in air and 6.488 g of magnesium oxide were produced.

   a How many moles of magnesium and of oxygen are present in 6.488 g of magnesium oxide?

   b What is the empirical formula of magnesium oxide?

3 What are the empirical formulae of the following molecules?

   a cyclohexane C_6H_{12},

   b dichloroethene $C_2H_2Cl_2$,

   c benzene C_6H_6?

4 M_r for ethane-1,2-diol is 62.0. It is composed of carbon, hydrogen and oxygen in the ratio by moles of 1 : 3 : 1. What is its molecular formula?

Moles in solutions and moles of gases

A solution consists of a solvent with a solute dissolved in it, see Figure 2.1.

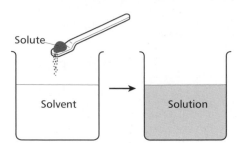

Fig 2.1 *A solution contains a solute and a solvent*

HINT

You will not get a solution with a concentration of 1 mol dm^{-3} by adding 1 mol of solute to 1 dm^3 of solvent. You add the solvent to the solute until you have 1 dm^3 of solution.

2.3.1 The units of concentration

- The concentration of a solution tells us how much solute is present in a known volume of solution.
- Concentrations of solutions are measured in the units moles per cubic decimetre, mol dm^{-3}.
- 1 mol dm^{-3} means there is 1 mole of solute per cubic decimetre of solution; 2 mol dm^{-3} means there are 2 moles of solute per cubic decimetre of solution and so on.

2.3.2 Finding the concentration in mol dm^{-3}

Example:
1.17 g of sodium chloride was dissolved in water to make 500 cm^3 of solution.

What is the concentration in mol dm^{-3}? A_r Na = 23.0, A_r Cl = 35.5

The mass of 1 mole of sodium chloride, NaCl, is 23.0 + 35.5 = 58.5 g.

$$\text{Number of moles} = \frac{\text{mass in g}}{\text{mass of 1 mole in g}}$$

So 1.17 g of NaCl contains $\frac{1.17}{58.5}$ mol = 0.02 mol.

This is dissolved in 500 cm^3, so 1000 cm^3 (1 dm^3) will contain 0.04 mol of NaCl.

So the concentration = 0.04 mol dm^{-3}.

2.3.3 The number of moles in a given volume of solution

You often have to work out how many moles are present in a particular volume of a solution of known concentration. The general formula for the number of moles in a solution of concentration M mol dm^{-3} and volume V cm^3 is:

$$\text{Number of moles in solution} = \frac{M \times V}{1000}$$

This is an example of how we reach this formula in steps:

How many moles are present in 25 cm^3 of a solution of concentration 0.10 mol dm^{-3}?

From the definition:
1000 cm^3 of a solution of 1.0 mol dm^{-3} contains 1 mol.

HINT

1 decimetre = 10 cm, so one *cubic* decimetre, 1 dm^3, is 10 cm × 10 cm × 10 cm = 1000 cm^3. It is the same as 1 litre (1 l or 1 L).

The small negative sign in mol dm^{-3} means 'per' and is sometimes written using a slash, mol/dm^3.

So 1000 cm^3 of a solution of 0.10 mol dm^{-3} contains 0.10 mol.

So 1.0 cm^3 of a solution of 0.10 mol dm^{-3} contains $\dfrac{0.10}{1000}$ mol = 0.0001 mol

So 25.0 cm^3 of a solution of 0.10 mol dm^{-3} contains $25.0 \times 0.0001 = 0.0025$ mol.
Using the formula gives the same answer:

$$\text{Number of moles in solution} = \frac{M \times V}{1000}$$
$$= \frac{0.10 \times 25}{1000} = 0.0025$$

2.3.4 Moles of gases

A mole of *any* gas has the same volume under the same conditions of temperature and pressure. At room temperature (about 25°C) and pressure, the volume of a mole of gas is approximately 24 000 cm^3 (24 dm^3). So, one mole of sulphur dioxide gas, SO_2 (mass 64.1 g) has the same volume as one mole of hydrogen gas, H_2 (mass 2.0 g).

This may seem very unlikely at first sight, but it is the space between the gas molecules that accounts for the volume of a gas. Even the largest gas particle is extremely small compared with the space in between the particles.

For example, how many moles of carbon dioxide gas (CO_2) are present in a volume of 240 cm^3 at room temperature and pressure? What is the mass of this volume of gas? (A_r C = 12.0, A_r O = 16.0).

1 mol of CO_2 has a volume of 24 000 cm^3, so

$$\text{Number of moles in 240 cm}^3 = \frac{240}{24\,000} = 0.01 \text{ mol}$$

1 mol of CO_2 has a mass of 44.0 g, so 0.01 mol has a mass of $44.0 \times 0.01 = 0.44$ g

240 cm^3 of hydrogen would also contain 0.01 mole but in this case the mass would be 0.02 g.

2.3.5 Summary

Learn and be able to use the following:

- The number of moles in a given mass of a solid $= \dfrac{\text{mass in grams}}{\text{mass of 1 mole in grams}}$

- The number of moles of solute in a given volume of solution $= \dfrac{M \times V}{1000}$, where M = concentration in mol dm^{-3} and V = volume of solution in cm^3.

- Number of moles in a given volume of gas is approximately $\dfrac{V}{24\,000}$ at room temperature and pressure, where V = volume of gas in cm^3.

QUICK QUESTIONS

1 What is the concentration in mol dm^{-3} of:
   a 0.50 mol acid in 500.0 cm^3 of solution,
   b 0.250 mol acid in 2000.0 cm^3 of solution,
   c 0.20 mol solute in 20.0 cm^3 of solution?

2 How many moles of solute are there in
   a 20.0 cm^3 of a 0.10 mol dm^{-3} solution,
   b 50.0 cm^3 of a 0.50 mol dm^{-3} solution,
   c 25.0 cm^3 of a 2.0 mol dm^{-3} solution?

3 0.234 g of sodium chloride was dissolved in water to make 250.0 cm^3 of solution. What is the concentration in mol dm^{-3}?

4 How many moles are there in the following volumes of hydrogen at room temperature and pressure?
   a 480 cm^3,
   b 120 cm^3,
   c 36 000 cm^3.

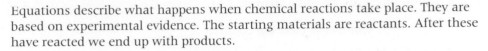

2.4 Equations

Equations describe what happens when chemical reactions take place. They are based on experimental evidence. The starting materials are reactants. After these have reacted we end up with products.

Reactants → Products

When chemists first experimented with how elements reacted together, they found that elements reacted in fixed ratios by mass. Once the idea of atoms and molecules had been established, they realised that atoms and molecules react together in simple whole number ratios. For example, two hydrogen molecules react with one oxygen molecule to give two water molecules.

2 hydrogen molecules : 1 oxygen molecule : 2 water molecules

The ratio in simple whole numbers in which the reactants react (and the products are produced) is called a **stoichiometric** relationship.

We can build up a stoichiometric relationship from experimental data by working out the number of moles that react together and the number of moles produced. This leads us to a balanced symbol equation.

2.4.1 Balanced symbol equations

Balanced symbol equations use the formulae of reactants and products:

- There are the same number of atoms of each element on both sides of the arrow. (This is because atoms are never created or destroyed in chemical reactions.)
- They tell us about the *amounts* of substances that react together and are produced.

2.4.2 Writing balanced equations

When sodium burns in chlorine it forms sodium chloride. We can build up a balanced symbol equation from this information and from the formulae of the reactants and product: Na, Cl_2, $NaCl$.

1. Write the word equation:

$$\text{sodium} + \text{chlorine} \rightarrow \text{sodium chloride}$$

2. Write in the correct formulae:

$$Na + Cl_2 \rightarrow NaCl$$

This is not balanced because there are 2 chlorine atoms on the reactants side (left hand side) but only 1 on the products side (right hand side)

3. To get two chlorine atoms on the right hand side put a 2 in front of the NaCl:

$$Na + Cl_2 \rightarrow 2NaCl$$

Now the chlorine is correct but there is only one sodium atom on the left hand side. If we now multiply the Na by 2, the equation is balanced:

$$2Na + Cl_2 \rightarrow 2NaCl$$

We can add state symbols. The equation tells us the numbers of moles of each of the substances that are involved. From this we work out the masses that will react together:

$2Na(s)$	$+$	$Cl_2(g)$	$\rightarrow$	$2NaCl(s)$
2 moles		1 mole		2 moles
46.0 g		71.0 g		117.0 g

The total mass is the same on both sides of the equation. This is another good way of checking whether the equation is balanced.

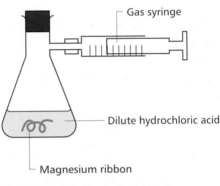

Fig 2.2 *Apparatus for collecting hydrogen gas*

Gas syringe

Dilute hydrochloric acid

Magnesium ribbon

NOTE

State symbols are letters, in brackets, which can be added to the formula in equations to show what state the reactants and products are in: (s) means solid; (l) means liquid; (g) means gas; (aq) means aqueous solution (dissolved in water).

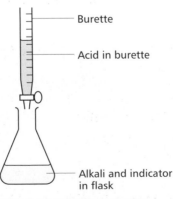

Burette

Acid in burette

Alkali and indicator in flask

Fig 2.3 *Apparatus for a titration*

Useful tips for balancing equations:

- Start with the correct formulae – you cannot change them to make the equation balance.
- You can only change the number of atoms by putting a number in front of formulae.
- If you cannot balance the equation after three or four steps then you probably have a formula wrong.
- The number in front of the symbol tells you how many moles are reacting.

2.4.3 Working out amounts

We can use a balanced symbol equation to work out how much product is produced from a reaction. For example, the reaction between magnesium and hydrochloric acid produces hydrogen gas (see Figure 2.2). (A_r Mg = 24.3, A_r H = 1.0, A_r Cl = 35.5)

Example 1

How much gas is produced by 0.061 g of magnesium ribbon and excess hydrochloric acid? (The word *excess* means there is more than enough acid to react with all the magnesium.)

First write the balanced symbol equation, and then the numbers of moles that react:

magnesium + hydrochloric acid → magnesium chloride + hydrogen

$$Mg(s) \; + \; 2HCl(aq) \; \rightarrow \; MgCl_2(aq) \; + \; H_2$$
$$\text{1 mol} \qquad \text{2 mol} \qquad \qquad \text{1 mol} \qquad \text{1 mol}$$

1 mol of Mg has a mass of 24.3 g because its $A_r = 24.3$. So, 0.061 g of Mg is 0.061/24.3 = 0.0025 mol.

From the equation, we can see that 1 mole of magnesium reacts to give 1 mole of hydrogen. Therefore, 0.0025 mol of Mg produce 0.0025 mol H_2.

1 mol of H_2 has a volume of 24 000 cm^3 (1 mol of any gas has a volume of 24 000 cm^3 at room temperature and pressure).

0.0025 mol of H_2 has a volume of 0.0025 × 24 000 = 60 cm^3.

2.4.4 Finding concentrations using titrations

We often do a titration to find the concentration of a solution, for example an acid.
We react the acid with an alkali using a suitable indicator.

We need to know:

- the concentration of the alkali
- the equation for the reaction between the acid and alkali.

The apparatus is shown in Figure 2.3.

The steps in a titration:

- Fill a burette with the acid of unknown concentration.
- Accurately measure an amount of the alkali using a calibrated pipette and pipette filler.
- Add the alkali to a conical flask with a few drops of a suitable indicator.
- Run in acid from the burette until the colour just changes, showing that the solution in the conical flask is now neutral.

Example 2

a) 25.0 cm^3 of a 0.10 mol dm^{-3} solution of sodium hydroxide, NaOH, was neutralised by 20.0 cm^3 of hydrochloric acid, HCl. What is the concentration of the acid?

First write a balanced symbol equation and then the numbers of moles that react:

$$NaOH(aq) \; + \; HCl(aq) \; \rightarrow \; NaCl(aq) \; + \; H_2O(l)$$

sodium hydroxide	hydrochloric acid	sodium chloride	water
1 mol	1 mol	1 mol	1 mol

So 1 mol of sodium hydroxide reacts with 1 mol of hydrochloric acid:

$$\text{Number of moles in solution} = \frac{M \times V}{1000}$$

So,

$$\text{number of moles of NaOH} = \frac{0.10 \times 25.0}{1000}$$

Let the concentration of acid be Y mol dm^{-3}:

$$\text{Number of moles of HCl} = \frac{Y \times 20.0}{1000}$$

Since we know there must be an equal number of moles of sodium hydroxide and hydrochloric acid for neutralisation, we can say:

Number of moles of NaOH = number of moles of HCl

So,

$$\frac{0.10 \times 25.0}{1000} = \frac{Y \times 20.0}{1000}$$

From this $Y = 0.125$ and the concentration of the acid is 0.125 mol dm^{-3}.

QUICK QUESTIONS

1 Balance the following equations:

   a $Mg + O_2 \rightarrow MgO$

   b $Ca(OH)_2 + HCl \rightarrow CaCl_2 + H_2O$

   c $Na_2O + HNO_3 \rightarrow NaNO_3 + H_2O$

2 Write down under the balanced equations the number of moles of each reactant and product that take part in the reaction.

3 What is the concentration of hydrochloric acid if 20.0 cm^3 is neutralised by 25.0 cm^3 of sodium hydroxide of concentration 0.20 mol dm^{-3}?

4 In the reaction:

   $$Mg(s) + 2HCl(aq) \rightarrow MgCl_2(aq) + H_2(g)$$

   2.43 g of magnesium was added to 100.0 cm^3 of 1.0 mol dm^{-3} hydrochloric acid.

   a Which reactant is in excess?

   b Would there be any magnesium left when the reaction finished? Explain your answer.

2.5 Equations using ions

NOTE

Cations are named because they are attracted to the cathode (−) and so they are positive. Anions go to the anode (+) and so are negative. This can be confusing if you are not careful. If you can remember that copper, like all metals, forms positive ions, then the sentence '**C**opper goes to the **c**athode' might help.

- An ionic compound (for example, sodium chloride) breaks up into ions if it dissolves in water.
- We can often write an equation using ions for a reaction that takes place in aqueous solution.
- Ions have charges – negatively charged ions are called **anions**, positively charged ones are called **cations**.
- An equation must balance and the charges on both sides of the equation must also balance.

Some examples of ionic equations are given below.

2.5.1 Displacement reactions

When magnesium is placed into a solution of blue copper sulphate, magnesium (which is a more reactive metal than copper) displaces the copper. Copper metal appears, and the solution gradually becomes colourless, see photo.

The balanced symbol equation is:

$$Mg(s) + CuSO_4(aq) \rightarrow MgSO_4(aq) + Cu(s)$$

magnesium   copper sulphate   magnesium sulphate   copper

But, since both copper sulphate and magnesium sulphate exist as ions when dissolved in water, we can write:

$$Mg(s) + Cu^{2+}(aq) + SO_4^{2-}(aq) \rightarrow Mg^{2+}(aq) + SO_4^{2-}(aq) + Cu(s)$$

We can cancel out any ions(s) that are on both sides of the arrow:

$$Mg(s) + Cu^{2+}(aq) + \cancel{SO_4^{2-}(aq)} \rightarrow Mg^{2+}(aq) + Cu(s) + \cancel{SO_4^{2-}(aq)}$$

We end up with:

$$Mg(s) + Cu^{2+}(aq) \rightarrow Mg^{2+}(aq) + Cu(s)$$

Notice that the total charge (2^+) is the same on both sides.

Ions that take no part in the reaction, like the sulphate ions that we cancelled out, are called **spectator ions**.

Another example is the reaction between zinc and copper chloride solution.

Since zinc chloride and copper chloride exist as ions in solution we can write:

$$Zn(s) + Cu^{2+}(aq) + \cancel{2Cl^-(aq)} \rightarrow Zn^{2+}(aq) + \cancel{2Cl^-(aq)} + Cu(s)$$

Cancelling the ions common to both sides (the spectator ions):

$$Zn(s) + 2Cu^{2+}(aq) + 2Cl^-(aq) \rightarrow Zn^{2+}(aq) + 2Cl^-(aq) + Cu(s)$$

$$Zn(s) + Cu^{2+}(aq) \rightarrow Zn^{2+}(aq) + Cu(s)$$

Again the total charge, 2^+, is the same on both sides.

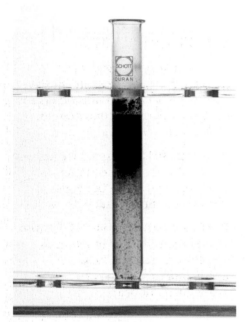

Magnesium displaces copper from copper sulphate solution

2.5.2 Acid reactions

It is very useful to know the typical reactions of acids and be able to write the equations for them because they turn up in all branches of chemistry. Strong acids break up completely into ions when they are in solution in water. The cation is the hydrogen ion; the anion depends on the acid.

Acids react to form salts. Three common acids found in the laboratory form salts with the names shown in the margin.

Acid	Type of salt	Anion
Hydrochloric acid, HCl	chloride	Cl^-
Sulphuric acid, H_2SO_4	sulphate	SO_4^{2-}
Nitric acid, HNO_3	nitrate	NO_3^-

2.5.3 Making salts

All acids react to form salts as shown below and the reactions may be written as balanced symbol or ionic equations.

- **Reactive metal + acid → salt + hydrogen**

For example:

$$Mg(s) \;+\; H_2SO_4(aq) \;\rightarrow\; MgSO_4(aq) \;+\; H_2(g)$$

magnesium   sulphuric acid   magnesium sulphate   hydrogen

Putting in the aqueous ions:

$$Mg(s) + 2H^+(aq) + SO_4^{2-}(aq) \rightarrow Mg^{2+}(aq) + SO_4^{2-}(aq) + H_2(g)$$

Cancelling out the spectator ions:

$$Mg(s) + 2H^+(aq) + \cancel{SO_4^{2-}(aq)} \rightarrow Mg^{2+}(aq) + \cancel{SO_4^{2-}(aq)} + H_2(g)$$

Ionic equation: $Mg(s) + 2H^+(aq) \rightarrow Mg^{2+}(aq) + H_2(g)$

- **Metal carbonate + acid → salt + water + carbon dioxide**

For example:

$$Na_2CO_3(s) \;+\; 2HNO_3(aq) \rightarrow 2NaNO_3(aq) + H_2O(l) + CO_2(g)$$

sodium carbonate   nitric acid   sodium nitrate   water   carbon dioxide

Putting in the aqueous ions:

$$Na_2CO_3(s) + 2H^+(aq) + 2NO_3^-(aq) \rightarrow 2Na^+(aq) + 2NO_3^-(aq) + H_2O(l) + CO_2(g)$$

Cancelling out the spectator ions:

$$Na_2CO_3(s) + 2H^+(aq) + \cancel{2NO_3^-(aq)} \rightarrow 2Na^+(aq) + \cancel{2NO_3^-(aq)} + H_2O(l) + CO_2(g)$$

Ionic equation: $Na_2CO_3(s) + 2H^+(aq) \rightarrow 2Na^+(aq) + H_2O(l) + CO_2(g)$

- **Metal hydroxide + acid → salt + water**

For example:

$$NaOH(aq) \;+\; HNO_3(aq) \rightarrow NaNO_3(aq) + H_2O(l)$$

sodium hydroxide   nitric acid   sodium nitrate   water

Putting in the aqueous ions:

$$Na^+(aq) + OH^-(aq) + H^+(aq) + NO_3^-(aq) \rightarrow Na^+(aq) + NO_3^-(aq) + H_2O(l)$$

Cancelling out the spectator ions:

$$\cancel{Na^+(aq)} + OH^-(aq) + H^+(aq) + \cancel{NO_3^-(aq)} \rightarrow \cancel{Na^+(aq)} + \cancel{NO_3^-(aq)} + H_2O(l)$$

Ionic equation: $OH^-(aq) + H^+(aq) \rightarrow H_2O(l)$

- **Metal oxide + acid → salt + water**

For example:

$$CaO(s) \;+\; 2HCl(aq) \;\rightarrow\; CaCl_2(aq) + H_2O(l)$$

calcium oxide   hydrochloric acid   calcium chloride   water

Putting in the aqueous ions:

$$CaO(s) + 2H^+(aq) + 2Cl^-(aq) \rightarrow Ca^{2+}(aq) + 2Cl^-(aq) + H_2O(l)$$

Cancelling out the spectator ions:

$$CaO(s) + 2H^+(aq) + \cancel{2Cl^-(aq)} \rightarrow Ca^{2+}(aq) + \cancel{2Cl^-(aq)} + H_2O(l)$$

Ionic equation: $CaO(s) + 2H^+(aq) \rightarrow Ca^{2+}(aq) + H_2O(l)$

If the water is evaporated from the solutions remaining when these reactions have taken place, the metal cations bond with the anions and a solid salt forms.

HINT

Learn the formulae of acids because this will help you to remember the charges on ions. For example, from the formula of sulphuric acid H_2SO_4 you can work out that SO_4 must have a charge of 2^- since hydrogen always forms H^+ ions and there are two H^+ ions to each sulphate in sulphuric acid.

QUICK QUESTIONS

1 Copper displaces silver from a solution of silver nitrate, $AgNO_3$. Write a balanced symbol equation and then an ionic equation to show this reaction.

2 Write a balanced symbol equation and then an ionic equation to show the reaction between magnesium and sulphuric acid.

3 Write a balanced symbol equation and then an ionic equation to show the reaction between calcium carbonate and hydrochloric acid.

4 Write a balanced symbol equation and then an ionic equation to show the reaction between sodium hydroxide and hydrochloric acid.

NOTE

Although calcium oxide is an ionic compound, it does not dissolve in water and so there are no aqueous ions from this compound. It could be written

$$(Ca^{2+} + O^{2-})(s).$$

3 Chemical bonding and structure

3.1 Ionic bonding

Helium   Neon   Argon

Fig 3.1 Inert gases

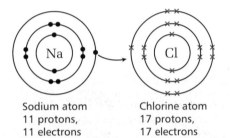

Sodium atom
11 protons,
11 electrons

Chlorine atom
17 protons,
17 electrons

Fig 3.2 A 'dot-and-cross' diagram to show the transfer of an electron from a sodium atom to a chlorine atom. Remember that electrons are all identical whether shown by a dot or a cross

3.1.1 How atoms bond together

The bonds between atoms always involve their outer electrons.

- Inert gases have full outer shells of electrons and are very unreactive.
- When atoms bond together they share, pool or transfer electrons to get full outer shells, making them more stable and less reactive, like the inert gases.
- There are three types of strong chemical bonds: **ionic**, **covalent** and **metallic**.

3.1.2 Ionic bonding

Ionic bonding occurs between metals and non-metals and involves transfer of electrons from metals to non-metals.

Sodium chloride

Sodium chloride, see Figure 3.2, has ionic bonding.

Sodium has 11 electrons (and 11 protons). The electron arrangement is 2,8,1.

Chlorine has 17 electrons (and 17 protons). The electron arrangement is 2,8,7.

- An electron is *transferred*. The single outer electron of the sodium atom moves into the outer shell of the chlorine atom.
- Each outer shell is now full.
- Both sodium and chlorine have an inert gas electron structure as in Figure 3.3.

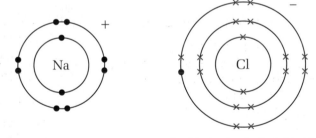

Na^+ Sodium ion
11 protons, 10 electrons,(2,8)

Cl^- Chlorine ion (called chloride)
17 protons, 18 electrons,(2,8,8)

Fig 3.3 The ions that result from electron transfer

- The two charged particles that result from this transfer are called **ions**.
- The sodium ion is positively charged, because it has lost a negative electron.
- The chloride ion is negatively charged, because it has gained a negative electron.
- The two ions are attracted to each other and to other oppositely charged ions in the sodium chloride compound by **electrostatic forces**.

So ionic bonding is the result of electrostatic attraction between oppositely charged ions. The attraction extends throughout the compound, as in Figure 3.4 making a structure called a **lattice**.

The formula of sodium chloride is NaCl, because we know that for every one sodium ion there is one chloride ion.

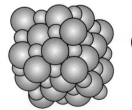

Chloride, Cl^-

Sodium ion, Na^+

Fig 3.4 The sodium chloride structure. This is an example of a **giant structure**. The strong bonding extends throughout the compound and because of this it will be difficult to melt

Magnesium oxide

Magnesium has 12 electrons. The electron arrangement is 2,8,2.
Oxygen has 8 electrons. The electron arrangement is 2,6.

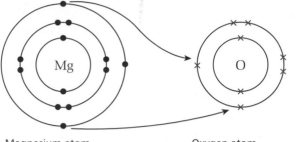

Magnesium atom
12 protons, 12 electrons

Oxygen atom
8 protons, 8 electrons

This time, two electrons are transferred from the magnesium atom. Each oxygen atom receives two electrons.

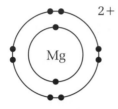 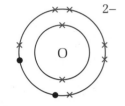

Mg^{2+} Magnesium ion
12 protons, 10 electrons (2,8)

O^{2-} Oxygen ion (called oxide)
8 protons, 10 electrons (2,8)

- The magnesium ion is positively charged, Mg^{2+}, because it has lost two negative electrons.
- The oxide ion, O^{2-}, is negatively charged, because it has gained two negative electrons.
- The formula of magnesium oxide is MgO.

3.1.3 Properties of ionically bonded compounds

- Ionic compounds are always solids. They have **giant structures** and therefore **high melting points**. This is because in order to melt an ionic compound, energy must be supplied to break up the lattice of ions.
- Ionic compounds **conduct electricity** when molten or dissolved in water (aqueous) but not when solid. This is because the ions that carry the current are free to move in the liquid state but are not free in the solid state, see Figure 3.5.
- Ionic compounds tend to be **brittle** and shatter easily

when given a sharp blow. This is because they form a lattice of alternating positive and negative ions, see Figure 3.6. A blow in the direction shown may move the ions and produce contact between ions with like charges.

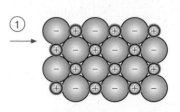 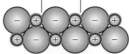

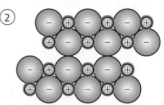

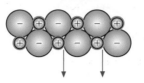

A small displacement causes contact between ions with the same charge...

...and the structure shatters

Shatters

Fig 3.6 *Breaking an ionic lattice*

QUICK QUESTIONS

1 Which of the following are ionic compounds and why?
   a CO, **b** KF, **c** CaO, **d** H_2O

2 Why do ionic compounds have high melting temperatures?

3 Under what conditions do ionic compounds conduct electricity?

4 Draw 'dot-and-cross' diagrams to show:
   a the ionic bonding between magnesium and fluorine,
   b the ionic bonding between sodium and oxygen.

5 What are the formulae of the compounds in **4**?

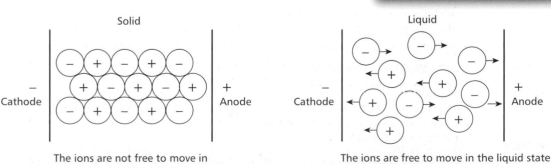

The ions are not free to move in the solid state

The ions are free to move in the liquid state and the compound conducts electricity

Fig 3.5 *Ionic liquids conduct electricity, ionic solids do not*

3.2 Covalent bonding

- Covalent bonds form between non-metal atoms.
- The atoms *share* some of their outer electrons so that each atom has a full outer shell of electrons.
- A covalent bond is a shared pair of electrons.

3.2.1 Covalent bonding to form molecules

A small group of covalently bonded atoms is called a **molecule**.

For example chlorine is a gas which is made of molecules, see Figure 3.7. Chlorine has 17 electrons and an electron arrangement 2,8,7. Two chlorine atoms make a molecule:

- The two atoms share one pair of electrons.
- Each atom now has a full outer shell.
- The formula is Cl_2.
- The molecule does not contain charged particles because no electrons have been transferred from one atom to another.

We can represent one pair of shared electrons in a covalent bond by a line, Cl–Cl.

Example

Methane gas is a covalent compound of carbon and hydrogen. Carbon has 6 electrons with electron arrangement 2,4 and hydrogen has just one electron.

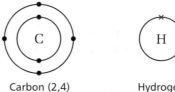

Carbon (2,4)   Hydrogen

In order for carbon to get a full outer shell, there are four hydrogen atoms to every carbon atom.

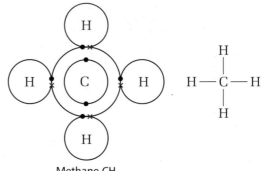

Methane CH_4

The formula of methane is CH_4.

3.2.2 Double covalent bonds

In a double bond, four electrons are shared. The two atoms in an oxygen molecule share two pairs of electrons, so that the oxygen atoms have a double bond between them, see Figure 3.8.

When you are drawing covalent bonding diagrams you may leave out the inner shells, because the inner shells are not involved at all. Other examples of molecules with covalent bonds are shown in Table 3.1.

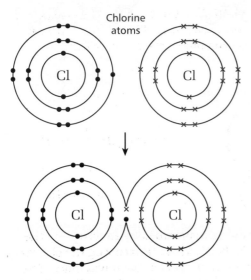

A chlorine molecule Cl_2

Fig 3.7 *Forming a chlorine molecule*

> **HINT**
>
> Notice that hydrogen has a full outer shell with only two electrons. (It is only filling the first shell to get the structure of the noble gas helium.)

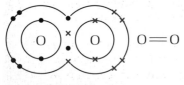

Oxygen O_2

Fig 3.8 *An oxygen molecule has a double bond*

All the examples in Table 3.1 below are neutral molecules. The atoms within the molecules are strongly bonded together, but the neutral molecules are not strongly attracted to each other.

3.2.3 Properties of substances with molecular structures

- Substances composed of molecules are gases, liquids or solids with low melting temperatures. (The strong covalent bonds are only *between the atoms in the molecules*.) The molecules do not need much energy to move apart from each other.
- They are poor conductors of electricity (there are no charged particles to carry the current).
- If they dissolve in water, the solutions are poor conductors of electricity. (Again there are no charged particles).

3.2.4 Dative covalent bonding

A single covalent bond consists of a pair of electrons shared between two atoms. In most covalent bonds, each atom provides one of the electrons. But, in some bonds, one atom provides both the electrons. This is called **dative covalent bonding**. It is also called **coordinate bonding**.
In a dative covalent bond:

- The atom that *receives* the electrons is an atom that does not have a full outer shell of electrons. We say the atom is electron deficient.
- The atom that is *donating* the electrons has a pair of electrons that is not being used in a bond, called a **lone pair**.

The ammonium ion
For example, ammonia, NH_3, has a lone pair of electrons:

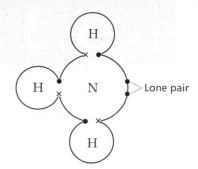

In the ammonium ion, NH_4^+, the nitrogen uses its lone pair of electrons to form a dative bond to an H^+ ion (a 'bare' proton with no electrons at all and therefore electron-deficient):

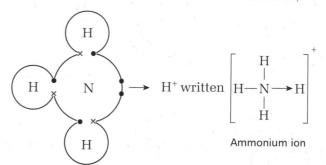

Ammonium ion

Dative covalent bonds are represented by an arrow →. The arrow points towards the atom that is receiving the electron pair. But this is only to show how the bond was made. The ammonium ion is completely symmetrical and all the bonds have exactly the same strength and length. Dative bonds have exactly the same strength and length as ordinary covalent bonds between the same pair of atoms.

The ammonium ion has *covalently* bonded atoms, but is a charged particle. Ions like this are called **complex ions**.

Table 3.1 Examples of covalent molecules. Only the outer shells are shown

Formula	Name	Formula	Name
H_2	Hydrogen Each hydrogen atom has a full outer shell with just two electrons	NH_3	Ammonia
HCl	Hydrogen chloride	C_2H_4	Ethene There is a carbon–carbon double bond in this molecule
H_2O	Water	CO_2	Carbon dioxide There are two carbon–oxygen double bonds in this molecule

QUICK QUESTIONS

1 What is a covalent bond?

2 Which of the following are covalent and why?
   a Na_2O,
   b SO_2
   c $MgCl_2$,
   d C_2H_4

3 Why are covalent molecules gases, liquids or low-melting solids?

4 Draw a dot-and-cross diagram for hydrogen sulphide, a compound of hydrogen and sulphur.

5 Draw a dot-and-cross diagram to show a water molecule forming a dative bond with a H^+ ion. Which is the electron-deficient atom?

3.3

The shapes of covalent molecules

NOTE

The electron pair repulsion theory may be called Valence Shell Electron Pair Repulsion Theory or VSEPR. The valence shell is another name for the outer shell.

NOTE

It is acceptable to draw electron diagrams and leave out the rings that indicate full outer shells.

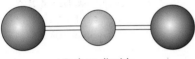

Carbon dioxide

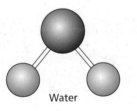

Methane

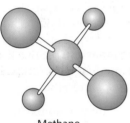

Water

Fig 3.9 *The shapes of the carbon dioxide, methane and water molecules*

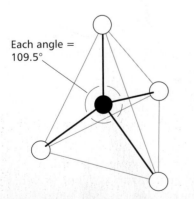

Each angle = 109.5°

Fig 3.10 *A tetrahedron has four points and four faces. It is a pyramid made up of four triangles*

Molecules are three dimensional and they come in many different shapes, see Figure 3.9.

3.3.1 Electron pair repulsion theory

We can predict the shape of a simple covalent molecule – for example, one consisting of a central atom surrounded by a number of other atoms – by using the ideas that:

- A group of electrons around an atom will repel all other electron groups.
- The groups of electrons will therefore take up positions as far apart as possible.

This is called the **electron pair repulsion theory**.

A 'group' of electrons may be:

- a set of two shared in a single bond
- a set of four shared in a double bond
- an unshared (lone) pair.

The shape of a molecule depends on the number of groups of electrons that surround the central atom. To work out the shape of any molecule you must first draw a dot-and-cross diagram.

1 Two groups of electrons

If there are two groups of electrons around the atom, the molecule will be **linear**. The furthest away from each other the two groups can get is 180° apart. Beryllium chloride, which is covalently bonded despite being a metal–non-metal compound, is an example of this:

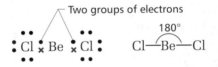

Carbon dioxide is similar, because there are again two groups of electrons. In this case each group has four electrons in a double bond between carbon and oxygen. The molecule is also linear.

2 Three groups of electrons

If there are three groups of electrons around the central atom, they will be 120° apart. The molecule is flat and the shape is called **trigonal planar**. Boron trifluoride is an example of this:

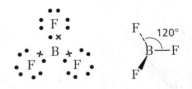

3 Four groups of electrons

If there are four groups of electrons, they are furthest apart when they are arranged so that they point to the four corners of a **tetrahedron** (a triangular based pyramid), see Figure 3.10.

Methane, CH_4, is an example. The angles here are 109.5°. This is a three-dimensional, not a flat arrangement, so the sum of the angles can be more than 360°.

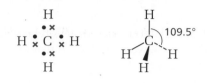

The ammonium ion is also shaped like a tetrahedron. It has four groups of electrons surrounding the nitrogen atom.

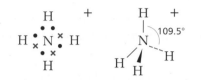

3.3.2 Molecules with lone pairs

Some molecules have unshared (lone) pairs of electrons. These are electrons that are not part of a bond. The lone pairs affect the shape of the molecule. Always draw the lone pairs in your dot-and-cross diagram, because otherwise you might overlook this. Water and ammonia are good examples of this effect.

Water, H₂O

Look at the 'dot-and-cross' diagram. There are four groups of electrons around the oxygen so the shape is based on a tetrahedron. However, two of the 'arms' of the tetrahedron are lone pairs that are not part of a bond. This results in a V-shaped or **angular** molecule.

The angles of a perfect tetrahedron, see Figure 3.10, are all 109.5° but lone pairs affect these angles. The *shared* pairs of electrons are attracted towards the oxygen nucleus and also the hydrogen nucleus. However, *lone* pairs are attracted only by the oxygen nucleus and are therefore pulled closer to it than the shared pairs. The lone pairs therefore repel more effectively than shared pairs, and 'squeeze' the hydrogens together, reducing the H–O–H angle. An approximate rule of thumb is 2° per lone pair. The actual bond angle in water is about 104.5°.

Ammonia, NH₃

Ammonia has four groups of electrons and one of the groups is a lone pair.

With four groups, the ammonia molecule, like the water molecule, has a shape based on a tetrahedron . In this case there are only three 'arms':

The lone pair squeezes the three shared pairs together and the bond angles are approximately 107°. The shape is described as **pyramidal**.

QUICK QUESTIONS

1 Draw 'dot-and-cross' diagrams of the molecules boron trifluoride and ammonia.

2 Use the diagrams you have drawn for question **1** to explain why the two molecules are different shapes.

3 Draw a 'dot-and-cross' diagram for the molecule silane, SiH_4 and describe its shape.

4 What is the H–Si–H angle in the silane molecule?

5 Explain why a water molecule is V-shaped rather than linear.

Electronegativity and the nature of bonds

The forces that hold atoms together are all about the attraction between positive and negative charges. In ionic bonding we have complete transfer of electrons from one atom to another. But, even in covalent bonds, the electrons shared by the atoms will not be evenly spread if one of the atoms is better at attracting electrons than the other. The ability of an atom to attract the electrons in a covalent bond towards itself is called **electronegativity**.

3.4.1 Electronegativity

Fluorine is better at attracting electrons than hydrogen. We say that fluorine is more electronegative than hydrogen.

Very electronegative atoms attract electrons because they have large shielded nuclear charges. The shielded nuclear charge is the nuclear charge after allowing for the shielding of the inner electrons, see Section 1.5.3. For example, fluorine has a shielded nuclear charge of +7 and hydrogen a shielded nuclear charge of +1.

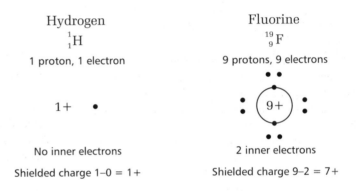

Hydrogen
$^{1}_{1}H$
1 proton, 1 electron

1+ •

No inner electrons

Shielded charge 1–0 = 1+

Fluorine
$^{19}_{9}F$
9 protons, 9 electrons

9+

2 inner electrons

Shielded charge 9–2 = 7+

As we go across a period in the Periodic Table, the nuclear charge increases from Group 1 to Group 7, while the shielding by the inner electrons remains the same, so the electronegativity of the element also increases, see Table 3.2

Table 3.2 *The nuclear charge increases across a period*

	Li	Be	B	C	N	O	F	
Nuclear charge	3	4	5	6	7	8	9	All have a shielding factor of 2 (2 electrons in the innner shell)
Shielded nuclear charge	1	2	3	4	5	6	7	

⎯Increasing electronegativity→

The size of the atom also affects electronegativity. The smaller the atom, the closer the nucleus is to the shared electrons and the greater its electronegativity. As we go up a group in the Periodic Table the shielded nuclear charge remains the same, but the outer electrons get closer to the nucleus, so electronegativity increases.

- The smaller the atom, the larger the electronegativity.
- The greater the shielded nuclear charge, the larger the electronegativity.

So, the most electronegative atoms are found at the top right hand corner of the Periodic Table (ignoring the inert gases which form few compounds). The most electronegative atoms are fluorine, oxygen and nitrogen followed by chlorine.

The Pauling scale is used to measure electronegativity. It runs from 0 to 4. The greater the number, the more electronegative the atom, see Table 3.3.

HINT

Think of electronegative atoms as having more 'electron pulling power'.

Table 3.3 *Trends in electronegativity*

Increasing electronegativity

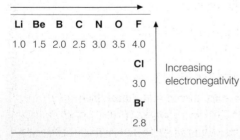

Li	Be	B	C	N	O	F
1.0	1.5	2.0	2.5	3.0	3.5	4.0

Cl
3.0

Br
2.8

Increasing electronegativity

- This adds to the strength of the bonding and is sometimes called 'delocalised' bonding.
- These 'spare' electrons are what make graphite conduct electricity (almost uniquely for a non-metal). An electron from the electrical circuit joins the pool at one end of a piece of graphite and a different electron leaves it at the other end – thus effectively allowing electrons to travel through the material.
- Carbon will only conduct along the hexagonal planes.

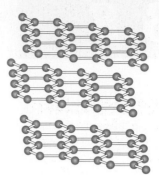

Fig 3.21 *The layers of hexagons in graphite*

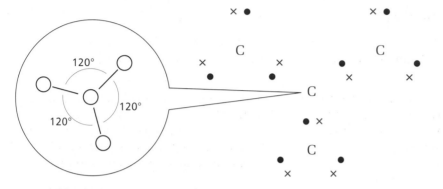

Fig 3.20 *A dot-and-cross diagram showing the three covalent bonds in graphite*

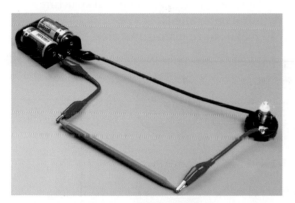

Graphite (pencil 'lead') conducts electricity

There is no covalent bonding *between* the layers. They are held together by the much weaker van der Waals' bonds, Figure 3.22. This weak bonding means that the layers can slide across one another making graphite soft and flaky. It is the 'lead' in pencils. The flakiness allows the graphite to be transferred from the pencil to the paper.

In fact other molecules such as oxygen can slide in between the layers of carbon and it is this that allows them to slide.

- Graphite is a soft material.
- It has a very high melting point and in fact it breaks down before it melts. This is because of the strong network of covalent bonds, which make it a giant structure.
- It conducts electricity along the planes of the hexagons.

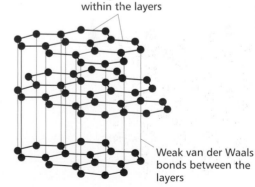

Strong covalent bonds within the layers

Weak van der Waals bonds between the layers

Fig 3.22 *van der Waals' forces between the layers of carbon atoms in graphite*

QUICK QUESTIONS

1 Carbon and graphite are allotropes. Explain the difference between allotropes and isotopes.

2 Why is graphite used as a lubricant?

3 Explain how graphite conducts electricity. How does it conduct differently from metals?

4 Why do both diamond and graphite have high melting points?

Metallic bonding

Metals are shiny elements made up of atoms that can easily lose up to three outer electrons, leaving positive metal ions.

For example, sodium, Na, 2,8,1 or $1s^2\,2s^2\,2p^6\,3s^1$ loses its one outer 3s electron; aluminium, Al, 2,8,3 or $1s^2\,2s^2\,2p^6\,3s^2\,3p^1$ loses its three outer electrons from the 3s and 3p orbitals.

3.8.1 Metallic bonding

The metal atoms in a metal element cannot transfer electrons (as happens in ionic bonding) unless there is a non-metal present. In an isolated piece of metal, they *pool* their outer electrons. A simple picture of metallic bonding is that metals consist of a lattice of positive ions existing in a freely moving 'sea' of outer electrons. The attraction of the ions for these electrons is what holds the structure together. Magnesium metal is shown in Figure 3.23.

- The number of electrons in the 'sea' depends on how many electrons have been lost by each metal atom.
- Think of this 'sea' as a giant orbital, spread over the whole metal structure, leaving the metal atoms as ions with full outer shells.
- The bonding spreads throughout so metals have giant structures.

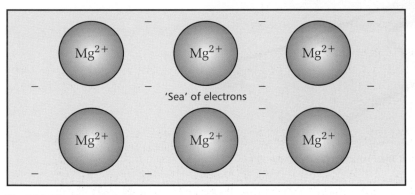

Fig 3.23 *The 'sea' of electrons in magnesium*

3.8.2 Properties of metals

Metals are good conductors of electricity and heat

The sea of moving electrons explains why metals are such good conductors of electricity. An electron from the negative terminal of the supply joins the electron pool at one end of a metal wire and at the same time a different electron leaves the wire at the positive terminal as in Figure 3.24.

Metals are also good conductors of heat. We say they have high thermal conductivities. The sea of electrons is also responsible for this.

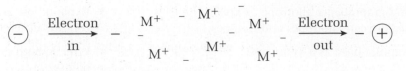

Fig 3.24 *The conduction of electricity by a metal*

Metals are strong

The sea of electrons also explains the strength of metals. The pool extends throughout the solid, so there are no individual bonds to break.

Metals are malleable and ductile

Metals are malleable (they can be beaten into shape) and ductile (they can be pulled into thin wires) After a small distortion, each metal ion is still in exactly the same environment as before so the new shape is retained, see Figure 3.25.

Contrast this with the brittleness of ionic compounds in Section 3.1.3.

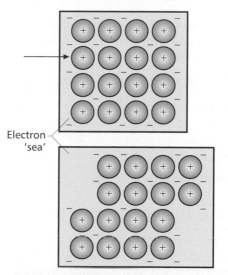

Electron 'sea'

Fig 3.25 The malleability and ductility of metals

Metals have high melting temperatures

Metals have high melting temperatures because they have giant structures. The sea of electrons acts as a bond that is spread throughout the atoms. This makes the atoms difficult to separate.

Both the strength and electrical conductivity of metals are made use of in electricity distribution

QUICK QUESTIONS

1 Give three physical differences between metals and non-metals.

2 Write the electron arrangement of a calcium atom, $_{20}^{40}Ca$.

3 How many electrons will a calcium atom lose to gain a full outer shell?

4 How many electrons will each calcium atom contribute to the pool of electrons that hold the metal atoms together?

3.9.1 Bonding

There are three extreme types of strong bonding that hold atoms together – ionic, covalent and metallic. All three involve the outer electrons of the atoms concerned:

- In covalent bonding the electrons are shared between non-metal atoms.
- In ionic bonding they are transferred from metal atoms to non-metal atoms.
- In metallic bonding they are pooled between metal atoms.

If we know what the compound is, we can usually tell the type of bonding from the types of atoms that it contains:

- metal atoms only – metallic bonding
- metal and non-metal – ionic bonding
- non-metal atoms only – covalent bonding.

The three types of bonding give rise to different properties.

Electrical conductivity

The property that best tells us what sort of bonding we have is electrical conductivity.

- Metallically bonded substances (metals and alloys) conduct electricity well in both the solid and liquid states. The current is carried by the mobile electrons in the sea or cloud that holds the metal atoms together, Topic 3.8, Figure 3.26.

Metal

Fig 3.26 *The conduction of electricity by a metal*

- Ionic compounds only conduct electricity well in the liquid state or when dissolved in water. They do *not* conduct when they are solid. The current is carried by the ions moving towards the electrode of opposite charge. The ions are free to move when the ionic compound is liquid or dissolved in water. In the solid state they are fixed rigidly in position in the ionic lattice, Figure 3.27.
- Covalently bonded compounds do not conduct electricity in either the solid or liquid state. This is because there are no charged particles to carry the current.

We can therefore decide what type of bonding a substance has by looking at how it conducts electricity, Table 3.4.

Table 3.4 *The pattern of electrical conductivity tells us about the type of bonding*

Type of bonding	Electrical conductivity		
	Solid	Liquid	Aqueous solution
Metallic	✓	✓	Does not dissolve
Ionic	✗	✓	✓
Covalent	✗	✗	✗

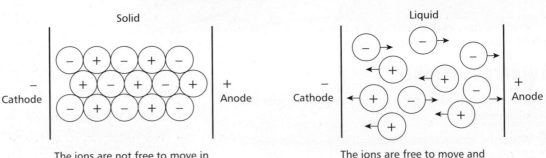

The ions are not free to move in the solid state

The ions are free to move and the compound conducts electricity

Figure 3.27 *Ionic liquids conduct electricity, but the solids do not*

3.9.2 Structure

Structure describes the arrangement in which atoms are held together in space. There are two extreme types – **molecular** and **giant**.

- A **molecular structure** is composed of molecules – small groups of atoms strongly held together by covalent bonding. The bonds *between* molecules are much weaker (usually over 100 times weaker than a covalent bond) and are called intermolecular forces. Examples of molecules include, Cl_2, H_2O, H_2SO_4 and NH_3.
- In a giant structure, the atoms are in a regularly repeating arrangement usually in three dimensions, often called a lattice. This lattice may be held together by any of the three types of strong bond – ionic, covalent or metallic.

Melting and boiling points

The property that best tells us what sort of structure a substance has is the melting (or boiling) point:

- Molecular compounds have low melting (and boiling) points.
- Giant structures have high melting (and boiling) points.

HINT

Any substance with a high melting point also has a high boiling point.

Table 3.5 *Summary of properties of substances with covalent, ionic and metallic bonding*

	Melting temperature T_m	Structure	Bond	Electrical conductivity		
				Solid	Liquid	Aqueous solution
	High	Giant	Ionic	No	Yes	Yes
	High	Giant	Covalent	No	No	No
	Low	Molecular	Covalent	No	No	No
	High	Giant	Metallic	Yes	Yes	– (does not dissolve)

We know that if a compound has a low melting (and boiling) point, it has a molecular structure. We know that all molecular compounds are covalently bonded. So all compounds with low melting (and boiling) points must have covalent bonding.

But, take care – a compound with covalent bonding may have either a giant or a molecular structure and therefore may have either a high or low melting (and boiling) point.

Intermolecular forces

When we melt and boil molecular compounds, we are breaking the intermolecular forces *between* the molecules, not the covalent bonds *within* them. So, the strength of the intermolecular forces determines the melting (and boiling) points.

There are three types of intermolecular force – in order of increasing strength:

- van der Waals, which act between all atoms;
- dipole–dipole forces, which act between molecules with permanent dipoles: $X^{\delta+}-Y^{\delta-}$;
- hydrogen bonds, which act between highly electronegative atoms (O, N or F) and hydrogen atoms covalently bonded to highly electronegative atoms.

Table 3.5 is a summary of the different properties of substances with covalent, ionic and metallic bonding

REMEMBER

- Melting points tell you about structure – giant structures have high melting points.
- The pattern of conductivity tells you about bonding.

QUICK QUESTIONS

The table below gives some information about four substances

Substance	Melting point/°C	Boiling point/°C	Electrical conductivity	
			As solid	As liquid
A	1083	2567	Good	Good
B	−182	−164	Poor	Poor
C	1723	2230	Poor	Good
D	993	1695	Poor	Poor

1 Which substances have giant structures?

2 Which substance is a gas?

3 Which substance is a metal?

4 Which substances are covalently bonded?

5 Which substance has ionic bonding?

1 Sulphur and sulphur compounds are common in the environment.

   a A sample of sulphur from a volcano contained 88.0% by mass of ^{32}S and 12.0% by mass of ^{34}S.

      (i) Complete the table below to show the atomic structure of each isotope of sulphur.

Isotope	Number of		
	protons	neutrons	electrons
^{32}S			
^{34}S			[2]

      (ii) Define the term *relative atomic mass*. [3]
      (iii) Calculate the relative atomic mass of the volcanic sulphur. Your answer should be given to three significant figures. [2]

   b Rotten eggs smell of hydrogen sulphide, H_2S, which is a poisonous gas.

      A *dot-and-cross* diagram of a hydrogen sulphide molecule is shown below; it shows outer electron shells only.

      H S H

      Draw a diagram to show the likely shape and bond angle of a hydrogen sulphide molecule. Explain how you have made your choice. [3]

   c Every year, between 20 and 50 million tonnes of sulphur are released into the atmosphere from the oceans in the form of DMS, a compound of carbon, hydrogen and sulphur. DMS causes the bracing feeling by the sea.

      DMS has the percentage composition by mass of C: 38.6%; H: 9.7%; S: 51.7%.

      Calculate the empirical formula of DMS. [2]

      [Total: 12]

      OCR, 4 Jun 2001

2 Lithium was discovered in 1817 by the Swedish chemist Arfvedson. Lithium exists naturally as a mixture of isotopes.

   a Explain the term *isotopes*. [1]

   b Which isotope is used as the standard against which relative atomic masses are measured? [1]

   c The mass spectrum below shows the isotopes present in a sample of lithium.

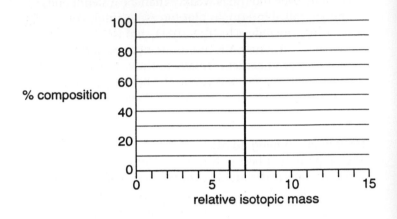

      (i) Use this mass spectrum to help you complete the table below for each lithium isotope in the sample.

Isotope	Percentage composition	Number of	
		protons	neutrons
^6Li			
^7Li			[3]

      (ii) Calculate the relative atomic mass of this lithium sample. Your answer should be given to three significant figures. [2]

   d The species responsible for the peaks in this mass spectrum are lithium ions, produced and separated in a mass spectrometer.

      (i) How are the electrons removed from lithium ions in a mass spectrometer? [1]
      (ii) How does a mass spectrometer separate the ions? [1]

   e The first ionisation energy of lithium is $+520\,kJ\,mol^{-1}$.

      (i) Define the term *first ionisation energy*. [3]
      (ii) The first ionisation energy of sodium is $+496\,kJ\,mol^{-1}$.

      Explain why the first ionisation energy of sodium is less than that of lithium. Your answer should compare the atomic structures of each element. [3]

      [Total: 15]

      OCR, 12 Jan 2001

3 Hydrogen chloride, HCl is a colourless gas which dissolves very readily in water forming hydrochloric acid.

[1 mol of gas molecules occupy 24.0 dm³ at room temperature and pressure (rtp).]

a At rtp 1.00 dm³ of water dissolved 432 dm³ of hydrogen chloride gas.

   (i) How many moles of hydrogen chloride dissolved in the water? [1]

   (ii) The hydrochloric acid formed has a volume of 1.40 dm³. What is the concentration in mol dm⁻³, of the hydrochloric acid? [1]

b In solution, the molecules of hydrogen chloride ionise.

$$HCl(aq) \rightarrow H^+(aq) + Cl^-(aq)$$

Describe a simple test to confirm the presence of chloride ions. [2]

c Hydrochloric acid reacts with magnesium oxide, MgO, and magnesium carbonate, MgCO₃.

For each reaction, state what you would see and write a balanced equation:

   (i) MgO [2]
   (ii) MgCO₃ [2]

[Total: 8]

OCR, 4 Jun 2001

4 Electrons are arranged in energy levels. The diagram below for the 7 electrons in a nitrogen atom is incomplete. It shows two electrons in the 1s level.

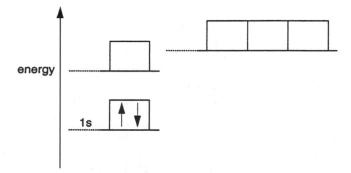

a Complete the diagram for the 7 electrons in a nitrogen atom by:

   (i) adding labels for the other sub-shell levels, [1]
   (ii) showing how the electrons are arranged. [2]

b Magnesium reacts with nitrogen forming magnesium nitride, which is an ionic compound.

   (i) Complete the electronic configuration for the 12 electrons in a magnesium atom. [1]
   (ii) What is the charge on each ion in magnesium nitride? [2]
   (iii) Complete the electronic configuration of each **ion** in magnesium nitride. [2]
   (iv) Deduce the formula of magnesium nitride. [1]

c Magnesium reacts with carbon dioxide forming a mixture of magnesium oxide, MgO, and carbon.

   (i) Write an equation, with state symbols, for this reaction. [2]
   (ii) When water is added to the mixture containing magnesium oxide, some of the magnesium oxide reacts to form a solution of magnesium hydroxide:

$$MgO(s) + H_2O(l) \rightarrow Mg(OH)_2(aq)$$

Predict the pH of this solution. [1]

[Total: 12]

OCR, 12 Jan 2001

5 Water is the most abundant compound on Earth. Much of the chemistry of water is influenced by its polarity and its ability to form hydrogen bonds.

a Polarity can be explained in terms of electronegativity.

   (i) Explain the term *electronegativity*. [2]
   (ii) Why are water molecules polar? [1]

b The polarity of water molecules results in the formation of hydrogen bonds.

   (i) Draw a diagram to show hydrogen bonding between two molecules of water. Your diagram must include dipoles and lone pairs of electrons. [4]
   (ii) State the bond angle in a water molecule. [1]

c State and explain **two** properties of **ice** that are a direct result of hydrogen bonding. [4]

[Total: 12]

OCR, 12 Jan 2001

6 The boiling points of water, hydrogen chloride and argon are shown in the table below.

Substance	H₂O	HCl	Ar
Boiling point/°C	100	−85	−186
Total number of electrons	10	18	18

a H₂O, HCl and Ar all have instantaneous dipoles (van der Waals' forces).

Outline how van der Waals' forces arise between molecules. [2]

b Liquid H₂O has additional intermolecular forces.

   (i) What are these forces? [1]
   (ii) Explain, with the aid of a diagram, how these forces arise between molecules of H₂O(l). [5]

c Liquid HCl also has additional intermolecular forces. What are these forces? [1]

d Explain the variation in boiling points shown in the table. [2]

[Total: 11]

OCR, 4 Jun 2001

45

7 Compare and explain the electrical conductivity of sodium chloride, diamond and graphite. In your answer, you should consider the structure and bonding of each of these materials.

In this question, 2 marks are available for the quality of written communication.

[Total: 13]

OCR, 4 Jun 2001

8 a State what is meant by:

(i) an *ionic bond*, [1]

(ii) a *covalent bond*. [2]

b Draw 'dot-and-cross' diagrams to show the bonding in sodium chloride and hydrogen chloride. You should show outer electron shells only. [3]

c (i) State what is meant by an *orbital*. [1]

(ii) Draw diagrams to show the shape of an s orbital and of a p orbital. [2]

(iii) Complete the table below to show how many electrons **completely** fill each of the following:

	Number of electrons
a p **orbital**	
a d **sub-shell**	
the third **shell** ($n = 3$)	

[3]

[Total: 12]

OCR, 4 Jun 2001

9 The table below shows the boiling points of the elements sodium to chlorine in Period 3 of the Periodic Table.

Element	Na	Mg	Al	Si	P	S	Cl
Boiling point/°C	883	1107	2467	2355	280	445	−35
Bonding							
Structure							

a (i) Complete the *bonding* row of the table using:
- **M** for *metallic* bonding,
- **C** for *covalent* bonding. [1]

(ii) Complete the *structure* row of the table using:
- **S** for *simple molecular structure*,
- **G** for a *giant structure*. [1]

b State what is meant by *metallic bonding*. You should draw a diagram as part of your answer. [3]

c Explain, in terms of their structure and bonding, why the boiling point of:

(i) phosphorus is much **lower** than that of silicon [2]

(ii) aluminium is much **higher** than that of magnesium. [2]

[Total: 9]

OCR, 4 Jun 2001

10 Gallium, atomic number 31, exists naturally as a mixture of its isotopes, ^{69}Ga and ^{71}Ga.

a Complete the table below to show the atomic structure of each isotope of gallium.

Isotope	Number of		
	protons	neutrons	electrons
^{69}Ga			
^{71}Ga			

[2]

b A mass spectrometer can be used to identify the isotopes in a sample of an element. The diagram below shows a mass spectrometer.

Complete the diagram by adding the names of the processes that take place in each of the four labelled regions.

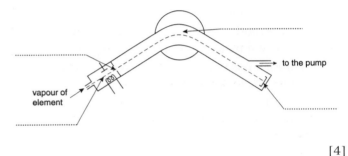

[4]

c A sample of gallium was analysed in a mass spectrometer to produce the mass spectrum below. The relative atomic mass of gallium can be calculated from this mass spectrum.

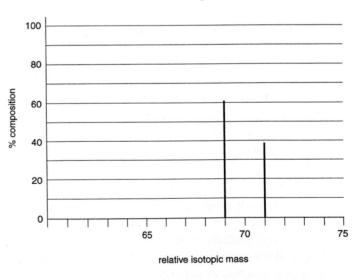

(i) Define the term *relative atomic mass*. [3]

(ii) Estimate the percentage composition of each isotope present in the sample. [1]

(iii) Calculate the relative atomic mass of this sample of gallium. Your answer should be given to three significant figures. [2]

[Total: 12]

OCR, 17 Jan 2003

11 Calcium carbonate is added to an excess of hydrochloric acid:

$$CaCO_3(s) + 2HCl(aq) \rightarrow CaCl_2(aq) + CO_2(g) + H_2O(l)$$

a Deduce **two** observations that you would expect to see during this reaction. [2]

b In this experiment, 0.040 g $CaCO_3$ is added to 25 cm^3 of 0.050 mol dm^{-3} HCl.

   (i) Explain what is meant by 0.050 mol dm^{-3} HCl. [2]

   (ii) Calculate how many moles of $CaCO_3$ were used in this experiment. [2]

   (iii) Calculate how many moles of HCl are required to react with this amount of $CaCO_3$. [1]

   (iv) Hence show that the HCl is in excess. [1]

c State **one** large-scale use of a named Group 2 compound that is being used to reduce acidity. [1]

[Total: 9]

OCR, 12 Jan 2001

12 Well over 2 000 000 tonnes of sulphuric acid, H_2SO_4, are produced in the UK each year. This is used in the manufacture of many important materials such as paints, fertilisers, detergents, plastics, dyestuffs and fibres.

The sulphuric acid is prepared from sulphur in a 3 stage process.

Stage 1:

   The sulphur is burnt in oxygen to produce sulphur dioxide:

   $$S + O_2 \rightarrow SO_2$$

Stage 2:

   The sulphur dioxide reacts with more oxygen using a catalyst to form sulphur trioxide:

   $$2SO_2 + O_2 \rightarrow 2SO_3$$

Stage 3:

   The sulphur trioxide is dissolved in concentrated sulphuric acid to form 'oleum', $H_2S_2O_7$, which is then diluted in water to produce sulphuric acid.

a 100 tonnes of sulphur dioxide were reacted with oxygen in stage 2.

   Assuming that the reaction was complete, calculate:

   (i) how many moles of sulphur dioxide were reacted; M_r: SO_2, 64.1. (1 tonne = 1×10^6 g) [1]

   (ii) the mass of sulphur trioxide that formed: M_r: SO_3, 80.1. [1]

b Construct a balanced equation for the formation of sulphuric acid from oleum. [1]

c The concentration of the sulphuric acid can be checked by titration. A sample of this sulphuric acid was analysed as follows.

   • 10.0 cm^3 of sulphuric acid was diluted with water to make 1.00 dm^3 of solution.

   • The diluted sulphuric acid was then titrated with aqueous sodium hydroxide, NaOH:

   $$H_2SO_4(aq) + 2NaOH(aq) \rightarrow Na_2SO_4(aq) + 2H_2O(l)$$

   • In the titration, 25.0 cm^3 of 0.100 mol dm^{-3} aqueous sodium hydroxide required 20.0 cm^3 of the **diluted** sulphuric acid for neutralisaton.

   (i) Calculate how many moles of NaOH were used. [1]

   (ii) Calculate the concentration, in mol dm^{-3}, of the **diluted** sulphuric acid, H_2SO_4. [2]

   (iii) Calculate the concentration, in mol dm^{-3}, of the original sulphuric acid sent for analysis. [1]

[Total: 7]

OCR, 12 Jan 2001

13 Iridium, atomic number 77, is a very dense material. Scientists believe that meteorites have deposited virtually all the iridium present on Earth. A fragment of a meteorite was analysed using a mass spectrometer and a section of the mass spectrum showing the isotopes present in iridium is shown below.

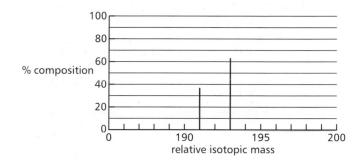

a Explain the term *isotopes*. [1]

b Use the mass spectrometer to help you complete the table below for each iridium isotope in the meteorite.

Isotope	Percentage composition	Number of protons	neutrons
^{191}Ir			
^{193}Ir			

[3]

c (i) Define the term *relative atomic mass*. [3]

   (ii) Calculate the relative atomic mass of the iridium in this meteorite. Give your answer to one decimal place. [2]

d Iridium reacts with fluorine to form a yellow solid **Y** with the percentage composition by mass: Ir, 62.75%; F, 37.25%.

   The empirical formula of **Y** can be calculated from this information.

   (i) Define the term *empirical formula*. [1]

   (ii) Calculate the empirical formula of **Y**. [2]

   (iii) Write a balanced equation for the reaction between iridium and fluorine. [1]

[Total: 13]

OCR, 29 May 2002

4 *The Periodic Table; introduction*

4.1 The Periodic Table

The Periodic Table is a list of all the elements in order of increasing atomic number. We can predict the properties of an element just from its position in the table. We can use it to explain the similarities of certain elements and the trends in their properties, in terms of their electronic structures.

4.1.1 The structure of the Periodic Table

The Periodic Table has been written in many forms including pyramids and spirals. The one shown at the end of the book is the most usual and useful one. Some areas of the Periodic Table are given names. These are shown in Figure 4.1.

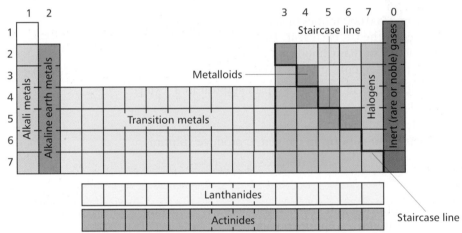

Fig 4.1 *Named areas of the Periodic Table*

4.1.2 The staircase line

The 'staircase' line, in Figure 4.1 divides metals (on its left) from non-metals (on its right). Elements that touch this line, such as silicon, have a combination of metallic and non-metallic properties. They are called **metalloids** or **semi-metals**. Silicon, for example, is a non-metal but it looks quite shiny and conducts electricity, although not as well as a metal.

4.1.3 The full form of the Periodic Table

The Periodic Table should really look like Figure 4.2. The conventional way of drawing it simply saves paper.

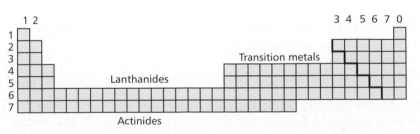

Fig 4.2 *The full form of the Periodic Table*

HINT

A copy of the Periodic Table can be found on p.169.

4.1.4 The s-, p-, d- and f-block areas of the Periodic Table

Figure 4.3 shows the elements described in terms of their electronic structures.

Areas of the table are labelled s-block, p-block, d-block and f-block.

- All the elements that have their outer electrons in s-orbitals are in the s-block, e.g. sodium, Na ($1s^2\ 2s^2\ 2p^6\ 3s^1$).
- All the elements that have their outer electrons in p-orbitals, e.g. carbon, C ($1s^2\ 2s^2\ 2p^2$) are called p-block, and so on.

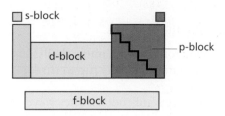

Fig 4.3 *The s-, p-, d- and f-block areas of the Periodic Table*

4.1.5 Groups

A **group** is a vertical column of elements. The elements in the same group form a chemical 'family' – they have similar properties. Elements in the same group have the same number of outer electrons. The groups were traditionally numbered I–VII in Roman numerals plus zero for the noble gases, missing out the transition elements. It is now common to number them in ordinary numbers.

4.1.6 Periods

Horizontal rows of elements are called **periods**. The periods are numbered starting from Period 1, which contains only hydrogen and helium. Period 2 contains the elements lithium to neon, and so on. There are trends in physical properties and chemical behaviour as we go across a period.

4.1.7 The placing of hydrogen and helium

The positions of hydrogen and helium vary in different versions of the Table.

Helium is usually placed above the inert gases (Group 0) because of its properties. But, it is not a p-block element; its electronic structure is $1s^2$. This makes it an s-block element.

Hydrogen is placed above Group 1 but separated from it. It usually forms singly charged H^+ ions like the Group 1 elements, but is not otherwise similar to them since they are all reactive metals and hydrogen is a gas. It can also form H^- ions and in some versions of the Periodic Table it is placed above the halogens.

QUICK QUESTIONS

1 From the elements, Br, Cl, Fe, K, Cs, Sb:
   a Pick out two elements
      (i) in the same period,
      (ii) in the same group,
      (iii) that are non-metals.

   b Pick out one element
      (i) that is a semi-metal,
      (ii) that is in the s-block.

2 From the elements Tl, Ge, Xe, Sr:
   a Pick out a noble gas,
   b The element described by Group 4, Period 4.

Periodicity

The Periodic Table reveals patterns in the properties of elements. For example, every time we go across a period we go from metals to non-metals. This is an example of **periodicity**. The word 'periodic' means recurring regularly.

4.2.1 Periodicity and properties

Periodicity is explained by the electron structures of the elements.

- Group 1, 2 and 3 are metals, with up to three electrons in their outer shells. They have giant structures. They give away their outer electrons (up to three) to form ionic compounds.
- Group 4, with four electrons in their outer shells, are semi-metals. They have giant structures. They only form covalent compounds.
- Groups 5 to 7 are non-metals with five, six or seven electrons in their outer shells. They either accept electrons (up to three) to form ionic compounds, or share their outer electrons to form covalent compounds.
- Group 0 are the noble gases – atoms that have full outer shells and are unreactive.

Table 4.1 shows some trends across Period 3. Similar trends are found in other periods.

Table 4.1 *Some trends across Period 3*

Group	1	2	3	4	5	6	7	0
Element	Sodium	Magnesium	Aluminium	Silicon	Phosphorus	Sulphur	Chlorine	Argon
Electron arrangement	[Ne] $3s^1$	[Ne] $3s^2$	[Ne] $3s^2 3p^1$	[Ne] $3s^2 3p^2$	[Ne] $3s^2 3p^3$	[Ne] $3s^2 3p^4$	[Ne] $3s^2 3p^5$	[Ne] $3s^2 3p^6$
Ion	Na^+	Mg^{2+}	Al^{3+}	None	P^{3-}	S^{2-}	Cl^-	None
	s-block			p-block				
	Metals less reactive ⟶			Semi-metal	Non-metals more reactive ⟶			Noble gas
Conductivity	Good			Slight	Poor			
Structure of element	Giant metallic			Giant molecular	Molecular			Atomic
Melting point, T_m/K	371	922	933	1683	317 (white)	392 (monoclinic)	172	84
Boiling point, T_b/K	1156	1380	2740	2628	553 (white)	718 (monoclinic)	238	87

4.2.2 Trends in electrical conductivity

The pattern is good conductivity on the left and poor conductivity on the right. This trend is due to the type of bonding. Metals (on the left) conduct well; the covalently bonded non-metals (on the right) do not conduct. Silicon, a semi-metal, conducts, but not as well as a metal.

4.2.3 Trends in melting and boiling temperature

There is a clear break in the middle of the table between elements with high melting points (on the left) and those with low melting points (on the right). These trends are because of the structure:

- Giant structures (found on the left) have high melting temperatures and boiling temperatures.

- Molecular or atomic structures (found on the right) have low melting temperatures and boiling temperatures.

4.2.4 Trends in reactivity

Metals

Sodium in Group 1 is the most reactive metal and the reactivity decreases as we move towards aluminium in Group 3. This is because as we move from Group 1 to Group 3, more electrons have to be lost to form a positive ion with a full outer shell of electrons.

- The elements become *less* reactive as we move from left to right.

Non-metals

The trend is less clear because some non-metal compounds are ionic and some are covalent. When they form ions the atoms are accepting electrons. This becomes easier as we move from phosphorus to chlorine. One reason for this is that phosphorus needs three electrons to gain a full outer shell whereas chlorine needs only one. Another is that chlorine has a higher shielded nuclear charge than phosphorus.

- The elements become *more* reactive as we move from left to right.

Elements have a wide variety of appearance and properties: gold, mercury and carbon (in the form of diamond)

QUICK QUESTIONS

1. For each of the following properties, say how it changes as we go from left to right across a period. Choose from 'increases', 'decreases' or 'no trend':
   a electrical conductivity,
   b melting point,
   c reactivity of metals.

2. Choose from 'left', 'right' or 'middle' to answer the following. Whereabouts in a period do we find:
   a elements that give away electrons;
   b elements that form covalent bonds only;
   c elements that exist as unbonded atoms?

Periodicity of atomic properties

Some key properties of atoms, such as size and ionisation energy are periodic.

4.3.1 Atomic radii

These tell us about the size of an atom. We cannot measure the radius of an isolated atom so we use half the distance between the centres of a pair of atoms. This differs depending on the type of bond between the atoms – covalent, metallic, van der Waals' etc. The covalent radius is most commonly used as a measure of the size of the atom.

(Even metals can form covalent molecules in the gas phase. Since noble gases do not bond covalently with one another, they do not have covalent radii and so they are often left out of comparisons of atomic sizes.)

Figure 4.4 is a plot of covalent radius against atomic number.

The graph shows:

- Atomic radius is a periodic property, because it decreases across each period and there is a jump when we start the next period.
- Atoms get larger as we go down any group.

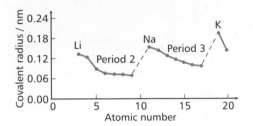

Fig 4.4 *The periodicity of covalent radii. The noble gases are not included as they do not form covalent bonds with one another*

4.3.2 Why the radii of atoms decrease across a period

We can explain this trend by looking at the electronic structures of the elements in a period, for example, sodium to chlorine, Period 3, as shown in Figure 4.5.

As we move from sodium to chlorine we are adding protons to the nucleus and electrons to the outer shell – the third shell. The charge on the nucleus increases from 11+ to 17+ (or 1+ to 7+ after allowing for the shielding of the inner shells, which remains the same). This increased charge pulls the electrons in closer to the nucleus. So the size of the atom *decreases* as we go across the period.

Atom	Na	Mg	Al	Si	P 2,8,5	S 2,8,6	Cl 2,8,7
Size of atom	2,8,1	2,8,2	2,8,3	2,8,4			
Atomic (covalent) radius /nm	0.156	0.136	0.125	0.117	0.110	0.104	0.099
Nuclear charge	11+	12+	13+	14+	15+	16+	17+
Shielded nuclear charge	1+	2+	3+	4+	5+	6+	7+

Fig 4.5 *The electronic arrangements in Period 3 showing the nuclear charge, and the shielded nuclear charge in red. Atomic radii are measured in nanometres (nm). 1 nm = 10^{-9} m*

4.3.3 Why the radii of atoms increase down a group

As we go down a Group 1 in the Periodic Table, each element has one extra complete shell of electrons than the one before. So, for example, the outer electron in potassium is in shell 4, while that in sodium is in shell 3. Both outer electrons experience the same shielded nuclear charge of 1+.

4.3.4 First ionisation energy

The first ionisation energy is the energy required to convert a mole of isolated gaseous atoms into a mole of singly positively charged gaseous ions, i.e. to remove one electron from each atom:

$$E(g) \rightarrow E^+(g) + e^-$$ where E stands for any element.

The first ionisation energies have periodic patterns. These are shown in Figure 4.6.

- The first ionisation energy increases across a period – alkali metals like sodium, Na, and lithium, Li, have the lowest values and the inert gases (helium, He, neon, Ne, and argon, Ar) have the highest values.
- The first ionisation energy decreases as we go down any group. Those for Group 1 and Group 0 are shown dotted in red on the graph.

We can explain these patterns by looking at electronic structures.

4.3.5 Why the first ionisation energy increases across a period

As we go along a period, the nuclear charge goes up, while the shielding effect of the inner electrons remains the same. Electrons are being added to the same shell (the same *distance* from the nucleus), see Figure 4.7. So it gets increasingly difficult to remove an electron. In sodium, for example, the outer electron feels a shielded nuclear charge of 1+ while in argon, each outer electron feels a shielded nuclear charge of 8+ and so argon has a higher ionisation energy.

4.3.6 Why the first ionisation energy decreases as we go down any group

All elements in the same group have the same shielded nuclear charge (which is the same as the group number). So, for example, the outer electron of all the elements in Group 1 experiences a shielded nuclear charge of 1+. All the elements in Group 2 experience a shielded charge of 2+ and so on.

The outer electrons get easier to remove as we go down a group *because they are further away* from the nucleus, see Figure 4.8.

4.3.7 Why there is a drop in ionisation energy from one period to the next

When we move from neon with electron arrangement 2,8 to sodium, 2,8,1 there is a sharp drop in the ionisation energy. This is because we start a new shell and so:

- The nuclear charge experienced by the outer electron is shielded by 10 (2 + 8) inner electrons and it becomes much easier to remove the outer electron.
- The outer electron is in shell 3 rather than shell 2 and is thus already further away from the nucleus.

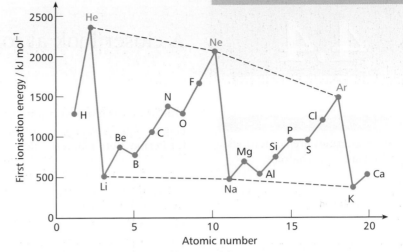

Fig 4.6 *The periodicity of first ionisation energies*

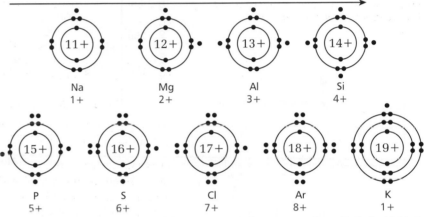

Fig 4.7 *The electronic structures of the elements sodium to potassium with their shielded nuclear charges in red*

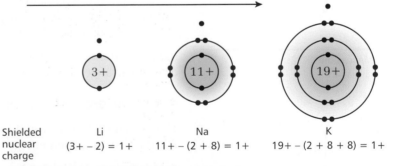

Fig 4.8 *The electronic structures of Group 1 elements*

QUICK QUESTIONS

1 What happens to the size of atoms as we go from left to right across a period ('increase', 'decrease' or 'no change')?

2 What happens to the first ionisation energy as we go from left to right across a period ('increase', 'decrease' or 'no change')?

3 What is the shielded charge felt by the outer electrons of all elements in Group 3?

4 What happens to the nuclear charge of the atoms as we go left to right across a period ('increase', 'decrease' or 'no change')?

5 Why do the noble gases have the highest first ionisation energy of all the elements in their period?

A closer look at ionisation energies

The graph of first ionisation energy against atomic number across a period (Figure 4.6, Topic 4.3) is not smooth. Figure 4.9 shows a section of the same plot for Period 3 on a larger scale.

Fig 4.9 *A graph of first ionisation energy against atomic number for the elements of Period 3*

It shows that:

- The first ionisation energy actually drops between Group 2 and Group 3, so that aluminium has a lower ionisation energy than magnesium.
- The ionisation energy drops again slightly between Group 5 (phosphorus) and Group 6 (sulphur).

Similar patterns occur in other periods. We can explain these if we look at the electron arrangements of the elements, covered in Topic 1.4.

4.4.1 The drop in first ionisation energy between Groups 2 and 3

This is to do with the orbital from which the first electron is removed. For the first ionisation energy:

- Magnesium, $1s^2 \, 2s^2 \, 2p^6 \, 3s^2$, loses a 3s electron.
- Aluminium, $1s^2 \, 2s^2 \, 2p^6 \, 3s^2 \, 3p^1$, loses the 3p electron.

The electron in the p sub-shell is already in a higher energy level than the s-electron, so it takes less energy to remove, Figure 4.10.

4.4.2 The drop in first ionisation energy between Groups 5 and 6

This is about the pairing of electrons. An electron in a pair will be easier to remove that one in an orbital on its own, because it is already being repelled by the other electron.

- Phosphorus, $1s^2 \, 2s^2 \, 2p^6 \, 3s^2 \, 3p^3$, has no paired electrons, because each p-electron is in a different sub-shell.
- Sulphur $1s^2 \, 2s^2 \, 2p^6 \, 3s^2 \, 3p^4$, has two of its p-electrons paired, and one of these will be easier to remove than an unpaired one, Figure 4.11.

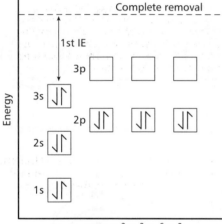

Magnesium $1s^2 \, 2s^2 \, 2p^6 \, 3s^2$

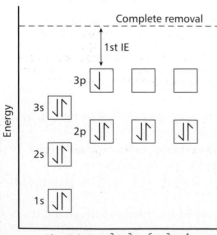

Aluminium $1s^2 \, 2s^2 \, 2p^6 \, 3s^2 \, 3p^1$

Fig 4.10 *The first ionisation energies of magnesium and of aluminium*

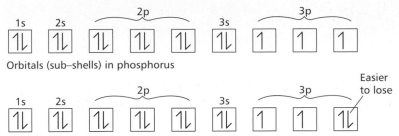

Orbitals (sub–shells) in phosphorus

Orbitals (sub–shells) in sulphur

Figure 4.11 *Electron arrangements of phosphorus and sulphur*

4.4.3 Successive ionisation energies

We have seen in Section 1.5.2 that if we remove the electrons from an atom one at a time, each one is harder to remove than the one before. Figure 4.12 is a graph of ionisation energy against number of electrons removed for sodium, electron arrangement 2,8,1.

We can see that there is a sharp increase in ionisation energy between the first and second electrons. This is followed by a gradual increase over the next eight electrons and then another jump before the final two electrons. Sodium, in Group 1 of the Periodic Table, has one electron in its outer shell (the easiest one to remove), eight in the next shell and two (very hard to remove) in the innermost shell.

Figure 4.13 is a graph of successive ionisation energies against number of electrons removed for aluminium, electron arrangement 2,8,3.

It shows three electrons that are relatively easy to remove – those in the outer shell and then a similar pattern to that for sodium.

If we plotted a graph for chlorine, the first seven electrons would be relatively easier to remove than the next eight.

So, the number of electrons that are relatively easy to remove tells us the group number in the Periodic Table. For example, the values of 906, 1763, 14 855 and 21 013 kJ mol^{-1} for the first five ionisation energies of an element, tell us that the element is in Group 2, because the big jump occurs after two electrons have been removed.

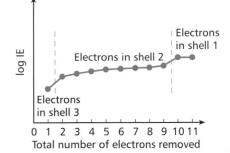

Fig 4.12 *Graph of successive ionisation energies against number of electrons removed for sodium. Note that the log of the ionisation energies (vertical scale) is plotted, rather than the ionisation energies, in order to fit the large range of values onto the scale*

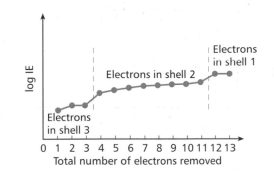

Fig 4.13 *Graph of successive ionisation energies against number of electrons removed for aluminium. Note that the log of the ionisation energies (vertical scale) is plotted, rather than the ionisation energies, in order to fit the large range of values onto the scale*

QUICK QUESTIONS

1 Write the electron arrangement in the form 1s^2, etc, for
  a beryllium, **b** boron.

2 If one electron is lost, what shell does it come from for
  a a beryllium atom, **b** a boron atom?

3 Why is the first ionisation energy of boron less than that of beryllium?

4 An element X has the following values for successive ionisation enthalpies:

  1093, 2359, 4627, 6229, 37 838, 47 285.

  a What group in the Periodic Table is it in?

  b Explain your answer to **a**.

5 The Periodic Table: Group 2

5.1 Redox reactions

Many of the reactions of Group 2 (and Group 7) elements and their compounds are redox reactions.

5.1.1 Oxidation and reduction

The word '**redox**' is short for reduction–oxidation. **Oxidation** was first used for reactions in which oxygen was added. For example in the reaction:

$$Mg(s) + \tfrac{1}{2}O_2(g) \rightarrow MgO(s)$$

magnesium has been oxidised to magnesium oxide. Oxygen is called an **oxidising agent. Reduction** described a reaction is in which oxygen was removed. For example in the reaction:

$$CuO(s) + H_2(g) \rightarrow Cu(s) + H_2O(l)$$

copper has been reduced and hydrogen is the **reducing agent.**

Hydrogen was often used to remove oxygen, so, the removal of hydrogen was called an oxidation and the addition of hydrogen was called a reduction. In the reaction:

$$Cl_2(g) + H_2(g) \rightarrow 2HCl(g)$$

chlorine is reduced, because hydrogen is added to it.

5.1.2 Gaining and losing electrons: redox reactions

If we describe what happens to the electrons in the above reactions, we get a much more general picture. When something is oxidised it loses electrons and when something is reduced it gains electrons.

loss of 2 electrons

$$Mg(s) + \tfrac{1}{2}O_2(g) \rightarrow (Mg^{2+} + O^{2-})(s) \qquad \text{Magnesium is oxidised.}$$

$$(Cu^{2+} + O^{2-})(s) + H_2(g) \rightarrow Cu(s) + H_2O(l) \qquad \text{Copper ions are reduced.}$$

gain of 2 electrons

The definition of oxidation and reduction we now use is:

Oxidation Is Loss of electrons. Reduction Is Gain of electrons.

The phrase **OIL RIG** makes the definition of oxidation and reduction easy to remember.

By this definition magnesium is oxidised by *anything* that removes electrons from it (not just oxygen) leaving a positive ion. For example, chlorine oxidises magnesium:

$$Mg(s) + Cl_2(g) \rightarrow (Mg^{2+} + 2Cl^-)(s)$$

Look at the chlorine. It has been reduced because it has gained electrons.

$$Mg(s) + Cl_2(g) \rightarrow (Mg^{2+} + 2Cl^-)(s)$$

reduction
gain of electrons

loss of electrons
oxidation

In a chemical reaction, if one species is oxidised (loses electrons), another *must* be reduced (gains them).

Redox reactions are sometimes called electron transfer reactions.

5.1.3 Oxidation numbers

We use **oxidation numbers** to see what has been oxidised and what reduced in a redox reaction. The abbreviation for oxidation number is Ox, though ON is also used. Oxidation numbers are also called **oxidation states.**

Each element in a compound is given an oxidation number. This tells us how many electrons it has lost or gained compared with the element in its uncombined state.

- Every element in its uncombined state has an oxidation number of zero.
- A positive number shows that the element has lost electrons and has therefore been oxidised.
- A negative number shows that the element has gained electrons and therefore been reduced.
- The more positive the number, the more the element has been oxidised. The more negative, the more it has been reduced.
- The numbers are written in Roman numerals and always have a sign unless they are zero, e.g. +II.

5.1.4 Rules for finding oxidation numbers

- Uncombined elements have oxidation number = 0
- Some elements always have the same oxidation numbers in their compounds:
  Group 1 metals, *always* +I.
  Group 2 metals, *always* +II.
  Al, *always* +III.
  H, +I, *except* in compounds with Group 1 or 2 metals (metal hydrides) where it is −I
  F, *always* −I.
  O, −II, *except* in peroxides and compounds with F, where it is −I, and superoxides where it is $-\frac{1}{2}$.
  Cl, −I, *except* in compounds with F and O, where it has positive values.
- The sum of all the oxidation numbers in a compound = 0, since all compounds are electrically neutral.
- The sum of the oxidation numbers of a complex ion = the charge on the ion.

Examples of redox reactions include burning, rusting and the extraction of iron in the blast furnace

QUICK QUESTIONS

1 The following questions are about the reaction:

$$Ca(s) + Br_2(g) \rightarrow (Ca^{2+} + 2Br^-)(s)$$

a Which element has gained electrons?

b Which element has lost electrons?

c Which element has been oxidised?

d Which element has been reduced?

e What is the oxidation number of Ca in $CaBr_2$?

2 What is the oxidation number of the metal M in each of the following:

a MCl, b M_2O_3, c MSO_4, d M?

Using oxidation numbers

Oxidation numbers are used:

- in the systematic naming system of inorganic compounds (ones not based on carbon chains);
- to work out in a redox reaction which elements have been oxidised and which reduced.

5.2.1 Naming inorganic compounds

Compounds with two elements

Inorganic compounds that contain only two elements start with the name of the metal followed by the name of the non-metal whose ending is changed to -ide. But copper, for example, has two oxides, CuO and Cu_2O and both would be called copper oxide in this system. We tell them apart by placing the oxidation number in brackets after the metal name:

CuO is copper(II) oxide because oxygen is always −II so copper must be +II to make the sum of the oxidation numbers in the compound = 0.

Cu_2O is copper(I) oxide because oxygen is always −II so each copper must be +I to make the sum of the oxidation numbers in the compound = 0.

Iron similarly forms two chlorides. Chlorine is always −I, so to make the sum of the oxidation numbers in a compound = 0:

$FeCl_2$ is iron(II) chloride
$FeCl_3$ is iron(III) chloride.

Molecular compounds

Molecular compounds are not usually named using oxidation numbers. For example, the chlorides of phosphorus, PCl_3 and PCl_5 are still usually called phosphorus trichloride and phosphorus pentachloride, rather than phosphorus(III) chloride and phosphorus(V) chloride.

Compounds with three elements

Salts made of complex ions, like sulphates, nitrates or carbonates have the ending -ate, which indicates that oxygen is present. For example potassium sulphate contains potassium, sulphur and oxygen. However, there are two compounds that contain these elements – K_2SO_4 and K_2SO_3. K_2SO_3 was called potassium sulph*ite*, using the ending -ite for the compound with the lower amount of oxygen. Now we use the oxidation numbers of the sulphur to tell them apart, because sulphur has a different oxidation state in each compound.

K_2SO_4 is potassium sulphate(VI) because here S has oxidation state +VI.

You can work this out because:
Oxidation number of each K in K_2SO_4 = +I; $2 \times +I = +2$
Oxidation number of each O in K_2SO_4 = −II; $4 \times -II = -8$
$\qquad\qquad\qquad\qquad\qquad\qquad\qquad\qquad$ Total = −6

So to make the sum of the oxidation numbers in a compound = 0, sulphur has an oxidation number of +VI.

K_2SO_3 is potassium sulphate(IV) because S has oxidation number +IV.

You can work this out this because:
Oxidation number of each K in K_2SO_3 = +I; $2 \times +I = +2$
Oxidation number of each O in K_2SO_3 = −II; $3 \times -II = -6$
$\qquad\qquad\qquad\qquad\qquad\qquad\qquad\qquad$ Total = −4

Copper(II) oxide is black whereas copper(I) oxide is red. Transition metals, such as copper, often show variable oxidation states in their compounds, which are often coloured

NOTE

This system for naming inorganic compounds is called the Stock notation.

So to make the sum of the oxidation numbers in a compound = 0, sulphur has an oxidation number of +IV.

- There is no need to include the oxidation numbers of elements whose oxidation numbers rarely change, like alkali metals (which are always +I) and fluorine (which is always −I).
- You do not need to include oxidation numbers if there is no chance of confusion. The full name for $CuSO_4$ is copper(II)sulphate(VI), but it is usually abbreviated to copper(II) sulphate or just copper sulphate.

It is more important to be able to work from the name to the formula, than to be able to name correctly a particular compound.

Oxidation numbers and ions

Elements in ions can also be given oxidation numbers. In this case, we have to remember that the sum of the oxidation numbers must add up to the charge on the ion.

For example, in the phosphate ion, PO_4^{3-}, the charge is −3.

The oxygen atoms each have an oxidation number of −II; Total = $4 \times -II = -8$.
So, the phosphorus, P, must have an oxidation number of +V, in order that the charge on the ion is −3.

5.2.2 Working out which elements are oxidised and which reduced

We can use oxidation numbers to work out which element has been oxidised and which reduced in a redox reaction.

Remember that 'Oxidation Is Loss of electrons (OIL) and Reduction Is Gain of electrons (RIG)'. When an element is oxidised it loses electrons and its oxidation number goes up. In the reaction below, copper, Cu, has been oxidised because its oxidation number has gone from 0 to +II:

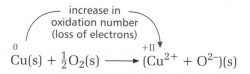

When an element is reduced, it gains electrons and its oxidation number goes down. In the reaction below, iron is reduced because its oxidation state has gone down from +III to +II:

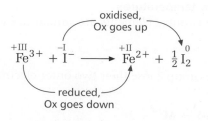

Even in complicated reactions, we can see which element has been oxidised and which reduced when we put in the oxidation numbers:

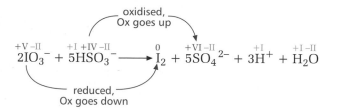

Iodine is oxidised and sulphur reduced. The oxidation states of all the other atoms have not changed.

5.2.3 Disproportionation

In **disproportionation** reactions, some of the atoms in a compound are reduced and some of the atoms *of the same element* are oxidised. In the example below, copper disproportionates because half the copper is reduced from +I to 0 (RIG) and half is oxidised from +I to +II (OIL).

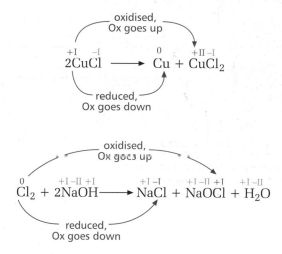

In the example above, chlorine disproportionates because half is oxidised from +I to +II (OIL) and half is reduced from 0 to −I (RIG).

QUICK QUESTIONS

1. Name these compounds using oxidations numbers:
   a $PbCl_2$,   b $PbCl_4$,   c $NaNO_3$,   d $NaNO_2$.

2. In the reaction $CuO + Mg \rightarrow Cu + MgO$, what are the oxidation numbers of oxygen before and after the reaction?

3. In the reaction $FeCl_2 + \frac{1}{2}Cl_2 \rightarrow FeCl_3$, what are the oxidation numbers of iron before and after the reaction?

4. Give the oxidation state of
   a S in SO_4^{2-},   b N in NO_3^-,   c N in NH_4^+.

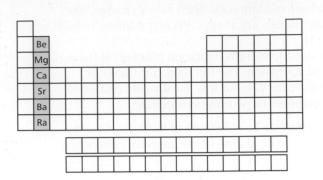

The elements in Group 2 are sometimes called the alkaline earth metals – their oxides and hydroxides are alkaline. Like Group 1, they are s-block elements. They are similar in many ways to Group 1, but they are less reactive. Beryllium is not typical of the group and is not considered here.

5.3.1 The physical properties of the Group 2 elements Mg to Ba

A summary of some of the physical properties of the elements from magnesium to barium is given in Table 5.1. Trends in properties are shown by arrows, which show the direction of increase.

Table 5.1 *The physical properties of Group 2, magnesium to barium*

	Atomic number Z	Electron arrangement	Metallic radius /nm	First + second IEs /kJ mol^{-1}	T_m/K	T_b/K	Density ρ/g cm^{-3}
Mg magnesium	12	[Ne]3s^2	0.160	738+ 1451 =2189	922	1380	1.74
Ca calcium	20	[Ar]4s^2	0.197	590+ 1145 =1735	1112	1757	1.54
Sr strontium	38	[Kr]5s^2	0.215	550+ 1064 =1614	1042	1657	2.60
Ba barium	56	[Xe]6s^2	0.224	503+ 965 =1468	998	1913	3.51

Electron arrangement
The elements have all got two electrons in an outer s-orbital. This s-orbital becomes further away from the nucleus as we go down the group.

Sizes of the atoms
The atoms get bigger as we go down the group. The atomic (metallic) radii increase because each element has an extra full shell of electrons compared with the one above it.

Melting temperatures and boiling temperatures
The melting and boiling points of Group 2 elements are similar to each other and there is no noticeable trend.

Ionisation energies
In *all* their reactions, elements in Group 2 lose their two outer electrons to form ions with two positive charges.

$$M \rightarrow M^{2+} + 2e^-$$

So, the sum of the first and the second ionisation energies is needed for ionisation. This sum decreases as we go down the group, because it takes less energy to remove the electrons as they become further and further away from the positive nucleus. (The shielded charge of the nucleus is the same ($+2$) for the whole group.)

In all their reactions, the metals become more reactive as we go down the group.

5.3.2 The chemical reactions of the Group 2 elements, Mg to Ba

Oxidation is loss of electrons, so in all their reactions the Group 2 metals are oxidised. The metals go from oxidation state 0 to oxidation state $+II$. These are redox reactions.

Reaction with oxygen

When we burn magnesium ribbon in air, the magnesium reacts with oxygen and is oxidised to magnesium oxide.

$$\overset{0}{2Mg(s)} + O_2(g) \rightarrow \overset{+II}{2MgO(s)}$$

We could equally write this:

$$\overset{0}{2Mg(s)} + O_2(g) \rightarrow \overset{+II}{2(Mg^{2+} + O^{2-})(s)}$$

$$\text{as magnesium oxide is ionic.}$$

All the metals form oxides, but the reaction gets more vigorous as we go down the group. This is partly because the ionisation energy decreases as we go down the group – the outer electrons are further away from the nucleus and easier to remove.

Magnesium and calcium form the 'normal' oxide, MO or ($M^{2+} + O^{2-}$), with oxygen.

Strontium and barium form a mixture of the normal oxide and the peroxide, MO_2, ($M^{2+} + O_2^{2-}$).

This is to do with the size of the metal ion and the oxide ions:

- The peroxide ion is larger than the oxide ion.
- The metal ions increase in size down the group.
- Strontium and barium ions are large enough for the peroxide ions to form a stable cluster around them.

Reaction with water

With water we see the same trend in reactivity – the metals get more reactive as we go down the group. These are also redox reactions.

Magnesium reacts very slowly with cold water (but rapidly with steam) to form an (alkaline) hydroxide and hydrogen.

For example:

$$\overset{0}{Mg(s)} + 2H_2O(l) \rightarrow \overset{+II}{Mg(OH)_2}(aq) + H_2(g)$$

Calcium reacts vigorously, even with cold water, and strontium and barium react even more vigorously.

5.3.3 Reactions with acids

The metals react with acids to give salts. Hydrogen is given off. The salt that is formed depends on the acid, see Section 2.5.3. Again the reaction is more and more vigorous as we go down the group.

For example:

$$\underset{\text{magnesium}}{Mg(s)} + \underset{\substack{\text{hydrochloric} \\ \text{acid}}}{2HCl(aq)} \rightarrow \underset{\substack{\text{magnesium} \\ \text{chloride}}}{MgCl_2(aq)} + \underset{\text{hydrogen}}{H_2(g)}$$

QUICK QUESTIONS

1 What is the oxidation number of all Group 2 elements in their compounds?

2 Why does it become easier to form 2^+ ions as we go down Group 2?

3 How would you expect the reaction of strontium with water to compare in reactivity with that of

a calcium,   b rubidium?

4 Explain your answer to 3.

5 Explain why the reaction Ca + Cl_2 → $CaCl_2$, is a redox reaction.

Compounds of Group 2 elements

The properties of the compounds of Group 2 elements are typically ionic. They have high melting and boiling temperatures.

5.4.1 Reactions with acid

Metal oxides

The metal oxides are bases which react with acids to form a salt and water only.

> **Metal oxide + acid → salt + water**

The salt depends on the acid – see Section 2.5.2.

For example:

$$MgO(s) \quad + \quad 2HCl(aq) \quad \rightarrow \quad MgCl_2(aq) \quad + H_2O(l)$$

Magnesium oxide   hydrochloric acid   magnesium chloride   water

Metal carbonates

The metal carbonates react with acids to form a salt, water and carbon dioxide.

> **Metal carbonate + acid → salt + water + carbon dioxide**

The salt depends on the acid – see Section 2.5.2.

For example:

$$MgCO_3(s) \;+\; 2HCl(aq) \;\rightarrow\; MgCl_2(aq) \;+\; H_2O(l) \;+\; CO_2(g)$$

Magnesium carbonate   hydrochloric acid   magnesium chloride   water   carbon dioxide

5.4.2 The industrial importance of Group 2 metals

Apart from magnesium, the metals are too reactive to be useful as elements.

Magnesium is used:

* in metal alloys because it is a very light (low density) metal;
* as a sacrficial anode, fastened to the sides of iron ships. (It releases electrons onto the iron surface and this stops the iron metal from forming positive ions, so the iron does not rust.);
* as 'monkey' metal – a cheap metal that is easy to cast (for example for pencil sharpeners).

5.4.3 The industrial importance of Group 2 compounds

Calcium carbonate

Limestone is mostly calcium carbonate ($CaCO_3$). Some 60 million tonnes are quarried each year in the UK. It is an important raw material.

Some uses of calcium carbonate

* cement and concrete
* manufacture of calcium oxide (lime)
* indigestion tablets
* in the blast furnace for making iron
* glass making.

Cement and concrete

Cement is made by heating limestone with clay to give a mixture containing calcium silicate and aluminium silicate. When mixed with water it forms a paste, which sets hard as it dries. Cement, mixed with water and sand or gravel, makes concrete which, when dry, has great strength in compression (i.e. when it is being squashed) although it is much weaker in tension (when it is being pulled).

The body (but not the blade or the screw) of metal pencil sharpeners is made of magnesium

Manufacture of calcium oxide – lime

When calcium carbonate is heated it breaks down to calcium oxide (lime) and carbon dioxide. This is called **thermal decomposition**:

$$CaCO_3(s) \rightarrow CaO(s) + CO_2(g)$$

calcium carbonate   calcium oxide
(limestone)   (lime)

Adding water to lime gives calcium hydroxide (slaked lime):

$$CaO(s) + H_2O(l) \rightarrow Ca(OH)_2(s)$$

calcium oxide   water   calcium hydroxide
(lime)   (slaked lime)

Calcium hydroxide (slaked lime)

This is a base and is used in agriculture to treat acidic soil.

acid + base → salt + water

For example, it will neutralise nitric acid:

$$Ca(OH)_2(s) + 2HNO_3(aq) \rightarrow Ca(NO_3)_2(aq) + 2H_2O(l)$$

calcium hydroxide   nitric acid   calcium nitrate   water

The limewater test

Limewater, $Ca(OH)_2(aq)$, is made by dissolving calcium hydroxide in water. It is an alkaline solution with a pH of about 12.

When carbon dioxide is bubbled into limewater, it reacts with it to form a milky white precipitate of calcium carbonate. This is the basis of the test for carbon dioxide:

$$Ca(OH)_2(aq) + CO_2(g) \rightarrow CaCO_3(s) + H_2O(l)$$

calcium hydroxide   carbon dioxide   calcium carbonate   water

If more carbon dioxide is bubbled into the milky solution, the calcium carbonate will eventually form soluble calcium hydrogencarbonate. The milkiness then clears:

$$CaCO_3(s) + H_2O(l) + CO_2(g) \rightarrow Ca(HCO_3)_2(aq)$$

calcium carbonate   water   carbon dioxide   calcium hydrogencarbonate

This reaction is the cause of hard water in limestone regions. Rain water is slightly acidic because it has dissolved carbon dioxide in it. As it trickles through limestone rocks, it reacts as above and dissolves calcium hydrogencarbonate. This is hard water.

Calcium hydrogencarbonate reacts with soap (sodium stearate) to form insoluble calcium stearate, known as scum.

Indigestion tablets

These often contain calcium carbonate. Calcium carbonate is called an antacid because it neutralises stomach acid, which is mainly hydrochloric acid, HCl:

$$CaCO_3(s) + 2HCl(aq) \rightarrow CaCl_2(aq) + CO_2(g) + H_2O(l)$$

Magnesium hydroxide, $Mg(OH)_2$

Magnesium hydroxide, like calcium carbonate, is used as an ingredient (an antacid) in indigestion tablets, to neutralise excess hydrochloric acid in the stomach:

$$Mg(OH)_2(s) + 2HCl(aq) \rightarrow MgCl_2(aq) + 2H_2O(l)$$

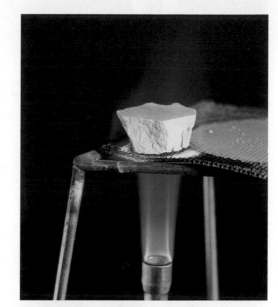

When calcium carbonate is heated with a hot flame it forms calcium oxide

When water is added to calcium oxide the reaction is so exothermic that the water turns to steam

QUICK QUESTIONS

1 Name the salt produced when
  a calcium oxide reacts with nitric acid;
  b strontium carbonate reacts with hydrochloric acid.

2 What is lime and how is it made?

3 Write the equation for the limewater test and underline the chemical that causes the milkiness if carbon dioxide is present.

4 Explain, with an equation, how magnesium carbonate could be used as an antacid.

The Periodic Table: Group 7

The halogens

The halogens – fluorine, chlorine, bromine and iodine

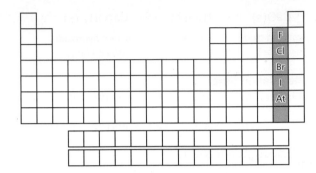

Group 7, on the right hand side of the Periodic Table, is made up of non-metals. As elements they exist as diatomic molecules – F_2, Cl_2, Br_2, I_2 etc. They are called the halogens.

6.1.1 Physical properties

The halogens vary in appearance, see photo. At room temperature fluorine is a pale yellow gas, chlorine a greenish gas, bromine a red-brown liquid and iodine a black solid – they get darker and denser as we go down the group. Astatine is both rare and radioactive and its chemistry has not been studied in any detail.

They all have a characteristic 'swimming-bath' smell.

Fluorine, at the top of the group, is not typical of the group and is not included in the Topic. It is the most electronegative element in the Periodic Table and is so reactive that it will combine directly with virtually all the other elements, including some of the noble gases.

The physical properties of chlorine, bromine and iodine are shown in Table 6.1.

Table 6.1 *The physical properties of chlorine, bromine and iodine*

	Atomic number Z	Electron arrangement	Electronegativity	Atomic (covalent) radius/nm	T_m/K	T_b/K
Cl	17	$[Ne]3s^23p^5$	3.0	0.099	172	238
Br	35	$[Ar]3d^{10}4s^24p^5$	2.8	0.114	266	332
I	53	$[Kr]4d^{10}5s^25p^5$	2.5	0.133	387	457

There are some clear trends shown by the arrows. These can be explained as follows:

- Electronegativity. Chlorine is very electronegative. (It readily attracts the electrons in covalent bonds.) The elements become less electronegative as we go down the group. This is because the shared electrons in the covalent bonds they form get further and further away from the halogen nucleus. At the same time these electrons feel the same shielded nuclear charge of +7, see Figure 6.1.
- Size of atoms. The atoms get bigger as we go down the group because each element has one extra full shell of electrons compared with the one above it.

- Melting and boiling temperatures. These increase as we go down the group. This is because larger atoms have more electrons and this makes the van der Waals forces between the molecules stronger. The lower the boiling temperature, the more volatile the element. So, chlorine, which is a gas at room temperature is more volatile than iodine, which is a solid.

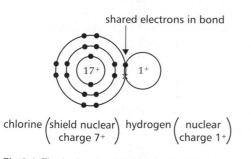

Fig 6.1 *The hydrogen chloride molecule*

6.1.2 Chemical reactivity

Halogens have seven electrons in their outer shell. They usually react by gaining electrons to become negative ions, with a charge of -1. So, these reactions are redox reactions - halogens are oxidising agents and are themselves reduced. For example:

$$Cl_2 + 2e^- \rightarrow 2Cl^-$$

gain of electrons

The halogens get less reactive as we go down the group. This is because it is gets harder to capture an electron as the outer shell gets further from the positive nucleus, see Figure 6.1. So, the **oxidising power** also decreases as we go down the group.

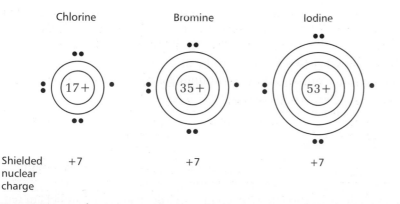

Fig 6.2 *The outer shell gets further from the nucleus as we go down the group*

QUICK QUESTIONS

1 Explain why chlorine is more electronegative than bromine.
2 Why is chlorine more volatile that iodine?
3 $2Na + Cl_2 \rightarrow 2NaCl$
   a Write the oxidation numbers above sodium and chlorine on both sides of the equation.
   b What is the oxidising agent in the reaction?
   c Explain your answer.
4 Why do all the halogens form molecules of formula X_2? Draw a dot-and-cross diagram to explain your answer.

Reactions of the halogens and their ions

6.2.1 Reaction with metals

The reactions of the halogens are redox reactions, see Topic 6.1. The halogen acts as an oxidising agent and is itself reduced to form a halide ion.

Halogens react directly with most metals to form ionic halides containing X^- ions, where X is any halogen.

For example if a clean piece of sodium is lowered into a gas jar of chlorine gas, it reacts immediately to form sodium chloride:

$$\underset{\text{sodium}}{\overset{0}{2Na(s)}} + \underset{\text{chlorine}}{\overset{0}{Cl_2(g)}} \rightarrow \underset{\text{sodium chloride}}{\overset{+I \quad -I}{2(Na^+ + Cl^-)(s)}}$$

6.2.1 Reaction with water

If chlorine gas is bubbled into water and the resulting solution tested with indicator paper, the paper will initially turn red, which shows that the solution is acidic, and then white which shows that it is a bleach.

Chlorine reacts with water to form to form chloric(I) acid (HClO), which is a bleach, and hydrochloric acid (HCl):

$$\overset{0}{Cl_2(g)} + H_2O(l) \rightarrow \overset{+I}{HClO(aq)} + \overset{-I}{HCl(aq)}$$

In this reaction, the oxidation number (in red) of one of the chlorine atoms increases from 0 to +I and that of the other decreases from 0 to −I. This is a redox reaction and also a disproportionation reaction, see Section 4.6.3.

The other halogens react similarly, but much more slowly as we go down the group, so that the reaction of iodine with water is undetectable with indicator paper.

In industry the reaction between chlorine and water takes place when chlorine is used to purify water for drinking and in swimming baths, to prevent life-threatening diseases. Chloric(I) acid is an oxidising agent and kills bacteria by oxidation. It is also a bleach.

6.2.3 Reaction with alkali

Chlorine reacts with cold, dilute sodium hydroxide to form a solution of sodium chlorate(I), NaOCl, which is a bleach, and sodium chloride. This is a redox reaction, and also a disproportionation reaction – see the oxidation numbers in red.

$$\overset{0}{Cl_2(g)} + 2NaOH(aq) \rightarrow \overset{+I}{NaOCl(aq)} + \overset{-I}{NaCl(aq)} + H_2O(l)$$

The other halogens behave similarly.

In industry sodium chlorate(I) is an oxidising agent and is the active ingredient in household bleaches.

6.2.4 Displacement reactions

Halogens will react with metal halides in solution in such a way that the halide in the compound will be displaced by a more reactive halogen but not by a less reactive one. Table 6.2 shows the pattern for halogen/halide displacement reactions.

Table 6.2 Displacement reactions between halogens and halogen ions. A tick means that the halogen will displace the halide from a compound.

halide halogen	Cl_2	Br_2	I_2
Cl^-	–	✗	✗
Br^-	✓	-	✗
I^-	✓	✓	–

So, bromide ions will be displaced by chlorine but not by iodine, for example:

$$\overset{0}{Cl_2}(aq) + 2\overset{-I}{NaBr}(aq) \rightarrow \overset{0}{Br_2}(aq) + 2\overset{-I}{NaCl}(aq)$$

We can write this as an ionic equation:

$$\overset{0}{Cl_2}(aq) + 2\overset{-I}{Br^-}(aq) \rightarrow \overset{0}{Br_2}(aq) + 2\overset{-I}{Cl^-}(aq)$$

The two colourless starting materials react to produce the red-brown colour of bromine.

In this redox reaction the chlorine is acting as an oxidising agent, by capturing electrons and oxidising $2Br^-$ to Br_2 (so the oxidation number of the bromine increases from $-I$ to 0). So, another way of looking at this is that the halogen with the greater oxidising power will always oxidise a halogen with less oxidising power:

chlorine   bromine   iodine
←increasing oxidising power—

In industry bromine is extracted from seawater, which contains Br^- ions, using chlorine as an oxidising agent.

6.2.4 Reaction of metal halides with silver ions

All metal halides (except fluorides) react with silver ions, for example in silver nitrate, to form a precipitate of the insoluble silver halide. For example:

$$Cl^-(aq) + Ag^+(aq) \rightarrow AgCl(s)$$

The reaction can be used as a test for halides because we can tell from the colour of the precipitate which halogen has formed it:

silver chloride (white)   silver bromide (cream)   silver iodide (pale yellow)

The last two colours are similar but if we add a few drops of concentrated ammonia solution, silver bromide dissolves but silver iodide does not. (Silver chloride also dissolves in ammonia solution.)

Plant for extracting bromine from seawater at Anglesey

QUICK QUESTIONS

1 When dilute sodium hydroxide solution is added to a solution of bromine water the brown colour of the bromine water disappears.

  a Write an equation to show why this happens

  b Add the oxidation numbers above the bromine atoms.

  c What sort of reaction is this?

  d Explain your answer to **c**.

2 a Which of the following mixtures would react?
    (i) $Br_2(aq) + 2NaCl(aq)$ (ii) $Cl_2(aq) + 2NaI(aq)$

  b Explain why you chose your answer.

  c Complete the equation for this reaction.

3 A few drops of silver nitrate were added to a solution of a sodium bromide.

  a What would you see?

  b Write the equation for the reaction.

  c What would happen if you now added a few drops of concentrated ammonia solution?

1 This question conccerns elements and compounds from Group 2 of the Periodic Table.

  a State the trend in reactivity of the Group 2 elements with oxygen. Explain your answer. [4]

  b The reactions of strontium are typical of a Group 2 element. Write the formulae for substances **A–D** in the flow chart below.

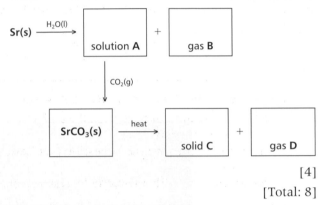

[4]

[Total: 8]

OCR, 29 May 2002

2 Chlorine and its compounds have many uses. Chlorine bleach is used to kill bacteria.

  a Chlorine bleach is made by the reaction of chlorine with aqueous sodium hydroxide:

$$Cl_2(g) + 2NaOH(aq) \rightarrow NaClO(aq) + NaCl(aq) + H_2O(l)$$

  (i) Determine the oxidation number of chlorine in: Cl_2, NaClO, NaCl. [3]

  (ii) The actual bleaching agent is the ClO^- ion. In the presence of sunlight, this ion decomposes to release oxygen gas.
  Construct an equation for this reaction. [1]

  b The sea contains a low concentration of bromide ions. Bromine can be extracted from sea water by first concentrating the sea water and then bubbling chlorine through this solution.

  (i) The chlorine oxidises bromide ions to bromine. Construct a balanced ionic equation for this reaction. [1]

  (ii) Suggest how bromine could be removed from the sea water after this oxidation. [1]

  c Phosgene is a compound of chlorine, carbon and oxygen, used to make polyurethanes and dyes. Phosgene has the percentage composition by mass: Cl, 71.7%; C, 12.1%; O, 16.2%.

  (i) Show that the empirical formula of phosgene is Cl_2CO. [2]

  (ii) The molecular formula of phosgene is the same as its empirical formula. Draw a posssible structure, including bond angles, for a molecule of phosgene. [2]

[Total: 10]

OCR, 12 Jan 2001

3 This question is about aluminium oxide, Al_2O_3.

  a Successive ionisation energies provide evidence for the arrangement of electrons in graphs.
  The graph below shows the 8 successive ionisation energies of **oxygen**.

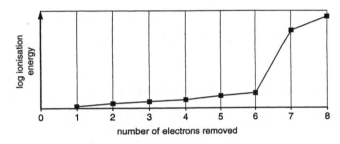

  (i) Write an equation, including state symbols, to represent the **second** ionisation energy of oxygen. [2]

  (ii) How does this graph provide evidence for the existence of two electron shells in oxygen? [2]

  b (i) Complete the electronic configuration for an **aluminium** atom.
  $1s^2$ [1]

  (ii) On the axes below, sketch a graph to show the **thirteen** successive ionisation energies of aluminium. [2]

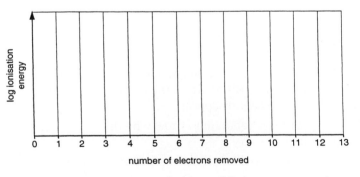

  c Aluminium oxide can be formed by reacting together aluminium and oxygen.

  (i) Write an equation, including state symbols, for this reaction. [2]

  (ii) The bonding in aluminium oxide is intermediate between ionic and covalent bonding. Explain why aluminium oxide has intermediate bonding. [3]

d Gemstones such as rubies, sapphires and topaz mainly contain aluminium oxide. Artificial rubies can be made by heating aluminium oxide with very small traces of transition metal oxides and cooling slowly. The traces of these oxides give the rubies their colours.

Calculate how many moles of Al_2O_3 are needed to make a 25.0 g ruby.

Assume that all the mass of this ruby is aluminium oxide. [2]

[Total: 14]

OCR, 29 May 2002

4 In this question, one mark will be awarded for the quality of written communication (QWC).

In the Periodic Table, describe and explain the trend in atomic radii shown by:

• the Group 2 elements Be–Ra
• the Period 3 elements Na–Ar. [8]

QWC [1]

[Total: 9]

OCR, 17 Jan 2003

5 The first six successive ionisation energies of an element D are shown in the table below.

Element	Ionisation energy/kJ mol^{-1}					
	1st	2nd	3rd	4th	5th	6th
D	1086	2353	4621	6223	37 832	47 278

a Define the term *first* ionisation energy. [3]

b Write an equation, with state symbols, to represent the **third** ionisation energy of element **D**. [2]

c Use the table to deduce which group of the Periodic Table contains element **D**. Explain your answer. [3]

[Total: 8]

OCR, 17 Jan 2003

6 The atomic radii of the elements Li to F and Na to Cl are shown in the table below.

Element atomic radius/nm	Li 0.134	Be 0.125	B 0.090	C 0.077	N 0.075	O 0.073	F 0.071
Element atomic radius/nm	Na 0.154	Mg 0.145	Al 0.130	Si 0.118	P 0.110	S 0.102	Cl 0.099

a Using **only** the elements in this table, select:

(i) an element with **both** metallic and non-metallic properties, [1]
(ii) the element with the largest first ionisation energy, [1]
(iii) an element with a giant molecular structure. [1]

b Explain what causes the general **decrease** in atomic radii across each period? [3]

c Predict and explain whether a sodium **ion** is *larger*, *smaller* or the *same size* as a sodium **atom**. [3]

[Total: 9]

OCR, 12 Jan 2001

Chains and rings

Basic concepts

Organic introduction

Organic chemistry is the chemistry of carbon compounds. Life on our planet is based on carbon and organic means 'to do with living beings'. Nowadays, we make our own carbon-based materials, like plastics and drugs, and there are large industries based on synthetic materials.

7.1.1 What is special about carbon?

Carbon can form very long chains (which may be branched) and rings. This is for two main reasons:

• A carbon atom has four electrons in its outer shell, so it forms four covalent bonds.
• Carbon–carbon bonds are relatively strong (see Table 7.1).

Table 7.1 *The bond energy of the carbon–carbon bond compared with some other elements*

Bond	Bond energy/kJ mol^{-1}
C—C	347
Si—Si	226
N—N	158
O—O	144

The carbon–hydrogen bond is also strong (413 kJ mol^{-1}) and hydrocarbon chains form the skeleton of most organic compounds, see Figures 7.1, 7.2 and 7.3.

7.1.2 Bonding in carbon compounds

In *all* stable compounds, carbon forms four covalent bonds and has eight electrons in its outer shell. It can do this by forming bonds in different ways:

• by forming four single bonds as in methane.

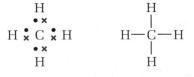

• by forming two single bonds and one double bond as in ethene.

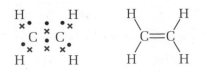

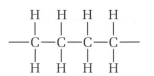

Fig 7.1 *Part of a hydrocarbon chain*

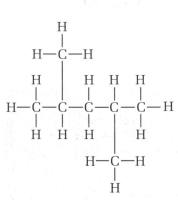

Fig 7.2 *A branched hydrocarbon chain*

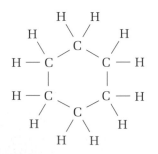

Fig 7.3 *A hydrocarbon ring*

- by forming one single bond and one triple bond as in ethyne.

7.1.3 Formulae of carbon compounds

The empirical formula

This formula just shows the simplest ratio of the atoms present. For example, ethane:

3.0 g of ethane contains 2.4 g of carbon, $A_r = 12.0$ and 0.6 g of hydrogen, $A_r = 1.0$. What is its empirical formula?

Number of moles of carbon = 2.4/12.0 = 0.2 mol of carbon

Number of moles of hydrogen 0.6/1.0 = 0.6 mol of hydrogen

Dividing through by the smallest number (0.2) gives C:H as 1:3

So the empirical formula of ethane is CH_3.

Look back at Topic 2.2 if you are not sure about this calculation.

The molecular formula

The molecular formula shows the numbers of each atom in the molecule. It is found from:

- the empirical formula
- the relative molecular mass of the empirical formula
- the relative molecular mass of the molecule.

For example:

The empirical formula of ethane is CH_3 and this group of atoms has a relative molecular mass of 15.0.

The relative molecular mass of ethane is 30.0, which is 2 × 15.0.

So, there must be two units of the empirical formula in every molecule of ethane.

The molecular formula is therefore $(CH_3)_2$ or C_2H_6.

7.1.4 Other formulae

We use other, different types of formulae in organic chemistry because, compared with inorganic compounds, organic molecules are more varied. We may want to know about the way the atoms are arranged within the molecule, as well as just the number of each atom present. There are different ways of doing this:

The displayed formula

This shows every atom and every bond in the molecule; — is a single bond, = a double bond.

For ethene, C_2H_4, the displayed formula is:

For ethanol, C_2H_6O, the displayed formula is:

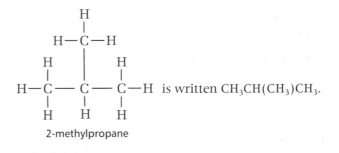

The structural formula

This is a shorthand form of the displayed formula.

- The formulae are written without showing the bonds.
- Each carbon is written separately, with the atoms or groups that are attached to it.

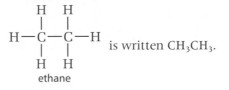

is written CH_3CH_3.

ethane

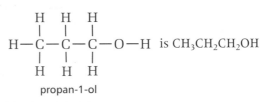

is $CH_3CH_2CH_2OH$

propan-1-ol

Branches in the carbon chains are shown in brackets:

is written $CH_3CH(CH_3)CH_3$.

2-methylpropane

QUICK QUESTIONS

The following questions are about a compound of carbon and hydrogen only in which 4.8 g of carbon combine with 1.0 g of hydrogen. The relative molecular mass is 58.0.

1 How many moles of carbon atoms in 4.8 g?

2 How many moles of hydrogen atoms in 1.0 g?

3 What is the empirical formula of this compound?

4 What is the molecular formula of this compound?

5 Draw the structural formula of the compound that has a branched chain.

More on formulae and molecular models

Skeletal notation

In this notation we do not draw the carbon atoms at all. We show only the carbon skeleton as straight lines, each of which represents a C—C bond, plus any functional groups. Butane is shown as an example:

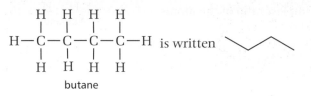

butane

- The carbon skeleton has no carbon or hydrogen atoms written in.
- We assume that (a) there is a carbon atom at each end and a carbon where the lines meet and (b) there are enough hydrogen atoms to make sure that every carbon forms four bonds.
- The skeleton is drawn to give a rough impression of bond angles. In a saturated carbon chain these are 109.5°.

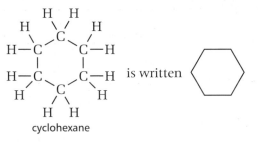

cyclohexane

Functional groups are added to the carbon skeleton:

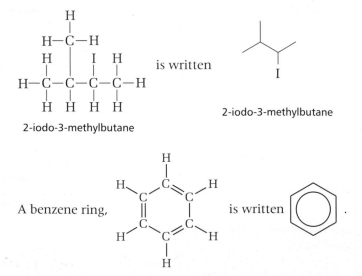

2-iodo-3-methylbutane

2-iodo-3-methylbutane

A benzene ring, is written

The type of formula that you meet with will depend on the information that you are dealing with.

None of the formulae that we saw in Topic 7.1 can show the true three-dimensional shape of organic molecules. This is done with molecular models (see photograph) or using computers.

There are two types of model most commonly used. They are called ball and stick and space filling. The ball and stick models emphasise the bonds, but the space-filling models probably look more like the molecule, if we could see it.

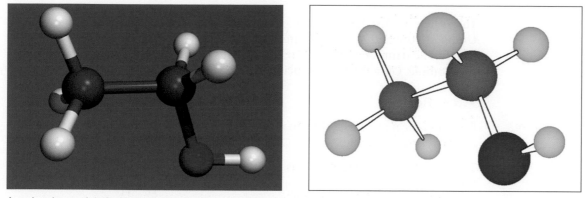

A molecular model of ethanol and a computer-generated model (both ball and stick)

Table 7.2 shows a selection of formulae with their computer-generated models.

Table 7.2 *Ways of representing some organic molecules*

Empirical formula	Molecular formula/name	Structural formula			Ball and stick representation	Space-filling representation
		Structural	Displayed	Skeletal		
CH_2	C_6H_{12} hex-1-ene	$CH_2CHCH_2CH_2CH_2CH_3$				
C_2H_6O	C_2H_6O ethanol	CH_3CH_2OH (or C_2H_5OH)				
C_3H_7Cl	C_3H_7Cl 2-chloropropane	$CH_3CHClCH_3$				

QUICK QUESTIONS

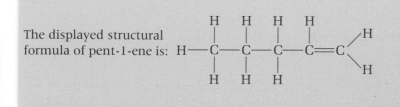

The displayed structural formula of pent-1-ene is:

1 Draw its shorthand structural formula.

2 Draw its skeletal formula.

3 What is the molecular formula?

4 What is the empirical formula?

The system we use for naming compounds was developed by the International Union of Pure and Applied Chemistry or **IUPAC**. It is used worldwide. Systematic names tell us about the structures of the compounds rather than just the formula. Only the basic principles are covered here.

7.3.1 Roots

A systematic name has a **root** that tells us the longest unbranched hydrocarbon chain or ring, see Table 7.3.

The syllable after the root tells us whether there are any carbon–carbon double bonds:

-ane means no double bonds, for example ethane — two carbon atoms and no double bond.

-ene means there is a double bond, for example ethene — two carbon atoms and one double bond

Table 7.3 *The roots used in naming organic compounds*

Number of carbons	Root
1	meth
2	eth
3	prop
4	but
5	pent
6	hex
7	hept
8	oct
9	non
10	dec

7.3.2 Prefixes and suffixes

Prefixes and suffixes describe the changes that have been made to the root molecule.

- Prefixes are added to the beginning of the root.
- A suffix is added to the end of the root.

Side chains are shown by a prefix, whose name tells us the number of carbons:
methyl CH_3—; ethyl C_2H_5—; propyl C_3H_7—; butyl C_4H_9—

For example [structure] is called methylbutane. The longest

methylbutane

unbranched chain is four carbons long, which gives us butane (as there are no double bonds) and there is a side chain of one carbon – a methyl group.

Table 7.4 *The suffixes and prefixes of some functional groups*

Family	Formula	Suffix	Prefix	Example
Alkenes		**-ene**		Prop**ene**, CH_2CHCH_3
Halogeno-alkanes	–X (X = F, Cl, Br, I)		Halogeno- (Fluoro-, chloro-, bromo-, iodo-)	Chloromethane, CH_3Cl
Alcohols	-OH	**-ol**	Hydroxy-	Ethan**ol**, C_2H_5OH
Carboxylic acids		**-oic acid**		Ethan**oic acid**, CH_3COOH
Aldehydes		**-al**		Ethan**al**, CH_3CHO
Ketones		**-one**		Propan**one**, CH_3COCH_3
Amines	-NH_2	**-amine**	Amino-	Ethyl**amine**, $CH_3CH_2NH_2$

Note that most groups have both suffixes and prefixes. Normally the suffix (in bold) is used but the prefix may be needed when a compound contains more than one functional group.

Functional groups

Reactive groups of atoms (called **functional groups**) are named by using a suffix or prefix as shown in Table 7.4.

Examples

Bromoethane [structure]

eth indicates that the molecule has a chain of two carbon atoms, **ane** that it is has no double or triple bonds and **bromo** that one of the hydrogen atoms of ethane is replaced by a bromine atom.

Propene

$$\underset{\underset{H}{|}}{\overset{\overset{H}{|}}{C}}=\underset{\underset{H}{|}}{\overset{\overset{H}{|}}{C}}-\underset{\underset{H}{|}}{\overset{\overset{H}{|}}{C}}-H$$

prop indicates a chain of three carbon atoms and **ene** that there is one C=C (double bond).

Methanol H—C—OH

Meth indicates a single carbon, **an** that there are no double bonds and **ol** an OH group (an alcohol).

7.3.3 Locants

With longer chains, we need to say where a side chain or a functional group is located on the main chain. For example, chlorobutane could refer to:

H—C—C—C—C—Cl or H—C—C—C—C—H

We use a number, called a **locant**, to tell us where the chlorine atom is on the chain – the first example is 1-chlorobutane and the second is 2-chlorobutane.

TAKE CARE
Don't get confused by the way the way the formula is drawn.

Br—C—C—C—H and H—C—C—C—Br

are both 1-bromopropane. The right-hand one is not 3-bromopropane (we always use the smallest possible number for locants).

Molecules with more than one locant
We may need more than one locant:

H—C—C—C—H (2-bromo-1-iodopropane)

Bromo is written before iodo, because we put the substituting groups in *alphabetical order*, rather than in the numerical order of the locants.

We can show that we have more than one of the same substituting group by adding prefixes as well as locants. Di-, tri- and tetra- mean two, three and four, respectively.

So, Cl—C—C—H is called 1,1-dichloroethane

and H—C—C—H is called 1,2-dichloroethane.

HINT
In chemical names, strings of numbers are separated by commas. A hyphen is placed between words and numbers.

It is much more important to be able to work out the structure of a molecule from its name than to name a given molecule. Further examples are given in Table 7.5.

Table 7.5 *Examples of systematic naming of organic compounds. Try covering up the name or structure to test yourself*

Structural formula	Name
H—C—C—C—H	2,2-dibromopropane
H—C—C—C—C—OH	2-bromobutan-1-ol **Note** The suffix -ol defines the end of the chain we count from
H—C—C—C—C—H	butan-2-ol
C=C—C—C—H	but-1-ene **Note** Not but-2-ene, but-3-ene or but-4-ene as we use the smallest locant possible

QUICK QUESTIONS
1 Draw the displayed formula of:
   a 2-chloropropene,   **b** but-2-ene.

2 What is the name of:
   a $CH_3CH_2CH_2Cl$,   **b** $CH_3CH(OH)CH_3$,
   c $CH_3CH_2CH=CHCH_3$

Functional groups, families and isomers

7.4.1 Functional groups

Most organic compounds are made up of a hydrocarbon chain that has one or more reactive groups attached to it. We call these reactive groups **functional groups,** see Table 7.4 in Section 7.3.2. The functional group reacts in the same way, whatever the length of the hydrocarbon chain. So, for example, if you learn the reactions of one alcohol, such as ethanol, you can apply this knowledge to any alcohol.

7.4.2 Homologous series

A homologous series is a family of organic compounds, with the same functional group, but different carbon chain length.

- Members of a **homologous series** have a **general formula**. For example the alcohols are $C_nH_{2n+1}OH$.
- The length of the carbon chain has little effect on the *chemical* reactivity of the functional group.
- The length of the carbon chain affects *physical* properties, like melting temperature, boiling temperature and solubility. In general small molecules are gases and larger ones liquids or solids.

In equations we often use the symbol R attached to the functional group to represent any member of the series. Think of R as meaning the <u>r</u>est of the molecule. For example R–OH represents any alcohol.

7.4.3 Isomers

Isomers have the same molecular formula, but their atoms are arranged differently. There are different types of isomerism in organic chemistry.

7.4.4 Structural isomerism

Structural isomers have either:

- functional groups attached to the main chain at different points or
- functional groups that are different or
- a different arrangement of the hydrocarbon chain (such as branching).

Examples
The functional group is attached to the main chain at different points.

The molecular formula C_3H_8O could represent:

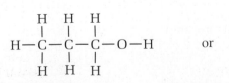

or

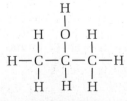

propan-1-ol   propan-2-ol

There are different functional groups.

The molecular formula C_2H_6O could represent:

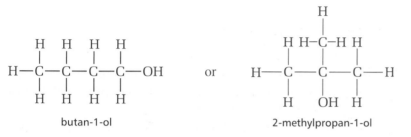

ethanol (an alcohol)   or   methoxymethane (an ether)

The hydrocarbon chain is arranged differently.

The molecular formula C_4H_9OH could represent:

butan-1-ol   or   2-methylpropan-1-ol

These isomers are called chain-branching isomers.

7.4.5 Geometrical (*cis–trans*) isomerism

Cis–trans isomerism can only occur when there is double bond in a molecule. If there is a group attached to each carbon atom of a carbon–carbon double bond, the groups may both be on the same side of the double bond (*cis*) or they may be on opposite sides (*trans*).

cis-1,2-dibromoethene   trans-1,2-dibromoethene

This happens because there is no rotation possible about the double bond. The carbon atoms in a single carbon–carbon bond will rotate, see photographs.

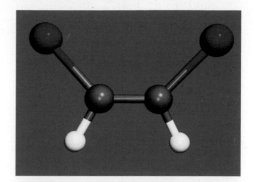
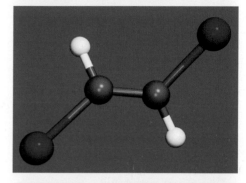
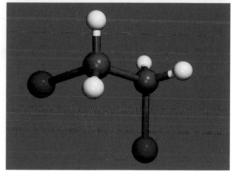

Models of cis-1,2-dibromoethene (top), trans-1,2-dibromoethene (middle) and 1,2-dibromoethane (bottom)

Rotation of the C–C bond is possible in 1,2-dibromoethane

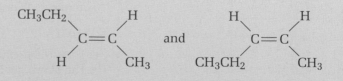

Table 7.6 *Some average bond energies*

Bond	Bond energy/kJ mol⁻¹
C–H	413
C–C	347
C–O	358
O–H	464
C–F	467
C–Cl	346
C–Br	290
C–I	228
C=C	612
C≡C	838
C=O	743
C–N	286
C=N	615
C≡N	887
N–H	391
N–O	214
O–O	144

NOTE

The actual C—O bond energy in ethanol is not exactly the same as the value in Table 7.6, which is the average over several compounds

Table 7.7 *Electronegativities of elements encountered in organic chemistry*

Element	Electronegativity
C	2.5
H	2.1
O	3.5
F	4.0
Cl	3.0
Br	2.8
I	2.5
N	3.0

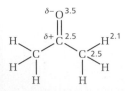

Fig 7.4 *Propanone, with electronegativities in red*

This section is about the *general* principles that decide how an organic compound reacts. The reactions of the different functional groups are dealt with in more detail in chapters 8 to 12.

There are two important factors in the reactivity of a molecule: bond enthalpies and polarity.

7.5.1 Bond enthalpies

Bond enthalpies (also called bond energies) tell us the amount of energy needed to break a particular bond, so they measure the strength of the bond. Table 7.6 includes some of the more common bond energies.

We would predict that the weakest bond in a molecule would be most likely to break. This is often, but not always, the case. For example, the bond energies in kJ mol⁻¹ are marked on the displayed formula of ethanol:

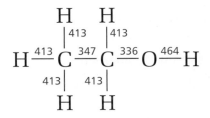

The C—O bond (336 kJ mol⁻¹) is the weakest bond and we would expect it to be the most likely to break. In many of the reactions of ethanol, this is what happens. But, there are reactions in which the O—H bond (464 kJ mol⁻¹) breaks, despite this being the strongest. The strength of the bond is therefore not the only factor.

7.5.2 Polarity

When two different atoms are covalently bonded, one of the atoms in the bond will always be more electronegative than the other, see Table 7.7. This will make the bond polar (see Section 3.4.2). Polarity is shown by the signs δ^+ and δ^-. For example in propanone, Figure 7.4, the C=O bond is very polar. Negatively charged reagents (called nucleophiles, see Section 7.6.1) attack the C$^{\delta+}$ atom; positively charged ones (called electrophiles, see Section 7.6.3) attack the O$^{\delta-}$ atom. The C—H bonds are not very polar because carbon and hydrogen have similar electronegativities and are unlikely to be attacked by positively charged or negatively charged reagents.

Bond enthalpy or polarity?

Sometimes the bond energy and polarity do not predict the same outcome. For example, look at the data for the carbon–halogen bonds, in Table 7.8.

As we go down the group from fluorine to iodine:

- The carbon–halogen bonds get weaker (and therefore *easier* to break).
- The bonds get less polar and therefore the carbon becomes *less easily* attacked by negatively charged reagents.

So bond energies predict C—F to be the *least* reactive, polarity predicts C—F to be the *most* reactive. In the reaction with OH⁻ ions CH₃I reacts the fastest and CH₃F not at all, so in this case bond energy is the more important factor.

Table 7.8 *Electronegativities and bond energies in carbon–halogen bonds*

Electronegativity	Bond energy/kJ mol^{-1}
2.5 4.0 C — F	467
2.5 3.0 C — Cl	346
2.5 2.8 C — Br	290
2.5 2.5 C — I	228

7.5.3 Hydrocarbon chains are unreactive

The bond energies in Table 7.6 show the C—C and C—H bonds to be among the strongest single bonds. The electronegativities in Table 7.7 show that the C—C is non-polar and the C—H bond relatively non-polar. Both these factors mean that the hydrocarbon skeleton of an organic molecule is unreactive. So reactions take place at the functional group rather than the carbon chain.

7.5.4 Double bonds

Carbon–carbon double bonds are areas of high electron density. A double bond has four electrons, compared with two in a single bond. The electrons are equally shared between the two carbon atoms. These electron-rich areas make these bonds open to attack by positively charged reagents (electrophiles) such as the hydrogen ion, H$^+$.

QUICK QUESTIONS

1 Draw the displayed structural formula of $CH_2CH_2CH_2Br$ and mark the atoms that are δ^+ and δ^-.

2 Where will this molecule be attacked by a nucleophile (a negatively charged species)?

3 Mark the bond energies on this molecule.

4 Which bond is
  a the strongest,
  b the weakest?

Types of reagent

One way of grouping reactions of organic molecules is by the type of chemical with which they react – called a chemical reagent.

Reagents may be divided into **nucleophiles, electrophiles** and **free radicals** (sometimes just called radicals).

7.6.1 Nucleophiles

Nucleophiles are defined as electron pair donors. Nucleophile means 'nucleus-loving', and as the nucleus is positive, nucleophiles must have at least a partial negative charge.

- A nucleophile is either a negatively charged ion or has an atom with a δ^- charge.
- It must also have a lone pair of electrons.
- It attacks a positively charged carbon atom in a molecule and forms a bond with it using this pair of electrons.

Examples of nucleophiles include:

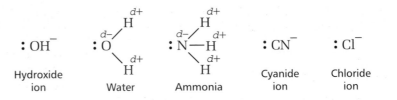

We use the symbol :Nu or :Nu$^-$ for a nucleophile in general. Notice that some are negatively charged while some are neutral overall.

7.6.2 How nucleophiles react

1. The nucleophile uses its lone pair of electrons to form a bond with the positively charged carbon atom to form an intermediate. If the nucleophile has a negative charge a negative ion is formed called a **carbanion**.

    We use 'curly arrows' to show the movement of electron pairs in organic reactions. Do not confuse them with the straight arrow that we use to show a dative bond.

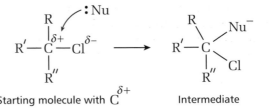

2. In the intermediate the carbon has five bonds (therefore it has ten electrons in its outer shell) so it needs to lose a pair of electrons. One way that this could happen is shown here:

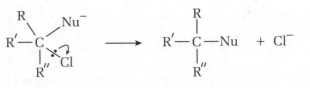

3. An electronegative atom or group of atoms (called the **leaving group**) takes the extra pair of electrons away. In this case the leaving group is a Cl^- ion.

7.6.3 Electrophiles

Electrophile means 'electron-loving'.

- Electrophiles tend to attack electron-rich areas of organic molecules like double bonds.
- They are positively charged ions or molecules that have an electron-deficient atom (shown by δ^+).
- Electrophiles are defined as electron pair acceptors.

Some examples of electrophiles include:

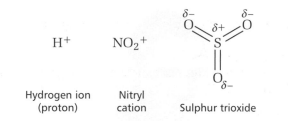

Hydrogen ion   Nitryl
(proton)   cation   Sulphur trioxide

The symbol El^+ or El is used to indicate any electrophile. Note that some are positively charged and some neutral overall.

7.6.4 How electrophiles react

1. First the electrophile is attracted to an electron-rich area of the molecule, such as a carbon–carbon double bond.

2. It then accepts a pair of electrons from the double bond and forms a single bond with one of the carbon atoms. This produces an intermediate:

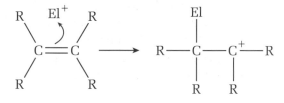

Notice that in the intermediate the carbon that is *not* bonded to the electrophile is forming only three bonds. It therefore has only six electrons in its outer shell and is

positively charged. If the electrophile has a positive charge, a positive ion is formed.

3. The resulting positive ion (sometimes called a **carbocation**) will then be attacked by a negative ion, which forms a bond using a lone pair of electrons. For example:

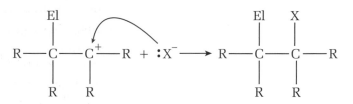

7.6.5 Free radicals

A free radical has an unpaired electron. A pair of free radicals is formed when a single covalent bond between two atoms breaks and one of the shared pair of electrons goes to each atom, for example:

$$Br—Br \rightarrow Br\cdot + Br\cdot$$

This is called **homolysis** (equal breaking) because one electron of the bond goes to each atom.

Most free radicals are extremely reactive. They attack any other molecules in order to gain another electron, for example:

$$Br\cdot + CH_4 \rightarrow \cdot CH_3 + HBr$$

Unless the reaction is between two free-radicals, a new free radical is always formed.

> **HINT**
>
> Another way in which a bond can break is called **heterolysis**. Both shared electrons go to one species and none to the other, so ions are formed rather than radicals. For example:
>
> $$H—Cl \rightarrow H^+ + :Cl^-$$
>
> The electrons both go to the chlorine atom as it is more electronegative than hydrogen.

QUICK QUESTIONS

These questions are about the following species:

$$:NH_3 \; , \; :\overline{O}H \; , \; Cl\overset{\bullet}{} \; , \; H^+$$

     A   B   C   D

1 Which one is a neutral nucleophile?

2 Which one is a negatively charged nucleophile?

3 Which one is a free radical?

4 Which one is an electrophile?

5 Which one has been formed by bond homolysis?

The yield of a chemical reaction

When we write an equation, it is implied that the reaction takes place and all the reactants are turned into products. In theory, we should be able to obtain all the products from our experiment. Our **yield** would then be 100%.

In practice this never happens. Even if all the reactants completely react together, we can never recover all the products. There will always be losses during the practical work that is carried out during the reaction. For example, when filtering there will always be some material left on the filter paper; when pouring there will always be droplets left behind in the original container and so on.

Filtering – this procedure always produces losses

In organic chemistry, yields are usually much lower than 100% for two more reasons:

- The reaction may be reversible and form an equilibrium mixture, see Section 15.1.1, so that not all of the reactants are converted into products.
- There may be two or even more alternative products that can be produced from the same starting materials.

7.7.1 Working out the yield of a reaction

The yield for any particular product of a chemical reaction is the number of moles of it we actually obtain, divided by the number of moles we could have obtained if all the reactant had been converted to product. It is usually expressed as a percentage. So:

$$\text{Yield} = \frac{\text{actual number of moles of product}}{\text{maximum possible number of moles of product}} \times 100\%$$

Example 1

The following equation is about the reaction between bromoethane and sodium hydroxide to produce ethanol:

$$CH_3CH_2Br + NaOH \rightarrow CH_3CH_2OH + NaBr$$

bromoethane			ethanol	
1 mol	1 mol		1 mol	1 mol

The equation shows us that if we start with 1 mol of bromoethane we should get 1 mol of ethanol. Working in grams, this means that 108.9 g of bromoethane should give 46.0 g of ethanol. But, some of the starting material is converted into ethene, $CH_2{=}CH_2$ by the following reaction:

$$CH_3CH_2Br + NaOH \rightarrow CH_2{=}CH_2 + NaBr + H_2O$$

If 1.089 g of bromoethane ($M_r = 108.9$) produces 0.40 g of ethanol ($M_r = 46$) what is the yield of ethanol?

Number of moles of bromoethane $= \dfrac{1.089}{108.9} = 0.01$

Therefore maximum possible number of moles of ethanol $= 0.01$

Number of moles of ethanol $= \dfrac{0.40}{46.0} = 0.0087$

Yield $= \dfrac{\text{actual number of moles of product}}{\text{maximum possible number of moles of product}} \times 100\%$

So, yield of ethanol $= \left(\dfrac{0.0087}{0.01}\right) \times 100\,\% = 87\%$

Example 2

Methane burns in the oxygen in air to form carbon dioxide and water, but some carbon monoxide and soot (carbon) may also form. The equation for complete combustion is:

$$\begin{array}{ccccccc} CH_4(g) & + & 2O_2(g) & \rightarrow & CO_2(g) & + & 2H_2O(l) \\ \text{1 mol} & & & & \text{1 mol} & & \\ \text{16.0 g} & & & & \text{44.0 g} & & \end{array}$$

In a laboratory experiment, methane was burnt and the carbon dioxide produced was weighed. 4.0 g of methane produced 5.5 g carbon dioxide. What is the yield of carbon dioxide?

Number of moles in 4.0 g of methane is $\dfrac{4.0}{16.0} = 0.25$

So, maximum number of moles of carbon dioxide $= 0.25$ (if reaction goes to completion)

Number of moles in 5.5 g of carbon dioxide is $\dfrac{5.5}{44.0} = 0.125$

Yield $= \dfrac{0.125}{0.25} \times 100\% = 50\%$

7.7.2 Improving the yield

Both in the laboratory and in industry, chemists try to produce the greatest possible yields in their reactions. They may try to do this by:

- Selecting reactions that do not lead to two (or more) different products.
- Choosing reaction conditions that force any equilibria in the direction of the required product.
- Improving their practical techniques to reduce any losses.

QUICK QUESTIONS

1 In Example 1 what is the yield if:

   a 2.18 g of bromoethane produce 0.75 g of ethanol?

   b 0.327 g of bromoethane produce 0.105 g of ethanol?

2 In Example 2 above what is the yield if 8.25 g of carbon dioxide is produced?

3 Suggest how the yield of carbon dioxide could be increased.

7.8 Molecular orbitals

A more sophisticated picture of bonding than 'dot-and-cross' diagrams uses the idea of **molecular orbitals**. An orbital is a volume of space where an electron charge is likely to be found, Section 1.4.4. This idea is particularly useful in organic chemistry.

7.8.1 Covalent bonding

When a covalent bond is formed, an atomic orbital from one atom overlaps an atomic orbital from the other atom to form a new molecular orbital, which spreads across both atoms. As with atomic orbitals, a single molecular orbital can hold up to two electrons. A bond is formed when electrons from atomic orbitals fill molecular orbitals.

- The shapes of *atomic* orbitals are called s, p and d – see Section 1.4.4.
- The shape of a *molecular* orbital depends on the atomic orbitals from which it was formed.
- There are two types of molecular orbitals, which have different shapes. They are called σ-(sigma) and π-(pi) orbitals.

7.8.2 σ-(sigma) orbitals

σ-orbitals always have rotational symmetry about a line joining the two atoms that are bonded together.

There are three ways in which σ- (sigma) orbitals may form:

1. Two s-orbitals can overlap

In hydrogen, H_2, for example, the two 1s-orbitals can overlap, as in Figure 7.5. The new orbital shows electrons concentrated *between* the nuclei. The new orbital has rotational symmetry about a line joining the nuclei, Figure 7.6.

1s atomic   1s atomic σ molecular orbital
orbital   orbital

Fig 7.5 *Molecular orbital picture of the hydrogen molecule, H_2*

Fig 7.6 *The shape of a σ-orbital is unaffected by rotation about the axis joining the nuclei*

2. An s- and a p-orbital can overlap

σ-orbitals may also be formed by overlap of an s- and a p-orbital as in hydrogen fluoride, HF, Figure 7.7.

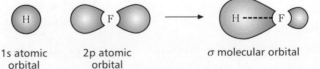

1s atomic   2p atomic σ molecular orbital
orbital   orbital

Fig 7.7 *A molecular orbital picture of the bonding in hydrogen fluoride, HF*

3. A pair of p-orbitals can also overlap

A pair of p-orbitals can also overlap to give a σ-orbital as in fluorine, F_2, Figure 7.8.

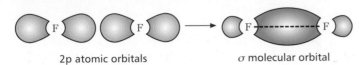

2p atomic orbitals σ molecular orbital

Fig 7.8 *A molecular orbital picture of the bonding in fluorine, F_2*

Note that a σ-orbital is formed when two p-orbitals approach along the line joining the nuclei of their atoms.

7.8.3 π-(pi) orbitals

π-orbitals do not have rotational symmetry. The electron cloud is above and below the line joining the nuclei.

For example, a pair of p-orbitals which are at right angles to the line joining the nuclei overlap as shown in Figure 7.9. The new orbital is called a π-orbital.

- π-orbitals only form where there is already a σ-orbital.
- Bonds formed from electrons in π-orbitals are weaker than those formed from σ-orbitals. The $\sigma + \pi$ combination is usually less than twice as strong as the σ alone.

Double bonds
Double bonds are composed of $\sigma + \pi$ bonds as in oxygen, O_2, Figure 7.10.

Triple bonds
Nitrogen, N_2 has a triple bond – a σ- and two π-orbitals as in Figure 7.11. Notice that there are orbitals holding electrons pairs that take no part in the bonding. These are called lone or unshared pairs. They exist in non-bonding orbitals.

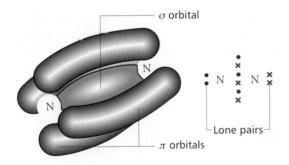

Fig 7.11 *Nitrogen, N_2 has one σ- and two π-molecular orbitals*

7.8.4 Delocalised orbitals

π-orbitals can spread over several atoms. In this case they are described as delocalised. The 'spare' electrons that are responsible for the electrical conduction of graphite (see Section 3.7.2) are in a delocalised π-orbital.

In the same way, we can think of the 'sea' of electrons that hold metals together as existing in a delocalised orbital that spreads over the whole metal structure (see Topic 3.8).

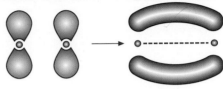

p atomic orbitals π molecular orbital

Fig 7.9 *Formation of a π-molecular orbital*

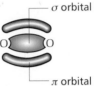

Fig 7.10 *σ and π molecular orbitals in oxygen, O_2*

QUICK QUESTIONS

1 Which of the following orbitals would lead to electron density *between* two nuclei;
   a p,
   b π,
   c σ,
   d s?

2 Which of the following orbitals would lead to electron density *above and below the line joining* two nuclei;
   a p,
   b π,
   c σ,
   d s?

3 Explain why a double bond between two atoms is usually less than twice as strong as a single bond between the same pair of atoms.

4 Suggest what type of orbital (σ or π) would be formed by overlap of an s-orbital with a d-orbital.

Hydrocarbons: alkanes

Alkanes

Alkanes are **saturated** hydrocarbons – they contain only carbon–carbon and carbon–hydrogen *single* bonds. They are among the least reactive organic compounds. They are used as fuels, lubricants and as starting materials for a range of other compounds, so they are very important to industry.

8.1.1 The general formula

The general formula for all chain alkanes is C_nH_{2n+2}. Hydrocarbons may be unbranched chains, branched chains or rings.

Unbranched chains

For example, pentane, C_5H_{12}:

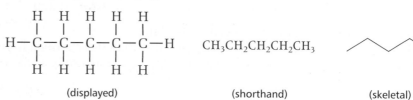

| (displayed) | (shorthand) | (skeletal) |

Unbranched chains are often called 'straight' chains – but the C—C—C angle is 109.5° so the chains are not actually straight.

Branched chains

For example, methylbutane, C_5H_{12}, which is an isomer of pentane:

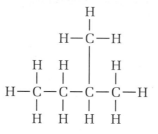

$CH_3CH_2CH(CH_3)CH_3$

| (displayed) | (shorthand) | (skeletal) |

Ring alkanes have the general molecular formula C_nH_{2n} as the 'end' hydrogens are not required.

For example, cyclohexane, C_6H_{12}:

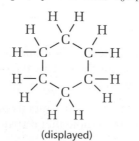

 C_6H_{12}

| (displayed) | (shorthand) | (skeletal) |

8.1.2 How to name alkanes

Straight chains

Alkanes are named from the root, which tells us the number of carbon atoms, and the suffix -ane, denoting an alkane, see Table 8.1.

Table 8.1 *Names of the first twelve alkanes*

Methane	CH_4
Ethane	C_2H_6
Propane	C_3H_8
Butane	C_4H_{10}
Pentane	C_5H_{12}
Hexane	C_6H_{14}
Heptane	C_7H_{16}
Octane	C_8H_{18}
Nonane	C_9H_{20}
Decane	$C_{10}H_{22}$
Undecane	$C_{11}H_{24}$
Dodecane	$C_{12}H_{26}$

Branched chains

When you are naming a hydrocarbon with a branched chain, you must first find the longest unbranched chain – sometimes a bit tricky, see the example below. This gives the root name. Then name the branches or **side chains** as prefixes – methyl-, ethyl-, propyl-, etc. Finally, add a locant to say which carbon each side chain is attached to.

Examples

Both the hydrocarbons below are the same, though they seem different at a first look.

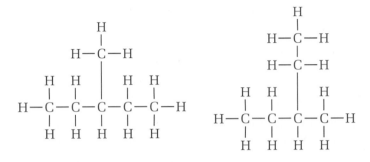

In both molecules, the longest unbranched chain (in red) is five carbons, so the root is pentane. The only side chain has one carbon so it is methyl-. It is attached at carbon number 3 so the full name is 3-methylpentane.

8.1.3 Structure

Isomerism

Methane, ethane and propane have no isomers but, after that, the number of possible isomers increases with the number of carbons in the alkane. For example butane, with four carbons, has two isomers while pentane has three:

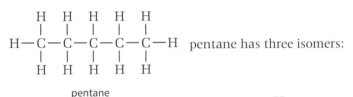

pentane   pentane has three isomers:

methylbutane   and   2,2-dimethylpropane

8.1.4 Physical properties

Alkanes are almost non-polar because the electronegativities of carbon (2.5) and hydrogen (2.1) are so similar. So, the only intermolecular forces between their molecules are weak van der Waals forces – and the larger the molecule the stronger the van der Waals forces.

This is why the boiling temperatures of alkanes increase as the chain length increases. The shorter chains are gases at room temperature. Pentane, with five carbons, is a liquid with a low boiling temperature ($T_b = 309K$). Then when we reach a chain length of about 18 carbons, the alkanes become solids at room temperature. The solids have a waxy feel.

Alkanes with branched chains have lower boiling points than straight chain alkanes with the same number of carbon atoms. This is because they do not pack together so well.

Alkanes are insoluble in water but mix with other relatively non-polar liquids.

Camping gas is a mixture of propane and butane. Polar expeditions use special gas mixtures with a higher proportion of propane, because butane is liquid below 272K (−1°C)

The effect of increasing chain length on the physical properties of alkanes

8.1.5 How alkanes react

Alkanes are unreactive. They have strong carbon–carbon and carbon–hydrogen bonds. Also, these bonds are almost non-polar so they are not attacked by nucleophiles or electrophiles.

QUICK QUESTIONS

1 Name the alkane $CH_3CH_2CH(CH_3)CH_3$.
2 Draw the displayed structural formula of 2-methylhexane.
3 Name an isomer of 2-methylhexane that has a straight chain.
4 Which of the two isomers will have the higher boiling point?
5 Explain your answer to 4.

Alkanes are quite unreactive. Their strong, non-polar bonds mean that they do not react with polar reagents (nucleophiles and electrophiles). They do not react with acids, bases, oxidising and reducing agents. But, they do burn and they will react with halogens under suitable conditions.

8.2.1 Combustion

The shorter chain alkanes burn completely in a plentiful supply of oxygen to give carbon dioxide and water.

For example, methane:

$$CH_4(g) + 2O_2(g) \rightarrow CO_2(g) + 2H_2O(l) \qquad \Delta H = -890 \, \text{kJ mol}^{-1}$$

These combustion reactions give out heat – they have large negative enthalpies of combustion, see Chapter 13. For this reason they are important to us as fuels. Examples include:

methane (natural or 'North Sea' gas),

propane ('camping' gas),

butane ('Calor' gas),

petrol (a mixture of hydrocarbons of approximate chain length C_8),

paraffin (a mixture of hydrocarbons of chain lengths C_{10} to C_{18}).

Incomplete combustion

In a limited supply of oxygen, the poisonous gas carbon monoxide, CO, is formed, for example:

$$C_3H_8(g) + 3\tfrac{1}{2}O_2(g) \rightarrow 3CO(g) + 4H_2O(l)$$

This is called incomplete combustion.

With even less oxygen, carbon (soot) is produced. This often happens with longer chain hydrocarbons, which need more oxygen to burn compared with shorter chains.

8.2.2 Reaction with halogens

When we put a mixture of an alkane and a halogen into bright sunlight, or shine a photoflood lamp onto the mixture, the alkane and the halogen will react to form a halogenoalkane. The ultraviolet component of the light starts the reaction. Alkanes do not react with halogens in the dark at room temperature.

For example, if you put a mixture of hexane and a little liquid bromine into a test-tube and leave it in the dark it stays red-brown (the colour of bromine). But, if you shine ultraviolet light onto it, the mixture becomes colourless, and misty fumes of hydrogen bromide appear.

A substitution reaction has taken place – one of the hydrogen atoms in the alkane has been replaced by a bromine atom and hydrogen bromide is given off as a gas. The main reaction is:

$$\underset{\text{hexane}}{C_6H_{14}(g)} + \underset{\text{bromine}}{Br_2(l)} \rightarrow \underset{\text{bromohexane}}{C_6H_{13}Br(l)} + \underset{\text{hydrogen bromide}}{HBr(g)}$$

Bromohexane is a halogenoalkane.

NOTE

You can test for hydrogen bromide by wafting the fumes from a bottle of ammonia over the mouth of the test tube – white fumes of ammonium bromide are formed. This test will also give a positive result for other hydrogen halides.

Chain reactions

The reaction above is called a **free-radical substitution.** It starts off a **chain reaction** which takes place in three stages – **initiation**, **propagation** and **termination**.

The reaction between any alkane and a halogen goes by the same mechanism.

For example, methane and chlorine:

$$CH_4(g) + Cl_2(g) \rightarrow CH_3Cl(g) + HCl(g)$$

Initiation

The first or initiation step of the reaction is the breaking of the Cl—Cl bond to form two chlorine **free radicals**, see Section 7.6.5:

$$Cl—Cl \xrightarrow{\text{UV light}} 2Cl\cdot$$

- The chlorine molecule absorbs the energy of a single quantum of ultraviolet (UV) light. The energy of one quantum of UV light is greater than the Cl—Cl bond energy, so the bond will break.
- The Cl—Cl bond breaks homolytically, i.e. one electron goes to each chlorine atom.
- This results in two separate chlorine atoms, written Cl·. They are called free radicals. The dot is used to show the unpaired electron.

The C—H bond needs more energy to break than is available in a quantum of ultraviolet radiation, so this bond does not break.

Propagation

This takes place in two stages.

1. Free radicals are highly reactive and take a hydrogen atom from methane to form hydrogen chloride. This leaves a methyl free radical.

$$Cl\cdot + CH_4 \rightarrow HCl + \cdot CH_3$$

2. The methyl free radical is also very reactive and combines with a chlorine atom from another chlorine molecule. Chloromethane is formed and this is a stable compound.

$$\cdot CH_3 + Cl_2 \rightarrow CH_3Cl + Cl\cdot$$

The effect of these two steps is to produce hydrogen chloride, chloromethane and a new Cl· free radical. This is ready to react with more methane and repeat the two steps. This is the chain part of the chain reaction. These steps may take place thousands of times before the radicals are destroyed in the termination stage.

Termination

Termination is the step in which the free radicals are removed. This can happen in any of the following three ways:

- $Cl\cdot + Cl\cdot \rightarrow Cl_2$ Two chlorine free-radicals react together to give a chlorine molecule.

- $\cdot CH_3 + \cdot CH_3 \rightarrow C_2H_6$ Two methyl free-radicals react together to give ethane.

- $Cl\cdot + \cdot CH_3 \rightarrow CH_3Cl$ A chlorine and a methyl free-radical react together to give chloromethane.

Other products of the chain reaction

Other products are formed as well as the main ones, chloromethane and hydrogen chloride.

- Some ethane is produced at the termination stage, as shown above.
- Dichloromethane may be made at the propagation stage, if a chlorine radical reacts with some chloromethane that has already formed:

$$CH_3Cl + Cl\cdot \rightarrow \cdot CH_2Cl + HCl$$

followed by $\cdot CH_2Cl + Cl_2 \rightarrow CH_2Cl_2 + Cl\cdot$

With longer-chain alkanes there will be many isomers formed, because the Cl· can replace *any* of the hydrogen atoms.

Chain reactions are not very useful because they produce such a mixture of products. They will also occur without light at high temperatures.

QUICK QUESTIONS

1 Write the equation for the complete combustion of butane, C_4H_{10}.

2 What stage of a free-radical reaction of bromine with methane is represented by:

   a $Br\cdot + Br\cdot \rightarrow Br_2$,

   b $CH_4 + Br\cdot \rightarrow CH_3\cdot + HBr$,

   c $\cdot CH_3 + Br_2 \rightarrow CH_3Br + Br\cdot$,

   d $Br_2 \rightarrow 2Br\cdot$?

Hydrocarbons: fuels

Petroleum

A vast amount of crude oil is converted into petrol and other fuels for vehicles

9.1.1 Crude oil

Crude oil is at present the world's main source of organic chemicals. It was produced over millions of years by the breakdown of plant and animal remains at the high pressures and temperatures deep below the sea. Because it originated so long ago, it is called a fossil fuel and is not renewable.

Crude oil is a mixture mostly of alkanes, both unbranched and branched. Crude oils from different sources have different compositions. The composition of a typical North Sea crude oil is given in Table 9.1.

Table 9.1 *The composition of a typical North Sea crude oil*

Product	Gases	Petrol	Naphtha	Kerosene	Gas oil	Fuel oil and wax
Approximate boiling temperature/K	310	310–450	400–490	430–523	590–620	above 620
Chain length	1–5	5–10	8–12	11–16	16–24	25+
Percentage present	2	8	10	14	21	45

Crude oil contains small amounts of other compounds, for example some that contain sulphur. These produce sulphur dioxide, SO_2, when they are burned. This is one of the causes of acid rain – it reacts with oxygen and water in the atmosphere to form sulphuric acid.

9.1.2 Fractional distillation of crude oil

To convert crude oil into useful products we have to separate the mixture. We do this by heating it and collecting the **fractions** that boil over different ranges of temperatures. Each fraction is a mixture of hydrocarbons that have a similar chain length and therefore similar properties, see Figure 9.1. The process is called **fractional distillation** and it is done in a **fractionating tower**.

• The crude oil is first heated in a furnace so that it vaporises.

• The vapours pass into a tower that is cooler at the top than at the bottom.

• They pass up the tower via a series of trays containing bubble caps until they arrive at a tray that is sufficiently cool (at a lower temperature than their boiling point). Then they condense to liquid.

• The mixture of liquids that condenses on each tray is piped off.

• The shorter chain hydrocarbons condense in the trays nearer to the top of the tower, where it is cooler, because they have lower boiling points.

• The thick residue that collects at the base of the tower is called tar or bitumen and is used for road surfacing.

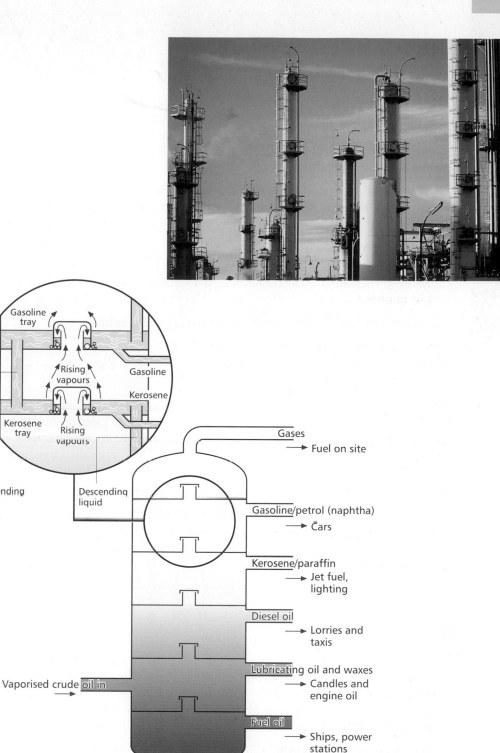

Crude oil is separated into fractions by distillation in cylindrical towers typically 8 m in diameter and 40 m high

Fig 9.1 *The fractional distillation of crude oil*

QUICK QUESTIONS

1 What is the molecular formula of heptane?

2 In which of the crude oil fractions named in Table 9.1 is heptane most likely to be found?

3 Write an equation for the formation of sulphur dioxide when sulphur is burned.

Industrial cracking

The petrol and naphtha fractions from the fractional distillation of crude oil are in huge demand in industry. The longer chain fractions are not as useful. Most crude oil has more of the longer chain fractions than is wanted and not enough of the petrol and naphtha fractions.

To meet the demand for the shorter chain hydrocarbons, many of the longer chain fractions are broken into shorter lengths (cracked). This has two useful results:

- Shorter, more-useful chains are produced
- Some of the products are alkenes, see Topic 10.1, which are more reactive than alkanes. They are used as chemical feedstock and are converted to other compounds.

There are a number of different ways of carrying out **cracking**.

9.2.1 Thermal cracking

This reaction involves heating alkanes to a high temperature, under high pressure. Carbon–carbon bonds break homolytically – one electron from the pair in the bond goes to each carbon atom. So two shorter chains are produced, each ending in carbon atom with an unpaired electron. These are called free radicals, Section 7.6.5.

As there are not enough hydrogen atoms to produce two alkanes, one of the new chains must have a carbon–carbon double bond, for example:

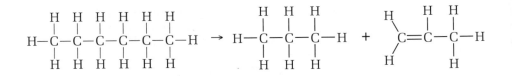

Any number of carbon–carbon bonds may break and the chain does not necessarily break in the middle.

9.2.2 Catalytic cracking

Catalytic cracking takes place at a lower temperature (approximately 800 K) using a zeolite catalyst, consisting of silicon dioxide and aluminium oxide. Zeolites have a honeycomb structure with an enormous surface area. They are also acidic. This form of cracking is used mainly to produce motor fuels and also **aromatic** compounds, see Figure 9.2.

In the laboratory, cracking may be carried out in the apparatus shown in Figure 9.3, using lumps of aluminium oxide as a catalyst.

The products are mostly gases, showing that they have chain lengths of less than C_5 and the mixture decolourises bromine solution, showing that it contains alkenes, Topic 10.2.2.

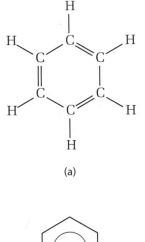

(a)

(b)

Fig 9.2 *Aromatic compounds are based on the benzene ring, C_6H_6. Although it appears to have three double bonds (a), the electrons in these are spread around the ring to make a very stable compound, usually represented as in (b). This is an example of delocalised bonding, see Section 7.8.4*

9.2.3 Isomerisation and reforming

A number of other processes are carried out on the products of fractional distillation and cracking to make better motor fuels. These include isomerisation and reforming.

Isomerisation

Straight chain alkanes make relatively poor motor fuels. They cause 'knocking' in the engine by detonating rapidly rather than burning steadily. Branched chains burn more smoothly which promotes efficient combustion. To produce branched chain alkanes, we heat straight chain alkanes under pressure with a platinum catalyst. For example:

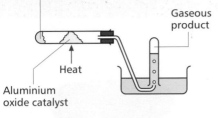

Fig 9.3 *Laboratory cracking of alkanes*

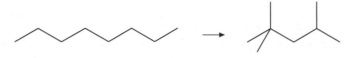

Reforming

In this process, straight chain alkanes are heated under pressure with a catalyst of platinum and alumina. This removes hydrogen in steps and we end up with cyclic hydrocarbons – cycloalkanes and arenes.

For example:

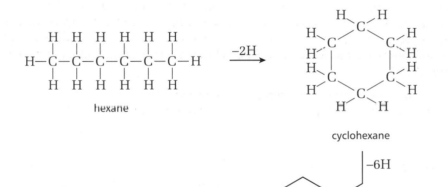

QUICK QUESTIONS

1 Complete the word equation for the cracking of decane:

   decane → octane + ?

2 In the laboratory cracking of alkanes, how can you tell that the products have shorter chains than the starting materials?

3 Why would we not crack octane industrially?

4 How may the temperature required for cracking be reduced?

5 Give two economic reasons for cracking long chain alkanes.

Crude oil and the environment

During the twentieth century crude oil became more and more important to the way of life in industrialised countries. It started by providing us with fuel and lubricants, and then became (from the 1940s onwards) a starting point for synthetic materials – including a variety of plastics tailor-made for different purposes, as well as drugs, dyes, etc. (we call this chemical feedstock). We depend on the products of crude oil for our way of life. Currently the majority of crude oil is used for fuels. As crude oil is used up, we will need to conserve it for use as chemical feedstock, rather than using it up as fuel.

9.3.1 Crude oil-based fuels

Crude oil-based fuels are produced by the distillation and cracking of crude oil, see Topics 9.1 and 9.2. They are alkanes which include methane (CH_4), natural gas; butane (C_4H_{10}), bottled gas; and octane (C_8H_{18}), a constituent of petrol. These all burn in air to give out large quantities of heat.

For example:

$$C_4H_{10} + 6\tfrac{1}{2}O_2 \rightarrow 4CO_2 + 5H_2O \qquad \Delta H = -2877 \text{ kJ mol}^{-1}$$
butane

The heat given out is the difference between the energy that has to be put in to break the bonds in the reactants and the energy that is given out when the bonds are formed in the products, Section 13.9.1. These fuels give out a lot of heat when one gram is burnt. We say they have a high **energy density**. Butane gives out about 50 kJ per gram when burned. Fuels used for transport need to have a high energy density because we need a large amount of energy from the least possible mass.

All hydrocarbon fuels produce polluting products when they burn. These include:

- carbon monoxide – a toxic gas
- unburnt hydrocarbons – these may form photochemical smogs
- carbon dioxide – a greenhouse gas
- nitrogen oxides (from the chemical reaction of nitrogen and oxygen in the air) – these contribute to acid rain
- sulphur dioxide (from the combustion of sulphur-containing impurities) – these also contribute to acid rain.

Crude oil is a fossil fuel. It has taken over a million years to be produced from plant and animal decay. It cannot be renewed in the short term so we are developing alternative sources of energy.

9.3.2 Biofuels

Biofuels are fuels that are obtained from fast-growing plants so they are renewable. Some biofuels can be used as they are, for example straw or wood can be burnt directly. Others crops such as sugar and rape-seed oil need chemical treatment to turn them into useable sources of energy.

Ethanol

Ethanol, C_2H_5OH, when made from fermentation of sugar and other carbohydrates obtained from plants, is a biofuel. It burns in oxygen to form carbon dioxide and water:

$$C_2H_5OH + 3O_2 \rightarrow 2CO_2 + 3H_2O \qquad \Delta H = -1367 \text{ kJ mol}^{-1}$$

Ethanol has an energy density of about 30 kJ per gram, significantly less than

Crude oil is the starting material for many plastics

alkane fuels (typically around 50 kJ per gram). With a little modification, normal car engines can run on pure ethanol or ethanol/petrol mixtures. This has been done in Brazil, for example, to reduce the need to import crude oil.

An ethanol-fuelled car

Biodiesel

Biodiesel is a fuel made from rape-seed oil (rape is a yellow flowered crop commonly seen in the spring). Biodiesel can replace diesel fuel in vehicles and is being used in trials for more widespread adoption in the future.

9.3.3 Hydrogen

Hydrogen (mixed with carbon monoxide) is the gas once used in our homes for cooking and heating. The mixture was called town gas and was produced by heating coke, C, with steam, H_2O.

Hydrogen can be also be made from the electrolysis of water. If the electricity used in electrolysis can be supplied from a renewable source, such as solar or wind power, this will make hydrogen a renewable fuel. When hydrogen is burned it produces fewer pollutants than hydrocarbon fuels because it burns to form water only (although nitrogen oxides are still produced at the high temperatures of the combustion).

Field of rape

$$H_2 + \tfrac{1}{2}O_2 \rightarrow H_2O \qquad \Delta H = -286 \text{ kJ mol}^{-1}$$

Cars can be designed to run on hydrogen, either by burning it in a conventional engine or by using it to generate electricity in a fuel cell to drive an electric motor. Hydrogen has a very high energy density, 143 kJ per gram. The main disadvantage is that like all gases it has a very large volume compared to a liquid fuel. Even when it is compressed in a cylinder, the container is very heavy, weighing much more than the gas it contains.

QUICK QUESTIONS

1 Explain the term 'fossil fuel'.

2 Why are fossil fuels considered to be non-renewable?

3 Write the equations for the complete combustion of
  a hydrogen,   b ethanol.

4 Give an advantage of ethanol over petrol as a car fuel.

5 Give a disadvantage of ethanol over petrol as a car fuel.

Hydrocarbons: alkenes

Alkenes

This polythene washing-up bowl began life as ethene

Alkenes are **unsaturated** hydrocarbons – they have one or more carbon–carbon double bonds and they are made of carbon and hydrogen only. The double bond makes them more reactive than alkanes. Ethene, the simplest alkene, is the starting material for a large range of products, including polymers such as polythene, pvc, polystyrene and Terylene fabric, as well as products like antifreeze and paints. Alkenes are produced in large quantities when crude oil is cracked.

10.1.1 The general formula

The homologous series of chain alkenes with one double bond has the general formula C_nH_{2n}.

10.1.2 How to name alkenes

We cannot have a carbon–carbon double bond if there is only one carbon. So, the

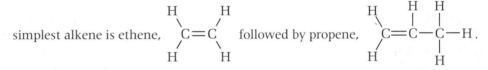

simplest alkene is ethene, followed by propene.

Isomers

Alkenes with more than three carbons can form different types of isomers and we name them according to the IUPAC system, see Topic 7.3.

As well as chain-branching isomers like those found in alkanes, alkenes can form two types of isomers that involve the double bond.

(a) those with the double bond in different positions

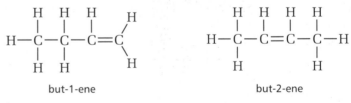

but-1-ene   but-2-ene

(b) *cis–trans*-isomers

Alkenes may have *cis–trans* isomers, see Section 7.4.5. For example, but-2-ene exists as *cis-* and *trans-* isomers. We can see this if the molecule is drawn with the correct bond angles.

cis-but-2-ene

trans-but-2-ene

10.1.3 Structure

The shape of alkenes

Ethene is a flat molecule. The geometry around each carbon atom is based on a trigonal planar shape, because each carbon has three groups of electrons round it. This should make the angle of each bond 120°. However, the H—C—H bond angles are in fact about 118° because the four electrons in the carbon–carbon double bond repel more than the pairs of electrons in the carbon–hydrogen single bonds. This is similar to the situation with lone pairs, see Section 3.3.2.

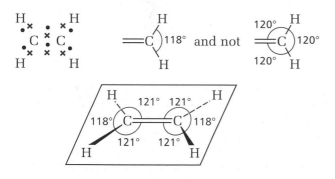

Unlike the C—C bonds in alkanes, there is no rotation about the double bond. You can see why this is if you look at the orbitals that make up the double bond – a σ-orbital from overlap of the p-orbitals along the line joining the nuclei and a π-orbital from the overlap of p-orbitals above and below this line. The orbitals are shown in Figure 10.1 and the photograph.

Fig 10.1 The bonding of ethene

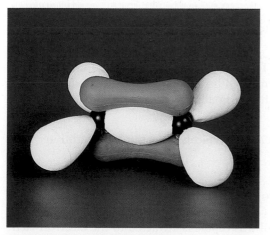

Model of ethene showing orbitals

Any molecules in which a hydrogen atom in ethene is replaced with another atom or group will have the same flat shape around the carbon–carbon double bond.

10.1.4 Physical properties of alkenes

The double bond does not greatly affect properties such as boiling and melting temperatures. van der Waals forces are the only intermolecular forces that act between the alkene molecules. This means that the physical properties of alkenes are very similar to those of the alkanes. The melting and boiling temperatures increase with the number of carbon atoms present, see Table 10.1. Alkenes are not soluble in water, because they are non-polar.

Table 10.1 *Melting and boiling temperatures of some alkenes*

Alkene	T_m/K	T_b/K
ethene	104	169
propene	88	226
but-1-ene	88	268
cyclohexene	170	357

10.1.5 How alkenes react

The double bond makes a big difference to the reactivity of alkenes when compared with alkanes. The bond energy for C—C is 347 kJ mol^{-1} and that for C=C is 612 kJ mol^{-1} so we might predict that alkenes would be less reactive than alkanes. There are three reasons why this is not the case:

- A double bond is made up of a σ-bond plus a π-bond see Topic 7.8. The σ-bond is the same as in the C—C single bond in alkanes, so the π-bond must have an energy of 612 − 347 which is only 265 kJ mol^{-1}. So it is relatively easy to break the π part of the carbon–carbon double bonds, and leave the σ part intact. This is what happens in most reactions of C=C and it is unusual for the carbon chain actually to break in two when alkenes react.
- When the π part of the double bond breaks, each of the carbon atoms is left needing to form a new bond. So, new groups can be added on.
- The C=C forms an electron-rich area in a molecule, which can easily be attacked by positively charged reagents (electrophiles, see Section 7.6.3).

So most of the reactions of alkenes are **electrophilic additions**.

QUICK QUESTIONS

1 What is the name of $CH_3CHCHCH_2CH_2CH_3$?

2 Draw the displayed formula for pent-2-ene.

3 The double bond in an alkene is attacked by
  a electrophiles,   **b** nucleophiles,
  c free radicals,   **d** bases.

4 The double bond in an alkene can be described as
  a electron-rich,   **b** electron-deficient,
  c positively charged,   **d** acidic.

5 Why is the H—C—H angle in ethene slightly less than 120°?

10.2.1 Combustion

Alkenes will burn in air:

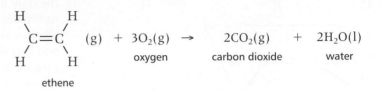

ethene

However, they are not used as fuels. This is because their reactivity makes them very useful for other purposes.

10.2.2 Electrophilic addition reactions

The reactions of alkenes are typically electrophilic additions, Section 10.1.5. The four electrons in the carbon–carbon double bond make it a centre of high electron density. Electrophiles are attracted to it.

HINT

Electrophiles have positively charged areas and will accept a pair of electrons.

Reaction of alkenes with halogens

Alkenes react rapidly with chlorine gas, or with solutions of bromine and iodine in an organic solvent, to give 1,2-dihalogenoalkanes.

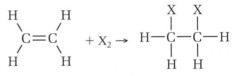

where X_2 is any halogen molecule. The halogen atoms *add* across the double bond.

The test for a double bond

This addition reaction is used to test for a carbon–carbon double bond. When a few drops of bromine solution (which is reddish-brown) are added to an alkene, the solution is decolourised because halogenoalkanes are colourless.

The mechanism

The mechanism by which bromine reacts is typical of electrophilic additions across a double bond.

- The electrophile attacks.
  At any instant, a bromine (or any other halogen) molecule is likely to have an instantaneous dipole: $Br^{\delta+}$—$Br^{\delta-}$. (An instant later, the dipole could be reversed $Br^{\delta-}$—$Br^{\delta+}$.) The $\delta+$ end of this dipole is attracted to the electron-rich double bond in the alkene – it is an electrophile.

- The double bond responds.
  The electrons in the double bond are attracted to the $Br^{\delta+}$. They repel the electrons in the Br—Br bond and this strengthens the dipole of the bromine molecule.

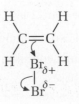

- A positive ion (a carbocation) is formed.
  Two of the electrons from the double bond form a bond with the $Br^{\delta+}$ and the other bromine atom becomes a Br^- ion. This leaves a carbocation, in which the carbon atom that is *not* bonded to the bromine has the positive charge.

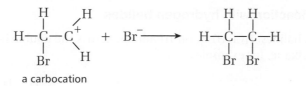

a carbocation

- A negative ion bonds to the carbon that has the positive charge.
  The carbocation is rapidly attacked by any negative ion. The only negative ion present in a non-aqueous solution will be the Br^-.

So the addition takes place in two steps:

1. formation of the carbocation by electrophilic addition;
2. rapid reaction with a negative ion.

Notice the difference:

- Halogens react with *alkanes* via homolytic fission of the X—X bond using ultraviolet light, followed by free-radical substitution, Section 7.6.5.
- Halogens react with *alkenes* via electrophilic addition that does not need ultraviolet light.

QUICK QUESTIONS

1 Write the equation for the complete combustion of propene.

2 What is the product of the reaction between propene and bromine?

3 Are the typical reactions of alkenes
  a electrophilic additions,
  b electrophilic substitutions or
  c nucleophilic substitutions?

4 The test for a carbon–carbon double bond is
  a a white precipitate with silver nitrate,
  b that limewater goes milky or
  c that bromine solution is decolourised?

More reactions of alkenes

10.3.1 Reaction with hydrogen halides

Hydrogen halides, HCl, HBr and HI add on across the double bond to form a halogenoalkane, for example:

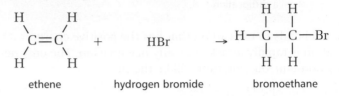

ethene   hydrogen bromide   bromoethane

The bond in hydrogen bromide breaks heterolytically (one electron from the shared pair in the bond goes to each atom) to give H^+ and Br^-. The H^+ ion is a good electrophile and forms a bond with two of the electrons in the carbon–carbon double bond. This leaves a positively charged ion that is rapidly attacked by the Br^- ion.

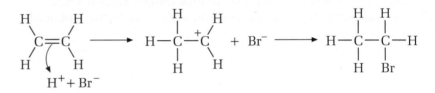

When hydrogen bromide adds on to ethene, bromoethane is the only possible product.

When the double bond is not in the middle of the chain, there are two possible products, because the bromine of the hydrogen bromide could bond to either of the carbon atoms of the double bond.

For example, propene:

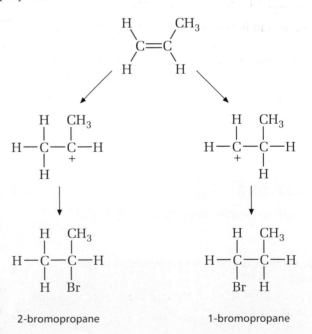

2-bromopropane   1-bromopropane

In fact the product is almost entirely 2-bromopropane.

10.3.2 Reaction with water

Water also adds on across the double bond in alkenes. The reaction is used industrially to make alcohols and is carried out with steam, using an acid catalyst such as phosphoric acid, H_3PO_4.

For example:

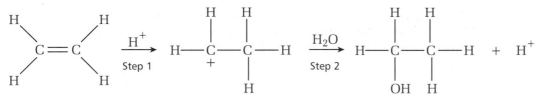

Notice how the H^+ ion, which comes from the phosphoric acid is used in step 1 and reformed in step 2 – it is acting as a catalyst.

10.3.3 Addition of hydrogen

Hydrogen reacts with alkenes by adding across the double bonds to make them into alkanes. This takes place at room temperature and pressure using a highly porous nickel catalyst called Raney nickel. For example:

This reaction is used in industry in the manufacture of margarines from vegetable oils. Vegetable oils are liquids containing long hydrocarbon chains with several double bonds – they are polyunsaturated, Figure 10.2.

They are 'hardened' to make margarines by reducing the number of double bonds. Oils with fewer double bonds have higher melting temperatures than polyunsaturated ones. Their molecules are more regularly shaped and pack together better making them harder to separate.

In industry the reaction is carried out at around 420 K and 500 kPa pressure using a powdered nickel catalyst. The reaction conditions are controlled so that only enough double bonds are hydrogenated to make margarine of the correct hardness. Unsaturated fats have dietary advantages over saturated ones.

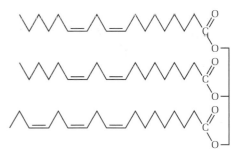

Fig 10.2 *A typical unsaturated vegetable oil before reaction with hydrogen*

QUICK QUESTIONS

1 What is the product of the reaction between ethene and hydrogen chloride?

2 Addition of hydrogen to alkenes produces

   a alcohols,   **b** alkanes,   **c** alkalis.

3 Suggest why it as an advantage for Raney nickel catalyst to be highly porous.

10.4 Polymerisation

10.4.1 Addition polymerisation

Alkenes can polymerise, joining together to form long chains with very high relative molecular masses (as much as 1 000 000). For example, ethene, C_2H_4, is the **monomer** and it polymerises to form poly(ethene):

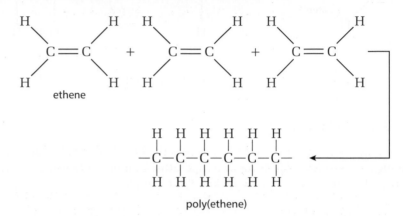

poly(ethene)

This reaction is **addition polymerisation**. The polymer is named poly(ethene) from the monomer but is usually called polythene. Despite the ending -ene the polymer is actually an alkane and is therefore unreactive.

The repeat unit of a polymer is the smallest group of atoms that is repeated over and over, see Figure 10.3.

Different forms of poly(ethene) can be made depending on the conditions of temperature, pressure and catalyst. These differ in chain length and also in the amount of branching.

Another polymer is poly(propene). This is formed from the monomer propene, CH_3CHCH_2:

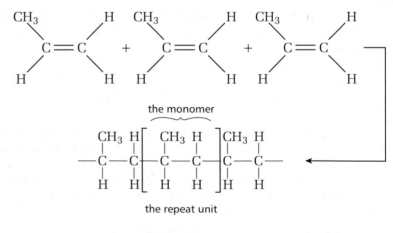

the monomer

the repeat unit

poly(propene)

The repeat unit is shown in brackets. In this case it is CH_3CHCH_2, the same as the monomer.

Table 10.2 is a summary of some polymers using monomers based on the ethene molecule, in which one of the hydrogen atoms is replaced by another group. The repeat unit is bracketed.

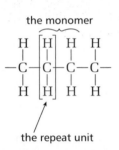

the monomer

the repeat unit

Fig 10.3 *In polythene the repeat unit is CH_2, (in square brackets) so in this case, the repeat unit is not the same as the monomer C_2H_4, (in red)*

Table 10.2 *Some polymers in everyday use. The repeat units for the polymers are in brackets*

Monomer	Polymer	Systematic chemical name	Common name or trade name (in capitals)	Typical uses
$CH_2{=}CH_2$	$-CH_2{-}[CH_2]{-}n$	poly(ethene)	polythene or polyethylene ALKATHENE	washing-up bowls, plastic bags
CH_3 $\vert$ $CH{=}CH_2$	$\begin{bmatrix} CH_3 \\ \vert \\ CH{-}CH_2 \end{bmatrix} n$	poly(propene)	polypropylene	rope
Cl $\vert$ $CH{=}CH_2$	$\begin{bmatrix} Cl \\ \vert \\ CH{-}CH_2 \end{bmatrix} n$	poly(chlorethene)	polyvinylchloride PVC	vinyl records
CN $\vert$ $CH{=}CH_2$	$\begin{bmatrix} CN \\ \vert \\ CH{-}CH_2 \end{bmatrix} n$	poly(propenenitrile)	polyacrylonitrile acrylic fibre COURTELLE	clothing
$CF_2{=}CF_2$	$-CF_2{-}[CF_2]{-}n$	poly(1,1,2,2-tetrafluoroethene)	TEFLON	coating cookware

This 'vinyl' record is made from pvc

10.4.2 Problems with plastics

Most plastics are not broken down by microbes quickly, and many not at all. They are not **biodegradable**. This is a problem that has become more obvious with time as more and more plastic litter is produced.

Buried plastics in landfill sites may take hundreds of years to decompose.

The solutions
We need to reduce the amount of plastic we use or to recycle it.

- **Mechanical recycling**
  The simplest form of recycling is called mechanical recycling. The first step is to separate the different types of plastics. (Plastic containers are now collected in recycling facilities for this purpose.) The plastics are then washed and once they are sorted they may be ground up into small pellets. These can be melted and remoulded. For example, recycled soft drinks bottles are used to make fleece clothes.

- **Feedstock recycling**
  Here, the plastics are heated to a temperature that will break the polymer bonds and produce monomers. These can then be used to make new plastics.

There are problems with recycling. Polythene is a thermoplastic polymer, which means that it will soften when heated, so it can be melted and re-used. This can only be done a limited number of times, however, because at each heating, some of the chains break and become shorter thus affecting the plastic's properties.

- **Burning**
  We can burn some plastics, such as poly(ethene) for fuel, but others produce toxic fumes in the gases given off. These gases include hydrogen chloride, from plastics, like PVC, which contain chlorine. This can be removed by passing the flue gases through water. The hydrogen chloride dissolves to form hydrochloric acid and this is then neutralised with sodium hydroxide. The process is called scrubbing.

Park bench made from recycled plastic

QUICK QUESTIONS

1 A sample of poly(thene) has an average relative molecular mass of 28 000. How many monomers are linked together to form the chain?

2 Identify (a) the monomer and (b) the repeat unit in each of the following:

(a)
$$-\overset{\overset{\displaystyle R}{\vert}}{C}-\overset{\overset{\displaystyle H}{\vert}}{\underset{\underset{\displaystyle H}{\vert}}{C}}-\overset{\overset{\displaystyle R}{\vert}}{\underset{\underset{\displaystyle H}{\vert}}{C}}-\overset{\overset{\displaystyle H}{\vert}}{\underset{\underset{\displaystyle H}{\vert}}{C}}-\overset{\overset{\displaystyle R}{\vert}}{\underset{\underset{\displaystyle H}{\vert}}{C}}-\overset{\overset{\displaystyle H}{\vert}}{\underset{\underset{\displaystyle H}{\vert}}{C}}-$$

(b)
$$-\overset{\overset{\displaystyle R}{\vert}}{C}-\overset{\overset{\displaystyle R}{\vert}}{\underset{\underset{\displaystyle H}{\vert}}{C}}-\overset{\overset{\displaystyle R}{\vert}}{\underset{\underset{\displaystyle H}{\vert}}{C}}-\overset{\overset{\displaystyle R}{\vert}}{\underset{\underset{\displaystyle H}{\vert}}{C}}-\overset{\overset{\displaystyle R}{\vert}}{\underset{\underset{\displaystyle H}{\vert}}{C}}-\overset{\overset{\displaystyle R}{\vert}}{\underset{\underset{\displaystyle H}{\vert}}{C}}-$$

1 Reagents used in organic chemistry may contain electrophiles, nucleophiles or free radicals.

    (i) Explain what is meant by each term.
    (ii) Give an example of each type of species.
    (iii) Write a balanced equation for a reaction that involves each species.

  a (i) *Electrophile*   [1]
      (ii) *Example*   [1]
      (iii) Write a balanced equation to illustrate electrophilic addition.   [1]

  b (i) *Nucleophile*   [1]
      (ii) *Example*   [1]
      (iii) Write a balanced equation to illustrate nucleophilic addition.   [1]

  c (i) *Free radical*   [1]
      (ii) *Example*   [1]
      (iii) Write a balanced equation to illustrate free-radical addition.   [1]

[Total: 9]

OCR, 12 Jun 2001

2 The structures of some saturated hydrocarbon compounds are shown below.

They are labelled **A, B, C, D, E** and **F**.

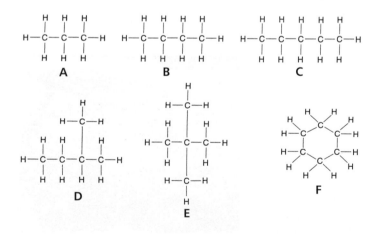

A   **B**   **C**

D   **E**   **F**

  a The general formula of an alkane is C_nH_{2n+2}.

    (i) Which of the compounds, **A** to **F**, has a formula that does **not** fit with this general formula? [1]
    (ii) **A, B** and **C** are successive members of the alkane series.
      What is the **molecular** formula of the next number in the series? [1]
    (iii) What is the **empirical** formula of compound **F**? [1]

b Three of compounds **A** to **F** are structural isomers of each other.

    (i) Identify, by letter, which of the compounds are the three structural isomers. [1]
    (ii) Explain what is meant by the term *structural isomer*. [1]

c (i) Which of the compounds, **A, B** or **C**, would you expect to have the highest boiling point? [1]
    (ii) Which of the compounds, **C, D** or **E**, would you expect to have the highest boiling point? [1]
    (iii) Explain your answers to **c**(i) and **c**(ii) in terms of intermolecular forces [3]

[Total: 10]

OCR, 12 Jun 2001

3 Ethene can be used to manufacture chloroethene $H_2C{=}CHCl$. This involves the following reactions:

step 1 $H_2C{=}CH_2 + Cl_2 \longrightarrow ClH_2C{-}CH_2Cl$

step 2 $ClH_2C{-}CH_2Cl \xrightarrow{500°C} H_2C{=}CHCl + HCl$

  a (i) State the type of mechanism involved in **step 1**. [2]
    (ii) Complete, with the aid of curly arrows, the mechanism involved in **step 1**. Show any relevant dipoles and charges.

$$H_2C{=}CH_2 \longrightarrow \qquad \longrightarrow ClH_2C{-}CH_2Cl$$

        Cl
        |
        Cl   [4]

b The chloroethene (also known as vinyl chloride) produced can be polymerised to form poly(chloroethene) or PVC.

Draw a section of the polymer, PVC, to show **two** repeat units. [1]

[Total: 7]

OCR, 17 Jan 2003

4 **a** (i) The brominated alkene, $C_3H_4Br_2$, has five posssible structural isomers.
      What is meant by the term *structural isomer*? [2]
    (ii) Two of the structural isomers of $C_3H_4Br_2$ are drawn below.
      Draw the other three **structural** isomers.

$$CH_3CH{=}CBr_2 \qquad CH_3CBr{=}CHBr$$
      1   **2**   [3]

    (iii) Name isomer **1**. [1]

b Isomer **2** in **a**(ii) shows *cis–trans* isomerism.

(i) Draw the *cis* and *trans* isomers of isomer **2**. [2]

(ii) State the approximate bond angle around each carbon atom involved in the C=C double bond of these *cis–trans* isomers. [1]

(iii) Isomer **1** does **not** show *cis–trans* isomerism. Explain why not. [1]

(iv) Identify **one** of your isomers, **3**, **4** or **5** in **a**(ii) that does show *cis–trans* isomerism. [1]

[Total: 11]

OCR, 17 Jan 2003

5 a Propene, C_3H_6, readily undergoes electrophilic reactions. Show, with the aid of curly arrows, the mechanism of the electrophilic addition reaction of propene with bromine.

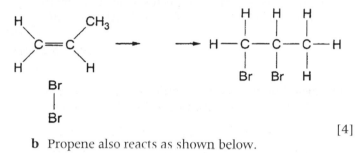

[4]

b Propene also reacts as shown below.

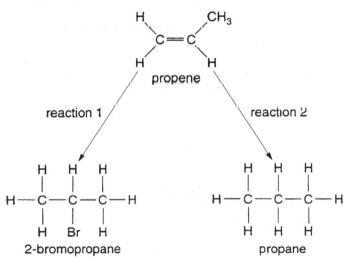

(i) State a suitable reagent for reaction 1. [1]

(ii) State a suitable reagent and conditions for reaction 2. [2]

(iii) In the presence of an acid catalyst, propene can react with steam to form a mixture of two alcohols. Draw the structures of the two alcohols. [2]

c The scientists Ziegler and Natta were awarded a Nobel Prize for chemistry in 1963 for their work on polymerisation. Part of this work involved the polymerisation of propene into poly(propene).

(i) What type of polymerisation forms poly(propene)? [1]

(ii) Draw a section of poly(propene) to show **two** repeat units. [1]

(iii) State **two** difficulties in the disposal of poly(propene). [2]

[Total: 13]

OCR, 17 Jan 2001

Alcohols

Alcohols: introduction

Alcohols have the functional group —OH attached to a hydrocarbon chain. They are relatively reactive. The most common alcohol is ethanol.

11.1.1 The general formula

The general formula of an alcohol is $C_nH_{2n+1}OH$. This is often shortened to ROH.

11.1.2 How to name alcohols

The name of the functional group (the —OH group) is normally given by the suffix '-ol'. (The prefix hydroxy- is used if some other functional groups are present.)

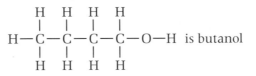 is butanol

Locants

With chains longer than ethanol, we need a locant to show where the —OH group is.

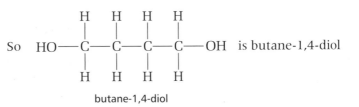 is propan-1-ol and ... is propan-2-ol.

If there is more than one —OH group we use di-, tri-, tetra- etc. to say *how many* —OH groups there are and locants to say *where* they are.

So HO—C—C—C—C—OH is butane-1,4-diol

butane-1,4-diol

and

CH₂OH
|
CHOH   is propane-1,2,3-triol.
|
CH₂OH

11.1.3 Structure

Classification of alcohols

Alcohols are classified as **primary** (1^0), **secondary** (2^0) or **tertiary** (3^0) according to how many other groups (R) are bonded to the carbon that has the —OH group.

Most beers contain around 5% ethanol

In a primary alcohol, this carbon has one R group (and therefore two hydrogen atoms).

H—C—C—C—O—H   propan-1-ol is a primary alcohol.

H—C—O—H   methanol where the carbon has no R groups, is counted as a primary alcohol.

A primary alcohol has the —OH group at the end of the chain.

In a secondary alcohol, the —OH group is attached to a carbon with two R groups (and therefore one hydrogen atom).

H—C—C—C—H   propan-2-ol, is a secondary alcohol.

A secondary alcohol has the —OH group in the body of the chain.

Tertiary alcohols have three R groups attached to the carbon that is bonded to the —OH (so this carbon has no hydrogen atoms).

H—C—C—C—H   2-methylpropan-2-ol is a tertiary alcohol.

A tertiary alcohol has the —OH group at a branch in the chain.

Shape

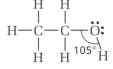

In alcohols, the oxygen atom has two bonding pairs of electrons and two lone pairs. The C—O—H angle is about 105° because the 109.5° angle of a perfect tetrahedron is 'squeezed down' by the presence of the lone pairs – see Section 3.3.2.

11.1.4 Physical properties

The —OH group in alcohols means that hydrogen bonding occurs between the molecules, see Figure 11.1.

> **HINT**
>
> Remember that hydrogen bonding takes place between an electronegative atom, like oxygen, and a hydrogen atom covalently bonded to an electronegative atom, see Topic 3.6.

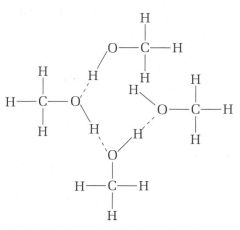

Fig 11.1 Hydrogen bonding in methanol

Boiling and melting temperatures

The hydrogen bonding in alcohols makes their boiling and melting temperatures much higher than those of alkanes of similar relative molecular mass. In other words they are less volatile. For example, butan-1-ol ($M_r = 74$) boils at 390 K while pentane ($M_r = 72$) boils at 309 K. Decanol is the first solid alcohol at room temperature. The first nine shorter chain alcohols are liquids.

Solubility

There is also hydrogen bonding between alcohols and water molecules. So, alcohols with relatively short carbon chains dissolve well in water. The first three alcohols mix completely with water. After this, the solubility in water decreases as the chain length increases.

Alcohols also mix well with non-polar solvents such as hydrocarbons – there is no hydrogen bonding involved in this case.

QUICK QUESTIONS

1 Draw the displayed formula and name the alcohol:

   $CH_3CHOHCH_3$

2 Why is the C—O—H angle less in alcohols than 109.5°?

3 Why do short-chain alcohols dissolve well in water?

11.2.1 How alcohols react

Figure 11.2 shows the bond energies and the electronegativities of the atoms of ethanol.

The C—C bonds and the C—H bonds are not polar, because the difference in electronegativities of the atoms is very small. Also these bonds are quite strong. On the other hand, both the C—O and the O—H bonds are strongly polar, $C^{\delta+}$—$O^{\delta-}$—$H^{\delta+}$, and it is around the C—O—H group that all the reactions take place.

There are two ways in which ethanol (and other alcohols) react:

• The O–H bond breaks.

• The C–O breaks – this is the more common.

In both cases the oxygen ends up with the negative charge. This is because the oxygen atom is so electronegative that it will always capture the electrons.

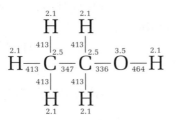

Fig 11.2 *Ethanol, showing the average bond energies and electronegativities*

11.2.2 Combustion

Alcohols burn completely to carbon dioxide and water if there is enough oxygen available. (Otherwise we can have incomplete combustion, see Section 8.2.1) This is the equation for the complete combustion of ethanol:

$$C_2H_5OH(l) + 3O_2(g) \rightarrow 2CO_2(g) + 3H_2O(l)$$

11.2.3 Reaction with sodium

Alcohols react as acids with alkali metals, such as sodium and potassium, to form hydrogen and compounds called metal alkoxides.

For example:

$$Na(s) + C_2H_5OH(l) \rightarrow C_2H_5O^-Na^+(s) + \tfrac{1}{2}H_2(g)$$

ethanol   sodium ethoxide

(Compare this reaction with metal + acid → salt + hydrogen)

In this reaction, the O—H bond of the alcohol breaks. The reaction is similar to the reaction of alkali metals with water, but is less vigorous.

Sodium ethoxide is a white, ionic solid and is left behind when the excess ethanol evaporates. It is a strong base (very alkaline).

If sodium is added to an organic compound and hydrogen is given off, this shows that an —OH group is present.

11.2.4 Substitution by halides

Here the C—O bond of the alcohol breaks, releasing an OH⁻ ion, which is replaced (substituted) by a halide ion, X⁻.

$$R—OH + X^- \rightarrow R—X + OH^-$$

Alcohols react with hydrogen halides (HCl, HBr, HI) to give halogenoalkanes. The rate of reaction is in the order HI > HBr > HCl.

The reaction is catalysed by strong acids. This makes it convenient to make the hydrogen halide in the reaction flask by the reaction of an alkali metal halide with concentrated sulphuric acid. So, we first add the acid to the alcohol in the reaction flask, then the metal halide. For example to make bromoethane, C_2H_5Br:

- The reaction to generate hydrogen bromide:

$$NaBr(s) + H_2SO_4(l) \rightarrow NaHSO_4(s) + HBr(g)$$

The reaction of hydrogen bromide with ethanol:

$$C_2H_5OH(l) + HBr(g) \xrightarrow{H^+ \text{ catalyst}} C_2H_5Br(l) + H_2O(l)$$

(We cannot use this method for hydrogen iodide as sulphuric acid oxidises iodide ions to iodine.)

Sulphuric acid is a dehydrating agent and this helps the loss of a molecule of water.

11.2.5 Esterification

Alcohols react with **carboxylic acids**, general formula RCOOH.

A molecule of water is lost and an **ester**, RCOOR, is produced. The general reaction is:

$$\text{alcohol} + \text{acid} \rightleftharpoons \text{ester} + \text{water}$$

For example:

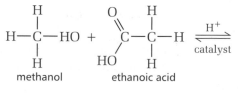

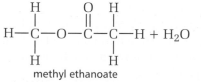

The reaction is catalysed by a strong acid, such as sulphuric acid. It is a reversible reaction and ends up at equilibrium with a mixture of reactants and products, see Chapter 15.

11.2.6 Elimination reactions

Elimination reactions are ones in which a small molecule leaves the parent molecule. In the case of alcohols, this molecule is always water, made from the –OH group and a hydrogen atom from the carbon next to the —OH group. So, the elimination reactions of alcohols are always dehydrations.

Dehydration

Alcohols can be dehydrated with hot concentrated sulphuric acid or by passing their vapours over heated aluminium oxide. An alkene is formed.

For example propan-1-ol is dehydrated to propene:

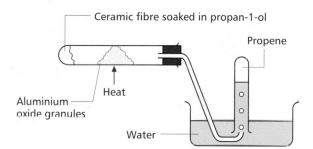

The apparatus used in the laboratory is shown in Figure 11.3.

With longer chain, or branched alcohols, a mixture of alkenes may be produced including ones with *cis* and *trans* isomers.

Phosphoric(V) acid is an alternative dehydrating agent.

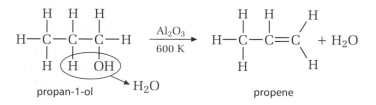

Fig 11.3 *Dehydration of an alcohol*

11.3.1 Selective oxidation

Combustion is complete oxidation but alcohols can be oxidised more gently and in stages. Primary alcohols are oxidised to **aldehydes**, RCHO. Aldehydes can be further oxidised to **carboxylic acids**, RCOOH.

For example:

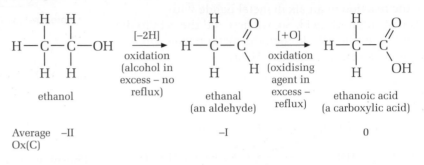

ethanol   ethanal (an aldehyde)   ethanoic acid (a carboxylic acid)

Average Ox(C)   –II   –I   0

Secondary alcohols are oxidised to **ketones**, R_2CO. Ketones are not oxidised further.

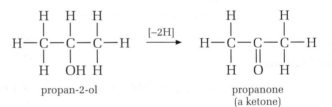

propan-2-ol   propanone (a ketone)

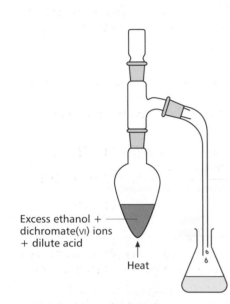

Fig 11.4 *Apparatus for the oxidation of ethanol to ethanal*

Excess ethanol + dichromate(VI) ions + dilute acid

Heat

Tertiary alcohols are not oxidised by this method. This is because oxidation would need a C—C bond to break, rather than a C—H bond (which is what happens when an aldehyde is oxidised). Ketones do not oxidise further for the same reason.

The experimental details

A solution of acidified potassium dichromate is often used as the oxidising agent. In the reaction, the orange dichromate(VI) ions are reduced to green chromium(III) ions.

To oxidise ethanol to ethanal

We use dilute acid and less dichromate than is needed for complete reaction. We heat the mixture gently in the apparatus shown in Figure 11.4. Ethanal (boiling point 294 K, 21°C) vaporises as soon as it is formed and distils over. This stops it from being oxidised further to ethanoic acid.

We often use [O] to represent oxygen from the oxidising agent, and the reaction is given by the equation:

$$C_2H_5OH(l) + [O] \rightarrow CH_3CHO(g) + H_2O(l)$$

To oxidise ethanol to ethanoic acid

We use concentrated acid and more than enough dichromate for complete reaction (the dichromate is in excess). We reflux the mixture in the apparatus shown in Figure 11.5.

While the reaction mixture is refluxing, any ethanol or ethanal vapour will condense and drip back into the flask until, eventually, it is all oxidised to the acid.

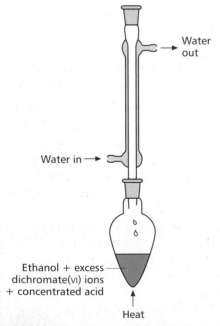

Water out

Water in

Ethanol + excess dichromate(VI) ions + concentrated acid

Heat

Fig 11.5 *Reflux apparatus for oxidation of ethanol to ethanoic acid. 'Reflux' means that vapour condenses and drips back into the reaction flask*

After refluxing for around 20 minutes, we can distil off the ethanoic acid, boiling point 391 K, 118°C, (along with any water) by rearranging the apparatus to that of Figure 11.6.

Using [O] to represent oxygen from the oxidising agent, the equation is:

$$C_2H_5OH(l) + 2[O] \rightarrow CH_3CO_2H \text{ (g)} + H_2O(l)$$

Notice that twice as much oxidising agent is used in this reaction compared with the oxidation to ethanal.

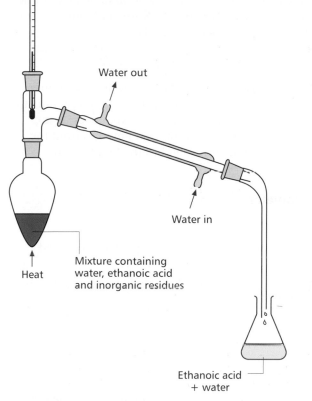

Water out

Water in

Heat

Mixture containing water, ethanoic acid and inorganic residues

Ethanoic acid + water

Fig 11.6 *Apparatus for distilling ethanoic acid from the reaction mixture*

Oxidising a secondary alcohol to a ketone

Secondary alcohols are oxidised to ketones by acidified dichromate.
We do not have to worry about further oxidation of the ketone.

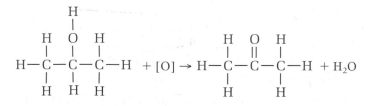

11.3.2 The importance of alcohols to industry

About one third of a million tonnes of ethanol and about a half a million tonnes of methanol are produced annually in the UK for a variety of uses including:

* as solvents
* as fuels or additives to fuels
* as intermediates in the manufacture of many other chemicals.

Alcohols are used as intermediates because they are easily made and easily converted into other compounds. Methanol is made from methane (natural gas) and is increasingly being used as a starting material for making other organic chemicals.

Ethanol

Ethanol, C_2H_5OH, is by far the most important alcohol. It is made by reacting ethene, from the cracking of crude oil, with steam using a catalyst of phosphoric acid. It is also made from sugars by fermentation, as in the production of alcoholic drinks.

Beers have about 5% ethanol and wines about 12%. Spirits, such as gin and whisky contain about 40% ethanol – these have been concentrated by distillation.

Making ethanol from crude oil

* Ethene is produced when crude oil fractions are cracked, see Topic 9.2.
* Ethene is hydrated, which means that water is added across the double bond

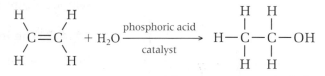

Making ethanol by fermentation

During fermentation, carbohydrates from plants are broken down into sugars, and then converted into ethanol by the action of enzymes from yeast.

Fermentation takes place at a little above room temperature, which is the optimum temperature for enzymes to work. Air is kept out of the fermentation vessels to prevent oxidation of ethanol to ethanoic acid (the acid in vinegar).

The key step is the breakdown of sugar in a process called **anaerobic respiration**:

$$\underset{\text{glucose (a sugar)}}{C_6H_{12}O_6(aq)} \xrightarrow{\text{enzymes}} \underset{\text{ethanol}}{2C_2H_5OH(aq)} + \underset{\text{carbon dioxide}}{2CO_2(g)}$$

Once the fermenting solution contains about 15% ethanol, the enzymes are unable to function and fermentation stops.

Fermentation was once the major source of ethanol for industrial use. In future, it may again become significant if and when we run out of crude oil. It is already used to produce ethanol for use as a petrol replacement in countries that have no deposits of crude oil.

QUICK QUESTIONS

1 State what happens in each case when the following alcohols are oxidised as much as possible, by potassium dichromate.
   a a primary alcohol,   **b** a secondary alcohol.

2 Why is a tertiary alcohol not oxidised by this method?

3 What is the difference between distilling and refluxing?

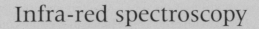

11.4 Infra-red spectroscopy

Infra-red (IR) spectroscopy is often used by organic chemists to help them identify compounds.

11.4.1 How infra-red spectroscopy works

The atoms joined by chemical bonds in molecules vibrate. A bond behaves rather like two balls (the atoms) joined by a spring (the bond). Stronger bonds vibrate faster (at higher frequency) and heavier atoms make the bond vibrate more slowly (at lower frequency). Every bond has its own unique natural frequency, which is in the infra-red region of the electromagnetic spectrum.

Fig 11.7 *Schematic diagram of an infra-red spectrometer*

When we shine a beam of infra-red radiation (heat energy) through a sample, the bonds in the sample absorb energy from the beam and vibrate more. But, any particular bond can only absorb radiation that has the same frequency as the natural frequency of the bond. Therefore, the radiation that emerges from the sample will be missing the frequencies that correspond to the bonds in the sample, Figure 11.7.

11.4.2 The infra-red spectrometer

In an infra-red spectrometer:

- A beam of infra-red radiation containing a spread of frequencies is passed through a sample.
- The radiation that emerges is missing the frequencies that correspond to the types of bonds found in the sample.
- The instrument plots a graph of the intensity of the radiation emerging from the sample – called transmittance – against the frequency of radiation.
- The frequency is expressed as a wavenumber, measured in cm^{-1}.

An infra-red spectrometer

11.4.3 The infra-red spectrum

A typical graph, called an infra-red spectrum is shown in Figure 11.8. The dips in the graph (confusingly, they are usually called peaks) represent particular bonds. Figure 11.9 shows the wavenumbers at which some bonds commonly found in organic chemistry are found, see also Table 11.1.

Table 11.1 *Characteristic infra-red absorptions in organic molecules*

Bond	Location	Wavenumber/ cm^{-1}
C—O	alcohols, esters	1000–1300
C=O	aldehydes, ketones, carboxylic acids, esters	1680–1750
O—H	hydrogen bonded in carboxylic acids	2500–3300 (broad)
N—H	primary amines	3100–3500
O—H	hydrogen bonded in alcohols, phenols	3230–3550
O—H	free	3580–3670

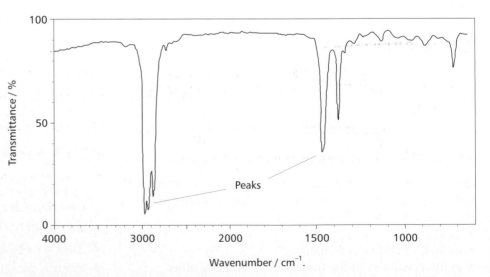

Fig 11.8 *A typical infra-red spectrum. Note that wavenumber gets smaller as we go from left to right*

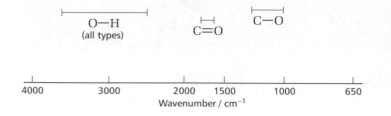

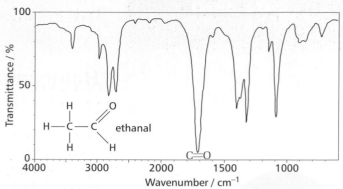

Fig 11.9 The ranges of wavenumbers at which some bonds absorb infra-red

These can help us to identify the functional groups present in a compound. For example:

- The O—H bond produces a broad peak at about 3300 cm^{-1} and this is found in both alcohols, ROH, and carboxylic acids, RCOOH.
- The C=O bond produces a peak at about 1725 cm^{-1}. This bond is found in aldehydes, RCHO, ketones, R_2CO and carboxylic acids, RCOOH.

Figures 11.10 to 11.12 show the infra-red spectra of ethanal, ethanol and ethanoic acid with the key peaks marked.

11.4.4 Using infra-red spectra

An infra-red spectrum can be run in less than a minute. It not only provides a lot of information to help a chemist identify the functional groups in a molecule, but it can also be used to investigate how a reaction is proceeding. For example, when a primary alcohol is oxidised to an aldehyde, an O—H bond in the alcohol disappears and is replaced by a C=O bond in the aldehyde.

- A sample of the reaction mixture is taken at intervals as the reaction proceeds and then the IR spectrum of the sample is run.
- At first it will show the peak caused by the O—H group of the alcohol at about 3300 cm^{-1}. This will gradually disappear and the peak at about 1725 cm^{-1} due to C=O will start to appear.
- When the alcohol peak has completely gone, the reaction has gone to completion.

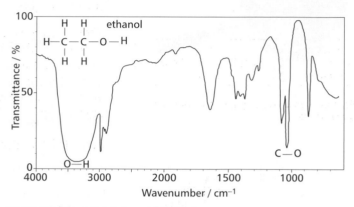

Fig 11.10 Infra-red spectrum of ethanal

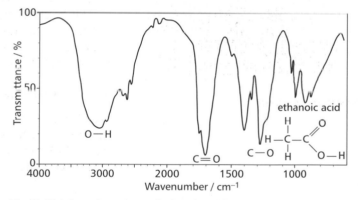

Fig 11.11 Infra-red spectrum of ethanol

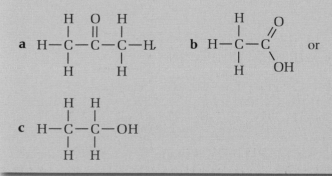

Fig 11.12 Infra-red spectrum of ethanoic acid

QUICK QUESTIONS

1 An organic compound has a peak in the IR spectrum at about 1725 cm^{-1}. Which of the following compounds could it be?

a H—C—C—C—H,   b H—C—C   or

c H—C—C—OH

2 Explain your answer to 1.

3 An organic compound has a peak in the IR spectrum at about 3300 cm^{-1}. Which of the compounds in question 1 could it be?

4 Explain your answer to 3.

5 An organic compound has peaks in the IR spectrum at 1725 and 3300 cm^{-1}. Which of the compounds in question 1 could it be?

Halogenoalkanes

Halogenoalkanes: introduction

The teflon non-stick coating on this pan is a halogenoalkane, poly(tetrafluoroethene)

Not many halogenoalkanes occur naturally but they are the basis of many synthetic compounds. Some examples of these are pvc, used to make drainpipes, Teflon, the non-stick coating on pans, and a number of anaesthetics. Halogenoalkanes have an alkane skeleton with one or more halogen (fluorine, chlorine, bromine or iodine) atoms in place of hydrogen atoms.

12.1.1 The general formula

The general formula of a halogenoalkane with a single halogen atom is $C_nH_{2n+1}X$, where X is the halogen. This is often shortened to R—X.

12.1.2 How to name halogenoalkanes

- The prefixes fluoro-, chloro-, bromo- and iodo- tell us which halogen is present.
- Locants are used if needed, to show on which carbon the halogen is.

1-chloropropane

1-iodopropane

2-bromo-2-methylpropane

- We use the prefixes di-, tri-, tetra-, etc. to show *how many* atoms of each halogen are present.
- When a compound contains different halogens they are listed in alphabetical order, *not* in order of the locant number.

For example:

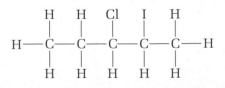

is 3-chloro-2-iodopentane not 2-iodo-3-chloropentane. (C is before I in the alphabet).

12.1.3 Structure

Halogenoalkanes may be:

primary, with a halogen at the end of the chain

$$H-\underset{\underset{H}{|}}{\overset{\overset{H}{|}}{C}}-\underset{\underset{H}{|}}{\overset{\overset{H}{|}}{C}}-\underset{\underset{H}{|}}{\overset{\overset{H}{|}}{C}}-\underset{\underset{H}{|}}{\overset{\overset{H}{|}}{C}}-Br \quad \text{1-bromobutane}$$

secondary, with a halogen in the middle of the chain

$$H-\underset{\underset{H}{|}}{\overset{\overset{H}{|}}{C}}-\underset{\underset{H}{|}}{\overset{\overset{H}{|}}{C}}-\underset{\underset{Br}{|}}{\overset{\overset{H}{|}}{C}}-\underset{\underset{H}{|}}{\overset{\overset{H}{|}}{C}}-H \quad \text{2-bromobutane}$$

tertiary, with a halogen at a branch in the chain.

$$H-\underset{\underset{H}{|}}{\overset{\overset{H}{|}}{C}}-\underset{\underset{Br}{|}}{\overset{\overset{CH_3}{|}}{C}}-\underset{\underset{H}{|}}{\overset{\overset{H}{|}}{C}}-H \quad \text{2-bromo-2-methylpropane}$$

These three compounds all have the molecular formula C_4H_9Br, so they are **isomers**.

12.1.4 Physical properties of halogenoalkanes

Solubility
- C—X bonds are polar, $C^{\delta+}$—$X^{\delta-}$, but not polar enough to make the halogenoalkanes soluble in water.
- The main intermolecular forces are dipole–dipole bonds.
- They mix with hydrocarbons so they can be used as dry-cleaning fluids and to remove oily stains. (Oil is a mixture of hydrocarbons.)

Boiling temperatures
The boiling temperatures depend on the number of carbon atoms and which halogen. There is a pattern. See Table 12.1.

- Boiling temperature increases with increased chain length.
- Boiling temperature increases as we go down the halogen group.

Halogenoalkanes have higher boiling temperatures than the corresponding alkanes because they have higher relative molecular masses and because they are more polar.

Table 12.1 Boiling temperatures of 1-halogenoalkanes / K

| | Halogen | | | | |
Parent alkane	F	Cl	Br	I	
methane	195	249	277	316	
ethane	235	285	312	345	Increasing T_b
propane	276	320	344	376	
butane	306	351	374	403	

Increasing T_b

12.1.5 How the halogenoalkanes react

There are two factors that decide how the C—X bond reacts, see Topic 7.5. These are:
- the $C^{\delta+}$—$X^{\delta-}$ bond polarity
- the C—X bond enthalpy.

Bond polarity
The halogens are more electronegative than carbon so the bond polarity will be $C^{\delta+}$—$X^{\delta-}$. The polarity of the bonds means that halogenoalkanes are attacked by **nucleophiles**, at the $C^{\delta+}$, see Section 7.6.2. The C—X bond becomes less polar as we go down the group.

As there are no double bonds we cannot get addition reactions. So when halogenoalkanes react the C—X bond breaks and the halogen is lost as an X^- ion, either in **nucleophilic substitution** or **elimination reactions**.

Bond enthalpies
C—X bond enthalpies are listed in Table 12.2. The bonds get weaker as we go down the group. This is because the shared electrons, which are close to the nucleus in fluorine, get further and further away from it as we go down the group.

Table 12.2 Carbon–halogen bond enthalpies

Bond	BE/kJ mol^{-1}	
C—F	467	
[C—H	413]	
C—Cl	346	stronger
C—Br	290	
C—I	228	

12.1.6 The reactivity of the C–X bond

The polarity of the C—X bond would predict that the C—F bond would be the most reactive – it is the most polar. The C—I bond would be the least reactive – it is the least polar. In fact the reverse is true. The bond enthalpies explain why iodo-compounds, with the weakest bonds, are the most reactive, and fluoro-compounds, with the strongest, are the least reactive.

QUICK QUESTIONS

1 These questions are about the following halogenoalkanes:
   (a) $CH_3CH_2CH_2CH_2I$,   (b) $CH_3CHBrCH_3$,
   (c) $CH_2ClCH_2CH_2CH_3$,   (d) $CH_3CH_2CHBrCH_3$
   a Draw the displayed formula for each halogenoalkane.
   b Name them.
   c Describe the halogenoalkanes above as primary, secondary or tertiary.
2 What is a nucleophile?
3 Why are halogenoalkanes attacked by nucleophiles?
4 Why do the halogenoalkanes get less reactive as we go up the halogen group?

One of the main ways that halogenoalkanes react is by **nucleophilic substitution** (substitution means the exchange of one atom or group for another).

12.2.1 The general equation

We can write a general equation for nucleophilic substitution, using :Nu⁻ to represent any negatively charged nucleophile:

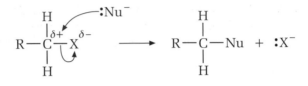

The nucleophile attaches itself to the $C^{\delta+}$ atom while the halogen leaves as a halide ion (taking the electrons of the C—X bond with it). The halide is called the **leaving group**, Section 7.6.2.

The rate of substitution depends on the halogen. Fluoro-compounds are unreactive owing to the strength of the C—F bond, then, as we go down the group the rate of reaction increases as the C—X bond strength decreases, Section 12.1.6).

Examples of nucleophilic substitution reactions
All these reactions are similar. Remember the basic pattern, shown above. Then work out the product with a particular nucleophile. This is easier than trying to remember the separate reactions.

12.2.2 Reaction of halogenoalkanes with aqueous sodium (or potassium) hydroxide

This reaction can take place at room temperature. Halogenoalkanes do not mix with water, so ethanol is used as a solvent in which the halogenoalkane and the aqueous sodium (or potassium) hydroxide both mix. This is a **hydrolysis** reaction.

The overall reaction is:

R—X + OH⁻ → ROH + X⁻ so an alcohol, ROH, is formed.

For example:

$$C_2H_5Br + OH^- \rightarrow C_2H_5OH + Br^-$$
bromoethane   ethanol

This is the mechanism:

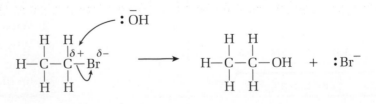

The same reaction occurs with water, still using ethanol as a solvent, but in this case it is much slower.

For example:

$$C_2H_5Br + H_2O \rightarrow C_2H_5OH + HBr$$

There is no colour change but we can show that halide ions, X^-, are formed by testing with aqueous silver nitrate mixed with ethanol. A precipitate forms – white for chloride ions, cream for bromide ions and pale yellow for iodide ions, see Section 6.2.4.

$$AgNO_3(aq) + X^-(aq) \rightarrow AgX(s) + NO_3^-(aq)$$
silver nitrate halide ion silver halide nitrate ion

This reaction can therefore be used to *identify* the halogen in the halogenoalkane.

We can use the same reaction to compare the *rates* at which the halogenoalkanes react, if we use water to hydrolyse the halogenoalkane. In this case we mix the silver nitrate solution with the reaction mixture and time how long it takes for a precipitate to form.

12.2.3 Reaction with ammonia

The reaction of halogenoalkanes with an excess concentrated solution of ammonia in ethanol is carried out under pressure. The reaction produces a **primary amine, RNH_2**.

$$RX + NH_3 \rightarrow RNH_2 + HX$$

This is the mechanism:

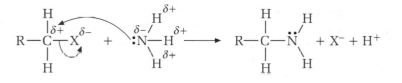

a primary amine

Ammonia is a nucleophile because it has a lone pair of electrons that it can donate (although it has no negative charge) and the nitrogen atom has a δ^- charge. Because ammonia is a neutral nucleophile, a proton, H^+, must be lost from the ammonia to form the neutral product – called a primary amine.

QUICK QUESTIONS

The equation represents the hydrolysis of a halogenoalkane by sodium hydroxide solution:

$$R\!-\!X + OH^- \rightarrow ROH + X^-$$

1 Why is the reaction carried out in ethanol?

2 What is the nucleophile?

3 Why is this a substitution?

4 Which is the leaving group?

5 Which would be the fastest reaction R—F, R—Cl, R—Br or R—I?

Elimination reactions and uses of halogenoalkanes

Halogenoalkanes typically react by nucleophilic substitution. But, under different conditions they react by **elimination**. A hydrogen halide is eliminated from the molecule, leaving a double bond in its place, so an alkene is formed.

12.3.1 OH⁻ ion acting as a base

We saw in Section 12.2.2 that the OH^- ion, from aqueous sodium or potassium hydroxide, is a nucleophile and its lone pair will attack a halogenoalkane at $C^{\delta+}$ to form an alcohol.

Under different conditions, the OH^- ion can act as a *base*. In this case we have an elimination reaction rather than a substitution. In the example below, bromoethane reacts with potassium hydroxide to form ethene. A molecule of hydrogen bromide, HBr, is eliminated in the process.

$$\underset{\text{(bromoethane)}}{H-\overset{\overset{\displaystyle Br}{|}}{\underset{\underset{\displaystyle H}{|}}{C}}-\overset{\overset{\displaystyle H}{|}}{\underset{\underset{\displaystyle H}{|}}{C}}-H} + KOH \longrightarrow \overset{H}{\underset{H}{}}C=C\overset{H}{\underset{H}{}} + KBr + H_2O$$

The conditions of reaction

The sodium (or potassium) hydroxide is dissolved in ethanol and mixed with the halogenoalkane. *There is no water present.* The mixture is heated. The experiment can be carried out using the apparatus shown in Figure 12.1.

The product is ethene, a gas that burns and also decolourises bromine solution, showing that it has a carbon–carbon double bond.

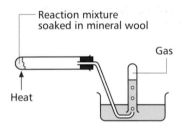

Reaction mixture soaked in mineral wool

Gas

Heat

Fig 12.1 *Apparatus for elimination of hydrogen bromide from bromoethane*

12.3.2 Substitution or elimination?

Since the hydroxide ion will react with halogenoalkanes as a nucleophile *or* as a base, there is competition between substitution and elimination. In general we produce a mixture of an alcohol and an alkene. For example:

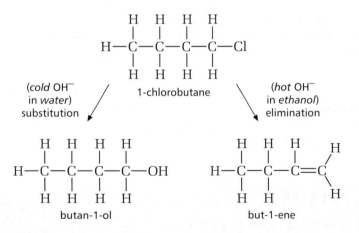

(*cold* OH⁻ in *water*) substitution

1-chlorobutane

(*hot* OH⁻ in *ethanol*) elimination

butan-1-ol

but-1-ene

The reaction that predominates depends on two factors – the reaction conditions (aqueous or ethanolic solution) and the type of halogenoalkane (primary, secondary or tertiary).

The conditions of the reaction

Hydroxide ions at room temperature, dissolved in water (aqueous), favour substitution.

Hydroxide ions at high temperature, dissolved in ethanol, favour elimination.

The type of halogenoalkane
Primary halogenoalkanes tend to react by substitution and tertiary ones by elimination. Secondary will do both.

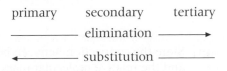

Until a few years ago, aerosol propellants often contained CFCs, and residues still remain in the atmosphere

12.3.3 Halogenoalkanes and the environment

Chlorofluorocarbons
- Chlorofluorocarbons are halogenoalkanes containing both chlorine and fluorine atoms but no hydrogen for example, CCl_3F, trichlorofluoromethane.
- They are also called CFCs.
- They are very unreactive.
- The short-chain ones are gases and were used, for example, as aerosol propellants, refrigerants, blowing agents for foams like expanded polystyrene, dry cleaning and de-greasing agents.

These gases eventually ended up in the atmosphere and there they decomposed to give chlorine atoms. These eventually decomposed ozone in the stratosphere, see Section 14.3.4, and this has caused a hole in the Earth's ozone layer. CFCs are now being phased out and replaced by other, safer, compounds including hydrochlorofluorocarbons (HCFCs) such as CF_3CHCl_2. However, a vast reservoir of CFCs remains in the atmosphere.

Anaesthetics
Another important halogenoalkane is fluothane, 1-bromo-1-chloro-2,2,2-trifluoroethane, Figure 12.2, which is an anaesthetic gas that has been used in over 500 million operations.

Fig 12.2 Fluothane. Can you see how the systematic name fits the IUPAC rules?

Plastics
Polyvinylchloride (pvc) is a widely used plastic. Its properties can be changed, depending on which additives are included during manufacture. It can be made flexible enough for tablecloths and rigid enough for drainpipes. The plastic is made by polymerising chloroethene, $CH_2{=}CHCl$, which used to be called vinyl chloride. The systematic name for pvc is poly(chloroethene).

Ptfe is a plastic made by polymerising tetrafluoroethene, $CF_2{=}CF_2$. One of its trade names is Teflon and it is found in the home as the non-stick coating on cooking pans.

Other uses
Halogen-containing organic compounds (usually chloro-compounds, because chlorine is the cheapest halogen) are used as solvents in industry. They are also involved as intermediates in reactions. This is because they are both easily made and easily converted into other materials.

QUICK QUESTIONS

1 In elimination reactions of halogenoalkanes, the OH^- group is acting as
   a a base,
   b an acid,
   c a nucleophile,
   d an electrophile?

2 Which of the following molecules is a CFC?
   a CH_3CH_2Cl, b $CF_2{=}CF_2$, c CF_3CH_2Cl.

3 Draw a section of the polymer pvc (poly(chloroethene)) showing six carbon atoms.

4 a Name the two possible products when 2-bromopropane reacts with hydroxide ions.
   b How could you show that one of the products is an alkene?

1 The table below shows information about some alcohols which form part of a homologous series.

Name	Formula	Boiling point/°C	Relative molecular mass
methanol	CH_3OH	65	32
ethanol	C_2H_5OH	78	46
propan-1-ol	C_3H_7OH	97	60
butan-1-ol	C_4H_9OH		74
pentan-1-ol	$C_5H_{11}OH$	138	
hexan-1-ol	$C_6H_{13}OH$	158	102

a (i) Identify the functional group common to all alcohols. [1]

(ii) What is the general formula for these alcohols? [1]

(iii) What is the formula of the next alcohol in the series? [1]

b Calculate the relative molecular mass of pentan-1-ol. [1]

c (i) Plot a graph of boiling point against number of carbon atoms in a molecule of the alcohol.

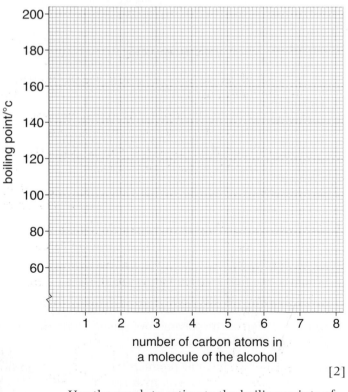

number of carbon atoms in a molecule of the alcohol [2]

Use the graph to estimate the boiling points of:

butan-1-ol, [1]

$C_8H_{17}OH$. [1]

(ii) State the connection between boiling point and the relative molecular mass of these alcohols. [1]

[Total: 9]

OCR, 17 Jan 2001

2 This question is about halogenoalkanes **A** to **D**, shown below.

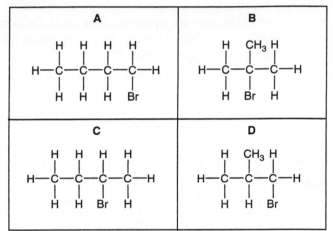

a Answer the questions that follow by using the appropriate letter **A**, **B**, **C** or **D**. Each letter may be used once, more than once or not at all.

(i) Which is 2-bromo-2-methylpropane? [1]

(ii) Which could react with hot aqueous sodium hydroxide to produce butan-2-ol? [1]

(iii) Which could react with hot aqueous sodium hydroxide to produce a tertiary alcohol? [1]

(iv) Which **two** could react with hot ethanolic sodium hydroxide to produce but-1-ene? [2]

b Compound **A** can react with ammonia to produce an amine.

(i) Complete the equation for this reaction:
$CH_3CH_2CH_2CH_2Br + NH_3 \rightarrow$ .... + ... [1]

(ii) Name the organic product. [1]

(iii) State a suitable solvent for this reaction. [1]

c Compound **D** can react with aqueous hydroxide ions OH^-. The hydroxide ion is a nucleophile.

(i) Define the term *nucleophile*. [1]

(ii) Draw a 'dot-and-cross' diagram of the OH^- ion. Show outer shell electrons only. [2]

(iii) Identify the organic product formed when compound **D** reacts with aqueous OH^- ions. [1]

[Total: 12]

OCR, 17 Jan 2003

3 Halogenoalkanes are useful synthetic reagents for the preparation of many important chemicals. Three reactions of bromoethane are shown below.

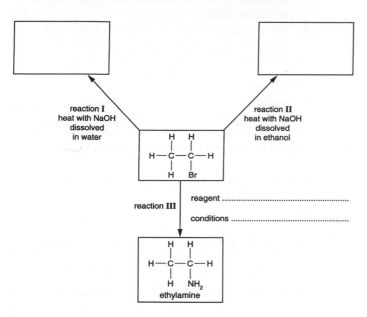

a (i) Identify the organic products in reactions **I** and **II** by writing their structural formulae in the relevant boxes. [2]

(ii) Name the **type** of reaction involved in: reaction **I**, reaction **II**. [3]

b Write, in the space provided in the reaction scheme above, the reagent and conditions required to convert bromoethane into ethylamine in reaction **III**. [2]

c (i) 2-bromobutane can react with ethanolic NaOH to form **two** structural isomers, each with a molecular formula of C_4H_8.

Draw and name each of the isomers. [4]

(ii) One of the isomers in **c**(i) can have *cis* and *trans* forms. In the boxes below, draw these *cis* and *trans* isomers. [2]

(iii) State **two** key structural features required for *cis–trans* isomerism to exist. [2]

[Total: 15]

OCR, 29 May 2002

4 An alcohol, **G**, has a relative molecular mass of 74 and has the following composition by mass: C, 64.9%; H, 13.5%; O, 21.6%.

a (i) Show that the empirical formula of **G** is $C_4H_{10}O$. [2]

(ii) Show that the molecular formula of **G** is the same as its empirical formula. [1]

b There are four structural isomers of $C_4H_{10}O$ that are alcohols. Alcohols can be classified as primary, secondary or tertiary. Complete the table following.

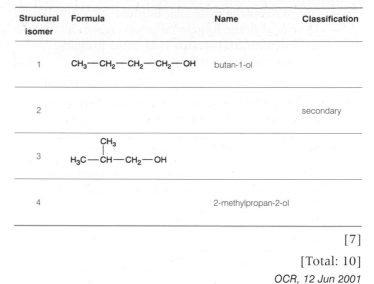

Structural isomer	Formula	Name	Classification
1	$CH_3-CH_2-CH_2-CH_2-OH$	butan-1-ol	
2			secondary
3	$H_3C-CH(CH_3)-CH_2-OH$		
4		2-methylpropan-2-ol	

[7]

[Total: 10]

OCR, 12 Jun 2001

5 Some reactions of 1-bromobutane $CH_3CH_2CH_2CH_2Br$, are shown below.

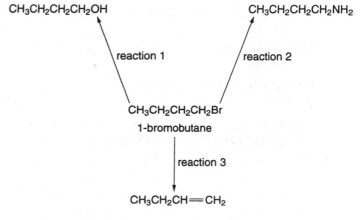

a For each of the reactions shown, name the reagent and the solvent used. [6]

b Under the same conditions, 1-chlorobutane was used in reaction 1 in place of 1-bromobutane.

What difference (if any) would you expect in the rate of reaction? Explain your answer. [2]

[Total: 8]

OCR, 12 Jun 2001

6 Menthol is a naturally occurring cyclic compound found in peppermint oil. It has been used in throat sprays and cough drops for many years.

The structural and skeletal formulae of menthol are shown below.

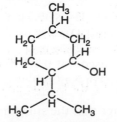
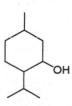

Structural formula of menthol   Skeletal formula of menthol

121

a (i) What is the molecular formula of menthol? [1]

(ii) Identify the functional group present in menthol and classify it as either primary, secondary or tertiary. [2]

b When menthol is reacted with hot concentrated sulphuric acid, H_2SO_4, two isomeric alkenes, each with formula $C_{10}H_{18}$, can be formed.

Draw the skeletal formula of each of the isomers formed. [2]

c Identify the organic product formed when menthol is reacted with ethanoic acid, CH_3COOH, in the presence of an acid catalyst. Draw its structure. [2]

[Total: 7]

OCR, 17 Jan 2003

7 A student was given the following instructions for the oxidation of an alcohol, C_3H_8O.

To 20 cm³ of water in a flask, carefully add 6 cm³ of concentrated sulphuric acid, and set up the apparatus as shown below.

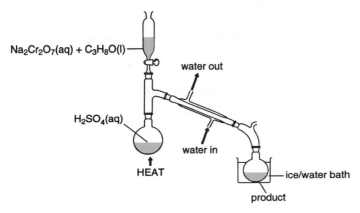

$Na_2Cr_2O_7(aq) + C_3H_8O(l)$
water out
$H_2SO_4(aq)$
water in
HEAT
ice/water bath
product

Make up a solution containing 39.3 g of sodium dichromate(VI), $Na_2Cr_2O_7$, in 15 cm³ of water, add 18.0 g of the alcohol C_3H_8O, and pour this mixture into the dropping funnel.

Boil the acid in the flask. Add the mixture from the dropping funnel at such a rate that the product is slowly collected.

Re-distil the product and collect the fraction that boils between 48°C and 50°C.

a Identify the possible isomers of the alcohol C_3H_8O. [2]

b The balanced equation for the reaction is:

$3C_3H_8O + Na_2Cr_2O_7 + 4H_2SO_4 \rightarrow 3C_3H_6O + Na_2SO_4 + Cr_2(SO_4)_3 + 7H_2O$

(i) The mass of $Na_2Cr_2O_7$ used was 39.3 g. Calculate how many moles of $Na_2Cr_2O_7$ were used. (The molar mass of $Na_2Cr_2O_7$ is 262 g mol⁻¹.) [1]

(ii) The amount of C_3H_8O used was 0.300 mol. Explain whether C_3H_8O or $Na_2Cr_2O_7$ was in excess. [1]

(iii) State the colour change that the student would observe during the reaction. [2]

c The student obtained 5.22 g of the carbonyl compound, C_3H_6O.

(i) Calculate how many moles of C_3H_6O were produced in the experiment. [2]

(ii) The theoretical yield of C_3H_6O is 0.300 mol. Calculate the percentage yield of C_3H_6O obtained by the student. [1]

d An **impure** sample of C_3H_6O obtained by a student was analysed using infra-red spectroscopy. The infra-red spectrum contained an absorption between 1680 and 1750 cm⁻¹. It also contained a broad absorption in the region 2550 to 3300 cm⁻¹ due to the impurity.

Refer to the Data Sheet provided on p.168.

(i) What does the absorption at between 1680 and 1750 cm⁻¹ indicate? [1]

(ii) What does the broad absorption in the region 2550 to 3300 cm⁻¹ indicate? [1]

(iii) Identify which of the alcohols in **a** was used by this student. Explain your answer. [1]

[Total: 12]

OCR, 29 May 2002

8 Many drinks have a characteristic smell. 2-Ethyl-3-methylbutanoic acid, $C_7H_{14}O_2$, gives rum its characteristic aroma.

a 2-Ethyl-3-methylbutanoic acid can be prepared in the laboratory by oxidation of 2-ethyl-3-methylbutan-1-ol $(CH_3)_2CHCH(C_2H_5)CH_2OH$.

(i) State the reagents and conditions that could be used for this oxidation. Describe what colour change you would see. [4]

(ii) State, with a reason, whether a reflux apparatus or a distillation apparatus should be used to produce the correct oxidation product. [2]

(iii) What is the molecular formula of 2-ethyl-3-methylbutan-1-ol? [1]

(iv) Using [O] to represent the oxidising agent, write a balanced eqation for this oxidation. [2]

(v) Identify a likely organic impurity which could be formed in this oxidation. [1]

b If 2-ethyl-3-methylbutan-1-ol were replaced by 3-ethyl-3-methylbutan-2-ol, oxidation would **not** occur in this experiment. Explain why not. [2]

[Total: 12]

OCR, 12 Jun 2001

9 Cyclohexene, C_6H_{10}, can be prepared from cyclohexanol, $C_6H_{11}OH$, by the dehydration method described below.

A reaction mixture of 10.0 g cyclohexanol and 4 cm³ of phosphoric acid, H_3PO_4, was placed in a round-bottomed flask and the apparatus arranged as shown below. An impure liquid, consisting of two immiscible layers, was collected after distillation.

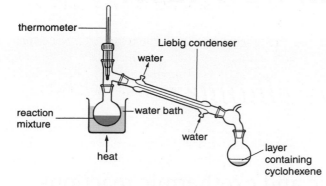

The upper organic layer was separated and dried. Finally it was re-distilled to yield 3.69 g of cyclohexene.

The equation for the preparation can be represented as either

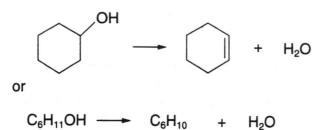

or

$$C_6H_{11}OH \longrightarrow C_6H_{10} + H_2O$$

Use the information above to answer the questions that follow.

a Suggest an impurity that could have been in the mixture after the first distillation. [1]

b (i) What is the relative molecular mass of cyclohexanol? [1]

    (ii) How many moles of cyclohexanol were used in the experiment? [1]

    (iii) How many moles of cyclohexene were produced in the experiment? [2]

    (iv) Calculate the percentage yield of cyclohexene in the experiment. [2]

c Suggest how infra-red spectroscopy could be used to show that the product was not contaminated with any unreacted cyclohexanol. Refer to the *Data Sheet on p.168* in your answer. [2]

[Total: 9]

OCR, 12 Jun 2001

13

Enthalpy changes

13.1

Endothermic and exothermic reactions

The amount of energy involved when a chemical reaction takes place is important for many reasons. For example:

- We can measure the energy value of fuels or the energy requirements for industrial processes.
- We can work out the theoretical amount of energy to break bonds and from this we can predict whether a reaction will take place or not.

The energy involved may be in different forms – light, electrical or, most usually, heat.

13.1.1 Thermochemistry

Thermochemistry is the study of heat changes during chemical reactions.

- When a chemical reaction takes place, chemical bonds break and new ones are formed.
- Energy must be *put in* to break bonds and energy is *given out* when bonds are formed, so most chemical reactions involve an energy change.
- The overall change may result in energy being given out or taken in.
- If at the end of the reaction, energy has been given out the reaction is **exothermic**.
- If at the end of the reaction, energy has been taken in, the reaction is **endothermic**.

13.1.2 Exothermic and endothermic reactions

Some reactions give out heat as they proceed. These are called **exothermic** reactions. Some reactions need to take in heat for the reaction to keep going. These are called **endothermic** reactions. For example the breakdown of limestone (calcium carbonate) to lime (calcium oxide) and carbon dioxide, Section 5.4.3, needs heat – it is an endothermic reaction. Another example is heating copper sulphate.

Blue copper sulphate crystals have the formula $CuSO_4.5H_2O$. The water molecules are bonded to the copper sulphate. In order to break these bonds and make white, anhydrous, copper sulphate, heat energy must be supplied. So, this reaction takes in heat and is endothermic:

$$CuSO_4.5H_2O \quad \rightarrow \quad CuSO_4 \quad + \quad 5H_2O$$

blue copper sulphate   anhydrous copper sulphate   water

When you add water to anhydrous copper sulphate, the reaction gives out heat:

$$CuSO_4 \quad + \quad 5H_2O \quad \rightarrow \quad CuSO_4.5H_2O$$

anhydrous copper sulphate   water   blue copper sulphate

> **HINT**
>
> The unit of energy is the joule, J. One joule represents quite a small amount of heat. For example, in order to bring to the boil enough water for a cup of tea you would need about 80 000 J which is 80 kJ.

In this direction the reaction is exothermic.

It is *always* the case that a reaction that is endothermic in one direction is exothermic in the reverse direction.

Another example of this is plant photosynthesis and respiration.

Photosynthesis
Plants make their food by photosynthesis. Photosynthesis is an endothermic reaction in which carbon dioxide and water react to form glucose and oxygen, driven by energy taken in from sunlight. The sunlight is absorbed by chlorophyll, the green pigment in plants:

$$6CO_2 + 6H_2O \rightarrow C_6H_{12}O_6 + 6O_2 \quad \text{(energy taken in from the sun)}$$

Respiration
The reverse of this reaction is respiration. Respiration is an oxidation reaction. Glucose and oxygen react to form carbon dioxide and water. Energy is given out as heat, so this is an exothermic reaction.

$$C_6H_{12}O_6 + 6O_2 \rightarrow 6CO_2 + 6H_2O \quad \text{(energy given out)}$$

Burning fuels
Another important oxidation reaction is burning fuels. These are exothermic reactions with a large heat output.

For example, coal is mostly carbon. Carbon gives out 393.5 kJ when one mole, 12 g, is burnt (oxidised) completely to carbon dioxide.

$$C + O_2 \rightarrow CO_2$$

Natural gas, methane, CH_4, gives out 890 kJ when one mole, 16 g, is burnt (oxidised) completely to carbon dioxide and water.

$$CH_4 + 2O_2 \rightarrow CO_2 + 2H_2O$$

Heating copper sulphate

During photosynthesis energy taken in from sunlight is absorbed by chlorophyll, the green pigment in plants. Photosynthesis is the original source of the energy in fossil fuels

QUICK QUESTIONS

$$CH_4 + 2O_2 \rightarrow CO_2 + 2H_2O$$

Natural gas, methane, CH_4, gives out 890 kJ when one mole is burnt completely.

1 How much heat would be given out when 8 g of methane is burnt completely?

2 The reaction $CO_2 + 2H_2O \rightarrow CH_4 + 2O_2$ does not take place under normal conditions. If it did, would you expect it to be exothermic or endothermic?

3 Explain your answer to **2**.

4 Approximately how much methane would have to be burnt to provide enough heat to boil a cup of tea:

   a 16 g,   **b** 1.6 g,   **b** 160 g?

The amount of heat given out or taken in by a reaction varies with the conditions – temperature, pressure, concentration of solutions etc. So we must state the conditions under which measurements are made. For example, we normally measure heat changes at constant pressure. (This makes sense as it means that we can use flasks open to the atmosphere.)

13.2.1 Enthalpy change, ΔH

When we measure a heat change at a fixed pressure and temperature, we call it an **enthalpy** change.

Enthalpy has the symbol H so enthalpy changes are given the symbol ΔH. The Greek letter Δ (delta) is used to indicate a *change* in any quantity.

There are standard conditions for measuring enthalpy changes:

- pressure of 100 kPa (approximately normal atmospheric pressure)
- temperature of 298 K (25°C, around normal room temperature).

We write an enthalpy change measured under standard conditions as $\Delta H^{\ominus}_{298}$ although we usually leave out the 298. $\Delta H^{\ominus}$ is pronounced 'delta H standard'.

It may seem strange to talk about measuring heat changes at a constant temperature because heat changes normally *cause* temperature changes. The way to think about this is to imagine the reactants at 298 K, see Figure 13.1. Mix the reactants and heat is produced (this is an exothermic reaction). This heat is given out to the surroundings.

We do not think of the reaction as being over *until the products have cooled back to 298 K*. The heat given out to the surroundings while the reaction mixture cools is the enthalpy change for the reaction, $\Delta H^{\ominus}$.

In an exothermic reaction the products end up with less energy than the starting materials, so ΔH is negative.

Some endothermic reactions that take place in aqueous solution absorb heat from the water and cool it down, for example, dissolving ammonium chloride in water.

Again we do not think of the reaction as being over *until the products have warmed up to the temperature at which they started*. In this case the solution has to take in heat from the surroundings to do this. Unless you remember this, it can seem strange that a reaction that is absorbing heat can get cold.

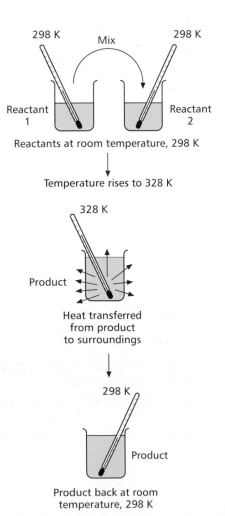

Reactants at room temperature, 298 K

Temperature rises to 328 K

Heat transferred from product to surroundings

Product back at room temperature, 298 K

Fig 13.1 *A reaction giving out heat at 298 K*

In an endothermic reaction the products end up with more energy than the starting materials, so ΔH is positive.

13.2.2 Enthalpy profile diagrams

We use enthalpy profile diagrams, sometimes called enthalpy (or energy) level diagrams, to represent enthalpy changes. They show the relative enthalpy levels of the reactants (starting materials) and the products. The vertical axis represents enthalpy and the horizontal axis, the extent of the reaction. We are usually only interested in the beginning, 100% reactants, and the end of the reaction, 0% reactants (and 100% products) so the horizontal axis is usually left without units.

Figure 13.2 shows a general enthalpy profile diagram for (a) an exothermic reaction (the products have less enthalpy than the reactants), and (b) an endothermic reaction (the products have less enthalpy than the reactants).

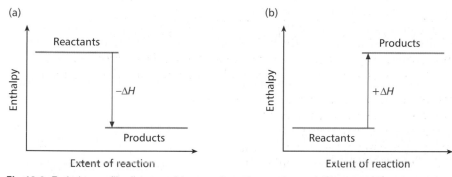

Fig 13.2 *Enthalpy profile diagrams (a) an exothermic reaction and (b) an endothermic reaction*

QUICK QUESTIONS

These questions are about the reaction:

$$CH_4(s) + 2O_2(g) \rightarrow CO_2(g) + 2H_2O(l)$$
$$\Delta H_{298}^{\ominus} = -890 \, kJ \, mol^{-1}$$

1 What does the symbol Δ mean?

2 What does the symbol H mean?

3 What does the 298 indicate?

4 What does the $-$ sign indicate?

5 Is the reaction exothermic or endothermic?

The general name for the enthalpy change for any reaction is the **standard molar enthalpy change of reaction, $\Delta H^{\ominus}$**. It is measured in kilojoules per mole, kJ mol^{-1} (molar means 'per mole'). We write a balanced symbol equation for the reaction and then find the heat change for the quantities in moles given by the reaction.

For example, ΔH for: $2NaOH + H_2SO_4 \rightarrow Na_2SO_4 + 2H_2O$ is the enthalpy change when 2 moles of NaOH react with 1 mole of H_2SO_4.

Heat and temperature

The words 'heat' and 'temperature' are often used to mean the same thing in daily conversation but in science they are quite distinct and you must be clear about the difference.

Temperature is a measure of the *average* kinetic energy of the particles in a system. As the particles move faster, their average kinetic energy increases and the temperature goes up. But it does not matter how many particles there are – temperature is independent of the *number* present. We measure temperature with a thermometer.

Heat is a measure of the *total* energy of all the particles present in a given amount of substance. It *does* depend on how much of the substance is present. The energy of every particle is included. There is no instrument that can measure heat directly.

So a bath of lukewarm water has much more heat than a red hot nail even though the temperature is less.

Heat always flows from high to low temperature, so heat will flow from the nail into the bath water, even though the water has much more heat than the nail.

13.3.1 Calculating the enthalpy change of a reaction

The enthalpy change of a reaction is the heat given out or taken in as the reaction heats up or cools down. There is no instrument that measures heat directly. To measure the enthalpy *change* we need to know three things:

- the mass of the substance that is being heated up or cooled down
- the temperature change
- the specific heat capacity of the substance.

The **specific heat capacity, c**, is the amount of heat needed to raise the temperature of 1 g of substance by 1 K. Its units are joules per gram per kelvin, or J g^{-1} K^{-1}. For example, the specific heat capacity of water is 4.2 J g^{-1} K^{-1} so it takes 4.2 joules to raise the temperature of 1 gram of water by 1 degree kelvin.

Then:

Enthalpy change = mass of substance $\times$ specific heat capacity $\times$ temperature change

$$\Delta H = m \times c \times \Delta T$$

13.3.2 The simple calorimeter

We can use the apparatus in Figure 13.3 to find the enthalpy change when a fuel burns.

The enthalpy change when one mole of substance in its standard state is completely burned in oxygen is called the **standard molar enthalpy change of combustion, $\Delta H_c^{\ominus}$**.

NOTE

The size of a degree kelvin is the same as the size of a degree celsius. Only the starting point of the scale is different.

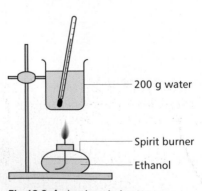

200 g water

Spirit burner

Ethanol

Fig 13.3 A simple calorimeter

We burn the fuel to heat a known mass of water and then measure the temperature rise of the water. We assume that all the heat from the fuel goes into the water.

The apparatus used is called a **calorimeter** (from the Latin *calor* meaning heat).

13.3.3 Working out the enthalpy change – an example

The calorimeter in Figure 13.3 was used to measure the enthalpy change of combustion of methanol:

$$CH_3OH(l) + 1\tfrac{1}{2}O_2(g) \rightarrow CO_2(g) + 2H_2O(l)$$

0.32 g (0.010 mol) of methanol was burned and the water temperature rose by 4 K.

$$\text{Heat change} = \Delta H = m \times c \times \Delta T$$
$$= 200 \times 4.2 \times 4 = 3360\,J$$

So 0.01 mol gives 3360 J
1 mol would give 336 000 J or 336 kJ
$\Delta H_c = -336\,kJ\,mol^{-1}$ (negative because heat is given out)

This value is less than half the accepted value since not all the heat reaches the water. This is because:

- There may be draughts that take heat away from the calorimeter.
- Heat is lost from the top and sides of the calorimeter.
- The beaker and the rest of the apparatus itself get heated rather than just the water.

- Not all the methanol burns completely to carbon dioxide. This is **incomplete combustion**. If there is not enough oxygen available, then we get some carbon monoxide and carbon formed. Soot (carbon) on the bottom of the beaker will show if this has happened.

The simple calorimeter can be used to *compare* the ΔH_c values of a series of similar compounds, as the errors will be similar for every experiment. We can improve the results by cutting down the heat loss as shown in Figure 13.4.

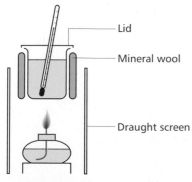

Fig 13.4 *An improved calorimeter*

More enthalpy calculations

13.4.1 The flame calorimeter

The flame calorimeter, shown in Figure 13.5, is an improved version of the simple calorimeters described in Topic 13.3. It is designed to reduce heat loss much further.

- The spiral chimney is made of copper. Copper is a very good conductor of heat and will conduct heat directly to the water.
- The flame is enclosed, so we don't have heat loss from draughts.
- The fuel burns in pure oxygen, rather than air, to make sure we have complete combustion.

We start by finding the heat capacity of the calorimeter – the number of joules to raise its temperature by 1 K. We burn a substance in the apparatus whose molar enthalpy change of combustion, $\Delta H_c^\ominus$, we already know accurately. We then use the results to work out the heat capacity of the calorimeter.

The following example shows you how to work out the heat capacity of a calorimeter, and then use it to find the enthalpy of combustion of methanol.

Benzoic acid ($M_r = 122.0$) is often used to calibrate calorimeters, as its enthalpy change of combustion $\Delta H_c^\ominus$ is accurately known. $\Delta H_c^\ominus$ for benzoic acid is $-3230\,kJ\,mol^{-1}$.

(a) Calibrating the calorimeter

1.22 g (0.010 mol) of benzoic acid was burned in a flame calorimeter and gave a temperature rise of 10.0 K.

$\Delta H_c^\ominus$ for benzoic acid is $-3230\,kJ\,mol^{-1}$. So burning 0.010 mol benzoic acid must produce 32.3 kJ of heat. This amount of heat raised the temperature of the calorimeter by 10.0 K.

The heat capacity of the apparatus is the heat needed to raise the temperature of the whole apparatus by 1.00 K, so:

Heat capacity of the calorimeter = $32.3/10.0\,kJ\,K^{-1} = 3.23\,kJ\,K^{-1}$

Heat losses will be similar for both the calibration and the experiment, so these will tend to cancel out.

(b) Finding the enthalpy change of combustion of methanol

0.320 g (0.010 mol) of methanol was burned in the same calorimeter and produced a temperature rise of 2.00 K.

Heat produced by the methanol = heat capacity of calorimeter
$$\times \text{ temperature change}$$
$$= 3.23\,kJ\,K^{-1} \times 2.00\,K$$
$$= 6.46\,kJ$$

0.010 mol methanol produces   6.46 kJ
1.00 mol methanol produces   646 kJ
$$\Delta H_c \text{ of methanol} = -646\,kJ\,mol^{-1}$$

The accepted value for methanol is $-726.0\,kJ\,mol^{-1}$ so this is a much better result than the one using the simplest calorimeter in Section 13.3.2.

13.4.2 Measuring enthalpy changes of reactions in solution

It is relatively easy to measure heat changes for reactions that take place in solution. The heat is generated in the solutions themselves and only has to be

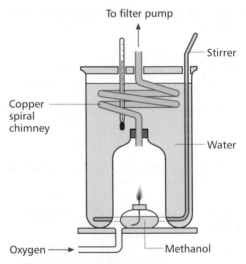

Fig 13.5 A flame calorimeter

To filter pump

Stirrer

Copper spiral chimney

Water

Oxygen

Methanol

Polystyrene beakers make good calorimeters because they are good insulators and have low heat capacities

kept in the calorimeter. We often use expanded polystyrene beakers for the calorimeters. These are good insulators (this reduces heat loss through their sides) and they have a low heat capacity so the beaker itself absorbs very little heat. We usually take the specific heat capacity of dilute solutions to be the same as that of water, $4.2\,J\,g^{-1}\,K^{-1}$.

Neutralisation reactions

Neutralisation reactions in solution are exothermic – they give out heat.
When an acid is neutralised by an alkali the equation is:

$$acid + alkali \rightarrow salt + water$$

When we find an enthalpy change for a reaction, we use the quantities in moles given by the balanced equation. For example, to find the molar enthalpy change of reaction for the neutralisation of hydrochloric acid by sodium hydroxide, we need to find the heat given out by the quantities in the equation:

$HCl(aq)$	$+$	$NaOH(aq)$	$\rightarrow$	$NaCl(aq)$	$+$	$H_2O(l)$
hydrochloric acid		sodium hydroxide		sodium chloride		water
1 mol		1 mol		1 mol		1 mol

Example

$50.0\,cm^3$ of $1.0\,mol\,dm^{-3}$ hydrochloric acid and $50.0\,cm^3$ of $1.0\,mol\,dm^{-3}$ sodium hydroxide solution were mixed in an expanded polystyrene beaker. The temperature rose by $6.6\,K$.

The total volume of the mixture is $100.0\,cm^3$, which has a mass of approximately $100.0\,g$.

> **HINT**
>
> Remember to use the *total* volume of the mixture, $100.0\,cm^3$. A common mistake is to use $50.0\,cm^3$.

Enthalpy change = mass of water $\times$ specific heat capacity of solution
$\times$ temperature change

$$\Delta H = m \times c \times \Delta T$$
$$= 100.0 \times 4.2 \times 6.6$$
$$= 2772\,J$$

Number of moles of acid (and also of alkali) $= \dfrac{M \times V}{1000}$,

where M is concentration in $mol\,dm^{-3}$ and V is volume in cm^3

$$= 1 \times 50.0/1000 = 0.050\,mol$$

so   1 mol would give $\dfrac{2772}{0.050}\,J$

$$= 55\,440\,J$$
$$= 55.44\,kJ$$

$\Delta H = -55.44\,kJ\,mol^{-1}$ (negative as heat is given out)

$\Delta H = -55\,kJ\,mol^{-1}$ (to 2 significant figures, see Section 16.5)

Displacement reactions

A metal that is more reactive than another will displace a less reactive one from a compound. If the compound will dissolve in water, then this reaction can be investigated using a polystyrene beaker as before.

For example, zinc will displace copper from a solution of copper sulphate. The reaction is exothermic:

$Zn(s)$	$+$	$CuSO_4(aq)$	$\rightarrow$	$ZnSO_4(aq)$	$+$	$Cu(s)$
1 mol		1 mol		1 mol		1 mol

We know from the equation that 1 mole of zinc reacts with 1 mole of copper sulphate.

Example

$0.50\,g$ of zinc was added to $25.0\,cm^3$ of $0.20\,mol\,dm^{-3}$ copper sulphate solution. The temperature rose by $10.0\,K$

Enthalpy change $= \Delta H = m \times c \times \Delta T$
$$= 25 \times 4.2 \times 10$$
$$= 1050\,J$$

A_r for zinc $= 65.4$, so $0.50\,g$ of zinc is $\dfrac{0.50}{65.4}$ moles $= 0.00764$ moles

Number of moles of copper sulphate in solution $= \dfrac{M \times V}{1000}$, where M is concentration

in $mol\,dm^{-3}$ and V is volume in $cm^3 = \dfrac{0.20 \times 25.0}{1000} = 0.0050\,mol$.

So, the zinc was in excess, and $0.0050\,mol$ of each reactant have taken part in the reaction, leaving some unreacted zinc behind.

Therefore, 1 mole of zinc would produce $\dfrac{1050}{0.0050}\,J = 210\,000\,J$.

So, ΔH for this reaction is $-210\,kJ\,mol^{-1}$ (to 2 significant figures, see Section 16.5).
The sign of ΔH is negative because heat is given out.

QUICK QUESTIONS

1 $0.74\,g$ ($0.01\,mol$) of propanoic acid was burned in the same calorimeter calibrated in example (a) in Section 13.4.1(a). The temperature rose by $5.00°C$. What is the enthalpy change of combustion of propanoic acid?

2 $50.0\,cm^3$ of $2.00\,mol\,dm^{-3}$ sodium hydroxide and $50.0\,cm^3$ of $2.00\,mol\,dm^{-3}$ hydrochloric acid were mixed in an expanded polystyrene beaker. The temperature rose by $11\,K$.

a Calculate ΔH for the reaction.
b How will this value compare with the accepted value for this reaction?
c Explain your answer to **b**.

13.5 Hess's Law

The enthalpy changes for some reactions cannot be measured directly. To find these we use an indirect approach. We use enthalpy changes that we *can* measure to work out enthalpy changes that we can't. To do this we use Hess's Law, first stated by Germain Hess, a Swiss-born Russian chemist, born in 1840.

13.5.1 The statement of Hess's Law

Hess's Law states that the total energy (or enthalpy) change for a chemical reaction is the same, *whatever route is taken,* **provided that the initial and final conditions are the same.** It is a consequence of a more general physical law – the Law of Conservation of Energy, which states that energy can never be created or destroyed.

13.5.2 Using Hess's Law

To see what Hess's Law means, look at the following example where ethyne is converted to ethane by two different routes.

Route 1. The reaction takes place directly – ethyne reacts with two moles of hydrogen to give ethane:

$$H-C{\equiv}C-H\ (g)\ +\ 2H_2(g)\ \rightarrow\ \underset{\text{ethane}}{H-\overset{\displaystyle H}{\underset{\displaystyle H}{C}}-\overset{\displaystyle H}{\underset{\displaystyle H}{C}}-H}\ (g)\quad \Delta H_1 = ?$$

ethyne

Route 2. The reaction takes place in two stages:

(a) Ethyne, C_2H_2, reacts with one mole of hydrogen molecules to give ethene, C_2H_4.
(b) Ethene, C_2H_4, then reacts with a second mole of hydrogen to give ethane, C_2H_6.

(a) $H-C{\equiv}C-H\ (g)\ +\ H_2(g)\ \rightarrow\ \underset{\text{ethene}}{C{=}C}\quad \Delta H_2 = -176\ \text{kJ mol}^{-1}$

ethyne

(b) $\underset{\text{ethene}}{C{=}C}\ (g)\ +\ H_2(g)\ \rightarrow\ \underset{\text{ethane}}{H-C-C-H}\quad \Delta H_3 = -137\ \text{kJ mol}^{-1}$

Hess's Law tells us that the total energy change is the same whichever route we take, direct or via ethene (or, in fact, any other route). We can show this on a diagram called a **thermochemical cycle**.

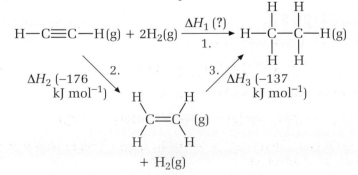

Hess's Law means that $\quad \Delta H_1 = \Delta H_2 + \Delta H_3$

The actual values are: $\quad \Delta H_2 = -176 \text{ kJ mol}^{-1}$
$$\Delta H_3 = -137 \text{ kJ mol}^{-1}$$
So $\quad \Delta H_1 = -176 + -137 = -313 \text{ kJ mol}^{-1}$

This method of calculating ΔH_1 is fine if we know the enthalpy changes for the other two reactions. There are certain enthalpy changes that can be looked up for a large range of compounds – these include the enthalpy change of formation, $\Delta H_f^{\ominus}$ and enthalpy change of combustion, $\Delta H_c^{\ominus}$.

Using the enthalpy changes of formation $\Delta H_f^{\ominus}$

The standard molar enthalpy change of formation $\Delta H_f^{\ominus}$ is the enthalpy change when a mole of compound is formed from its elements in their standard states under standard conditions.

Another theoretical way to convert ethyne to ethane could be via the elements carbon and hydrogen.

* Ethyne is first converted to its elements, carbon and hydrogen – this is the reverse of formation and the enthalpy change is the *negative* of the enthalpy change of formation. This is an example of a general rule. The reverse of a reaction has the negative of its ΔH value.

* Then the carbon and hydrogen react to form ethane – this is the enthalpy of formation for ethane.

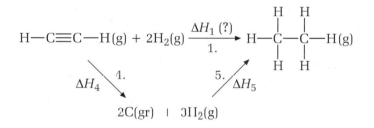

Hess's Law tells us that $\Delta H_1 = \Delta H_4 + \Delta H_5$

ΔH_5 is the enthalpy of formation, $\Delta H_f^{\ominus}$, of ethane while reaction 4 is the *reverse* of the formation of ethyne.

The values we need are: $\Delta H_f^{\ominus} C_2H_2 = +228 \text{ kJ mol}^{-1}$
and $\Delta H_f^{\ominus} C_2H_6 = -85 \text{ kJ mol}^{-1}$
So $\quad \Delta H_4 = -228 \text{ kJ mol}^{-1}$ (Remember to change the sign)
$$\Delta H_5 = -85 \text{ kJ mol}^{-1}$$
Thus $\quad \Delta H_1 = -228 + -85 = -313 \text{ kJ mol}^{-1}$

This was the result we got from the previous method, as we should expect from Hess's Law.

Notice that in reaction 4 there are two moles of hydrogen 'spare' as only one of the three moles of hydrogen is involved.

$$\text{H—C}{\equiv}\text{C—H(g)} \rightarrow 2\text{C(gr)} + \text{H}_2\text{(g)}$$

is the reaction we are considering , but we have:

$$\text{H—C}{\equiv}\text{C—H(g)} + 2\text{H}_2\text{(g)} \rightarrow 2\text{C(gr)} + 3\text{H}_2\text{(g)}$$

However this makes no difference. The 'extra' hydrogen *is not involved in the reaction* and it does not affect ΔH.

QUICK QUESTIONS

Quick questions for all the topics relating to Hess's Law and thermochemical cycles will be found at the end of Topic 13.8.

The enthalpy changes of combustion $\Delta H_c^\ominus$

The standard molar enthalpy of combustion $\Delta H_c^\ominus$ is the enthalpy change at standard state when a mole of substance is completely burned in oxygen.

13.6.1 Thermochemical cycles using enthalpy changes of combustion

We can look again at the thermochemical cycle we used fo find ΔH for the reaction

$$H-C\equiv C-H(g) + 2H_2(g) \longrightarrow H-\underset{\underset{\displaystyle H}{|}}{\overset{\overset{\displaystyle H}{|}}{C}}-\underset{\underset{\displaystyle H}{|}}{\overset{\overset{\displaystyle H}{|}}{C}}-H(g)$$

that we dealt with in Topic 13.5, but this time using enthalpy changes of combustion. In this case we can go via the combustion products, carbon dioxide and water.

All three substances, ethyne, hydrogen and ethane, burn readily, which means their enthalpy changes of combustion can be easily measured. The thermochemical cycle is:

$$3\tfrac{1}{2}O_2(g) + H-C\equiv C-H(g) + 2H_2(g) \xrightarrow[\text{1.}]{\Delta H_1} H-\underset{\underset{\displaystyle H}{|}}{\overset{\overset{\displaystyle H}{|}}{C}}-\underset{\underset{\displaystyle H}{|}}{\overset{\overset{\displaystyle H}{|}}{C}}-H(g) + 3\tfrac{1}{2}O_2(g)$$

$$6. \qquad 7. \qquad 2\times\Delta H_c^\ominus(H_2) \qquad 8.$$

$$\Delta H_c^\ominus(C_2H_2) \qquad\qquad \Delta H_c^\ominus(C_2H_6)$$

$$2CO_2(g) + 3H_2O(l)$$

HINT

1. Both reactions 6 *and* 7 have to occur to get from the starting materials to the combustion products. Do not forget the hydrogen.
2. In this case there are two moles of hydrogen so we need *twice* the value of ΔH_c which refers to one mole of hydrogen.

$$\Delta H_c^\ominus C_2H_2 = -1301 \text{ kJ mol}^{-1}$$
$$\Delta H_c^\ominus H_2 = -286 \text{ kJ mol}^{-1}$$
$$\Delta H_c^\ominus C_2H_6 = -1560 \text{ kJ mol}^{-1}$$

Putting in the values:

$$3\tfrac{1}{2}O_2(g) + H-C\equiv C-H(g) + 2H_2(g) \xrightarrow[\text{1.}]{\Delta H_1} H-\underset{\underset{\displaystyle H}{|}}{\overset{\overset{\displaystyle H}{|}}{C}}-\underset{\underset{\displaystyle H}{|}}{\overset{\overset{\displaystyle H}{|}}{C}}-H(g) + 3\tfrac{1}{2}O_2(g)$$

$$6. \qquad 7. \quad \begin{array}{c} 2\times-286 \text{ kJ mol}^{-1} \\ = -572 \text{ kJ mol}^{-1} \end{array} \qquad 8.$$

$$-1301 \text{ kJ mol}^{-1} \qquad\qquad -1560 \text{ kJ mol}^{-1}$$

$$-1873 \text{ kJ mol}^{-1} \quad 2CO_2(g) + 3H_2O(l) \quad +1560 \text{ kJ mol}^{-1}$$

To get the enthalpy change for reaction 1 we must go round the cycle in the direction of the red arrows. This means reversing reaction 8 and so we must change its sign.

So $\Delta H_1 = -1873 + 1560 \text{ kJ mol}^{-1}$

$\Delta H_2 = -313 \text{ kJ mol}^{-1}$ – once again , the same answer as before.

Notice that in reaction 1 there are $3\tfrac{1}{2}$ moles of oxygen on either side of the equation. They take no part in the reaction and do not affect the value of ΔH.

13.6.2 Finding $\Delta H_f^\ominus$ from $\Delta H_c^\ominus$

Enthalpy changes of formation of compounds are often difficult or impossible to measure directly as often the elements simply do not react directly to form the compound we are interested in.

For example the following equation represents the formation of ethanol from its elements

$$2C(gr) + 3H_2(g) + \tfrac{1}{2}O_2(g) \rightarrow C_2H_5OH(l)$$

This does not take place, but all the species concerned will readily burn in oxygen and their enthalpies of combustion can easily be measured.

The thermochemical cycle we need is

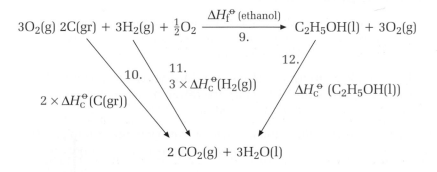

Putting in the values:

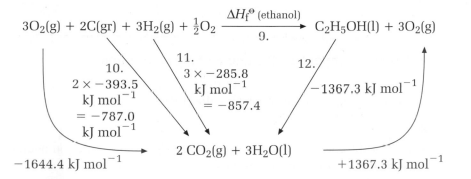

NOTE

The values we need are:

$\Delta H_c^\ominus (C(gr)) = -393.5 \text{ kJ mol}^{-1}$

$\Delta H_c^\ominus (H_2) = -285.8 \text{ kJ mol}^{-1}$

$\Delta H_c^\oplus (C_2H_5OH) = -1367.3 \text{ kJ mol}^{-1}$

Note that in reaction 9 there are 3 moles of oxygen on either side of the equation. They take no part in the reaction and do not affect the value of $\Delta H_f^\ominus$.

Note also that $\Delta H_c^\ominus (C(gr))$ is the same as $\Delta H_f^\ominus (CO_2(g))$ and $\Delta H_c^\ominus (H_2(g))$ is the same as $\Delta H_f^\ominus(H_2O(l))$.

To get the enthalpy change for reaction 9, we must go round the cycle in the direction of the red arrows. This means reversing reaction 12 and so we must change its sign.

So $\Delta H_9 = -1644.4 + 1367.3 \text{ kJ mol}^{-1} = -277.1 \text{ kJ mol}^{-1}$

$\Delta H_c^\ominus (C_2H_5OH(l)) = -277.1 \text{ kJ mol}^{-1}$

QUICK QUESTIONS

Quick questions for all the topics relating to Hess's Law and thermochemical cycles will be found at the end of Topic 13.8.

13.7

Representing thermochemical cycles

We can use **enthalpy diagrams** rather than **thermochemical cycles** to represent the enthalpy changes in chemical reactions. These show the energy (enthalpy) levels of the reactants and products of a chemical reaction on a vertical scale, so we can compare their energies. If a substance is of lower energy than another, we say it is energetically more stable.

13.7.1 The enthalpy of elements

So far we have considered enthalpy *changes,* not absolute values. When drawing enthalpy diagrams we need a zero to work from. We can then give absolute numbers to the enthalpies of different substances.

The enthalpies of all elements in their standard states (i.e. the states in which they exist at 298 K and 100 kPa) are taken as zero. 298 K (25°C) and 100 kPa are approximately normal room conditions.

This convention means that the standard state of hydrogen, for example, is H_2 and not H, because hydrogen exists as H_2 at room temperature and pressure.

Pure carbon can exist in a number of forms at room temperature including graphite, diamond and buckminsterfullerene ('buckyballs'). These are called **allotropes**. Graphite is the most stable of these and is taken as the standard state of carbon. It is given the special state symbol gr, so C(gr) represents graphite.

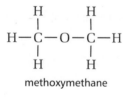

methoxymethane

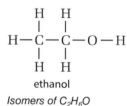

ethanol

Isomers of C_2H_6O

13.7.2 Thermochemical cycles and enthalpy diagrams

Here are some examples of reactions with their enthalpy changes presented both as thermochemical cycles and as **enthalpy diagrams**.

Example

What is $\Delta H^{\ominus}$ for the change from methoxymethane to ethanol (the compounds are a pair of isomers – they have the same formula but different structures)?

The standard molar enthalpy changes of formation of the two compounds are:

$$CH_3OCH_3 \quad \Delta H_f^{\ominus} = -184 \text{ kJ mol}^{-1}$$
$$C_2H_5OH \quad \Delta H_f^{\ominus} = -277 \text{ kJ mol}^{-1}$$

Using a thermochemical cycle

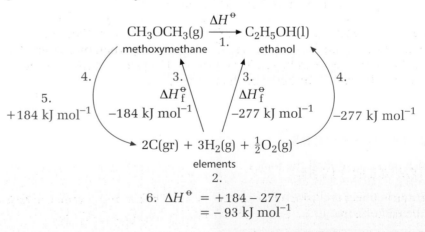

6. $\Delta H^{\ominus} = +184 - 277$
$= -93 \text{ kJ mol}^{-1}$

The steps below relate to the numbers in red on the thermochemical cycle.

1. Write an equation for the reaction.

2. Write down the elements in the two compounds with the correct quantities of each.

3. Put in the $\Delta H_f^\ominus$ values with arrows showing the direction, i.e. from elements to compounds.

4. Put in the arrows to go from starting materials to products via the elements (the red arrows).

5. Reverse the sign of $\Delta H_f^\ominus$ if the red arrow is in the reverse direction to the black arrow.

6. Go round the cycle in the direction of the red arrows and add up the ΔH values as you go.

Hess's Law tells us that this is the same as $\Delta H^\ominus$ for the direct reaction.

Using an enthalpy diagram

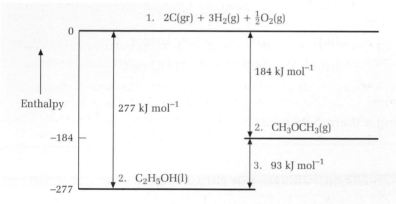

The steps below relate to the numbers in red on the enthalphy diagram.

1. Draw a line at level 0 to represent the elements.

2. Look up the values of $\Delta H_f^\ominus$ for each compound and enter these on the enthalpy diagrams, taking account of the signs – negative values are below 0, positive values are above.

3. Find the difference in levels between the two compounds. This represents the difference in their enthalpies.

4. $\Delta H^\ominus$ is the difference in levels taking account of the direction of change. Up is positive and down negative. From methoxymethane to ethanol is *down*, so the sign is negative and thus $\Delta H^\ominus$ is -93 kJ mol^{-1}.

Notice how the enthalpy level diagram makes it much clearer than the thermochemical cycle does, that ethanol has less energy than methoxymethane so it is the more energetically stable compound. The values of $\Delta H^\ominus$ for the reaction are the same whichever method we use.

QUICK QUESTIONS

Quick questions for all the topics relating to Hess's Law and thermochemical cycles will be found at the end of Topic 13.8.

More examples of Hess's Law

Here is a further example of how to use Hess's Law to find an unknown ΔH using firstly a thermochemical cycle and secondly an enthalpy diagram. The two methods, of course, give the same answer. You may find the thermochemical cycle a little easier to set out but the enthalpy diagram has the advantage of showing the relative enthalpy levels of the reactants and products.

Example

To find $\Delta H^{\ominus}$ for the reaction:

$$NH_3(g) + HCl(g) \rightarrow NH_4Cl(s)$$

The standard molar enthalpy changes of formation of the compounds are:

NH_3	$\Delta H_f^{\ominus}$	$= -46 \text{ kJ mol}^{-1}$
HCl	$\Delta H_f^{\ominus}$	$= -92 \text{ kJ mol}^{-1}$
NH_4Cl	$\Delta H_f^{\ominus}$	$= -314 \text{ kJ mol}^{-1}$

13.8.1 Using a thermochemical cycle

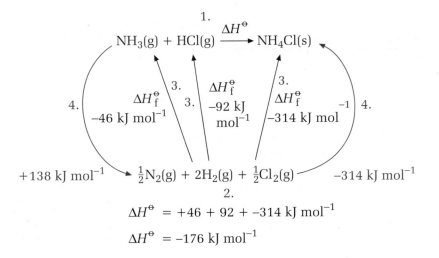

$$\Delta H^{\ominus} = +46 + 92 + -314 \text{ kJ mol}^{-1}$$

$$\Delta H^{\ominus} = -176 \text{ kJ mol}^{-1}$$

1. Write an equation for the reaction.

2. Write down the elements that make up the two compounds.

3. Put in the $\Delta H_f^{\ominus}$ values with arrows showing the direction, i.e. from elements to compounds.

4. Put in the arrows to go from the starting materials to products via the elements (the red arrows).

5. Reverse the sign of $\Delta H^{\ominus}$ if the red arrow is in the opposite direction to the black arrow.

6. Go round the cycle in the direction of the red arrows and add up the values of $\Delta H^{\ominus}$ as you go.

13.8.2 Using an enthalpy diagram

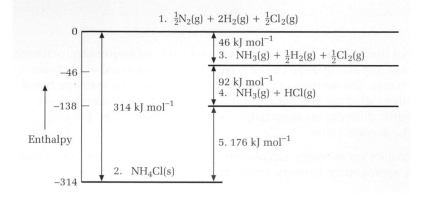

1. Draw a line at level 0 to represent the elements.

2. Draw in ammonium chloride $314 \, \text{kJ mol}^{-1}$ below this.

3. Draw a line representing ammonia $46 \, \text{kJ mol}^{-1}$ below the level of the elements. (There is still $\frac{1}{2} H_2$ and $\frac{1}{2} Cl_2$ left unused.)

4. Draw a line $92 \, \text{kJ mol}^{-1}$ below ammonia. This represents ammonia plus hydrogen chloride.

5. Find the difference in levels between the $(NH_3 + HCl)$ line and the NH_4Cl one. This represents $\Delta H^{\ominus}$ for the reaction. As the change from $(NH_3 + HCl)$ to NH_4Cl is 'downhill', $\Delta H^{\ominus}$ must be negative and so $\Delta H^{\ominus}$ is $-176 \, \text{kJ mol}^{-1}$.

Notice how the enthalpy level diagram makes it much clearer than the thermochemical cycle does, that ammonium chloride is more energetically stable than ammonia and hydrogen chloride. The values of $\Delta H^{\ominus}$ for the reaction are the same whichever method we use.

QUICK QUESTIONS

Compound	$\Delta H_f^{\ominus}/\text{kJ mol}^{-1}$
$CH_3COCH_3(l)$	-248
$CH_3CH(OH)CH_3(l)$	-318
$C_2H_4(g)$	$+52$
$C_2H_4Cl_2(l)$	-165
$C_2H_5Cl(l)$	-137
$HCl(g)$	-92
$CuO(s)$	-157
$ZnO(s)$	-348
$Pb(NO_3)_2(s)$	-452
$PbO(s)$	-217
$2NO_2(g)$	$+33$

Use the values of $\Delta H_f^{\ominus}$ in the table to calculate $\Delta H^{\ominus}$ for each of the reactions below using (a) thermochemical cycles and (b) enthalpy diagrams.

1 $CH_3COCH_3(l) + H_2(g) \rightarrow CH_3CH(OH)CH_3(l)$

2 $C_2H_4(g) + Cl_2(g) \rightarrow C_2H_4Cl_2 \, (l)$

3 $C_2H_4(g) + HCl(g) \rightarrow C_2H_5Cl(l)$

4 $Zn(s) + CuO(s) \rightarrow ZnO(s) + Cu(s)$

5 $Pb(NO_3)_2(s) \rightarrow PbO(s) + 2NO_2(g) + \frac{1}{2}O_2(g)$

Bond enthalpies

We have to put in energy to break a covalent bond – it is an endothermic change. The same amount of energy is given out when the bond is formed – this is an exothermic change. The amount of energy involved is called the **average bond enthalpy** (often called the bond energy). The same bond, for example C—H, may have slightly different bond enthalpies in different molecules, but we usually use the average value.

As bond enthalpies are averages, calculations using them for specific compounds will only give approximate answers. However, they are useful and quick and easy to use.

13.9.1 Using bond enthalpies to calculate enthalpy changes of reaction

We can use bond enthalpies to work out the enthalpy change of reactions, for example:

$$C_2H_6(g) + Cl_2(g) \rightarrow C_2H_5Cl(g) + HCl(g)$$

ethane   chlorine   chloroethane   hydrogen chloride

The bond enthalpies you will need for this example are given in Table 13.1

The steps are:

- First draw out the molecules and show all the bonds.

(Formulae drawn to show all the bonds are called displayed formulae.)

- Now imagine that all the bonds in the *reactants* break leaving separate atoms. Look up the bond enthalpy for each bond and add them all up. This will give you the total energy that must be *put in* to break the bonds and form separate atoms.

We need to *break* these bonds:

$6 \times$ C—H	6×413 kJ mol^{-1}	$= 2478$ kJ mol^{-1}
$1 \times$ C—C	1×347 kJ mol^{-1}	$= 347$ kJ mol^{-1}
$1 \times$ Cl—Cl	1×243 kJ mol^{-1}	$= 243$ kJ mol^{-1}
		$= 3068$ kJ mol^{-1}

So 3068 kJ mol^{-1} must be *put in* to convert ethane and chlorine to separate hydrogen, chlorine and carbon atoms.

- Next imagine the separate atoms join together to give the *products*. Add up the bond enthalpies of the bonds that must form. This will give you the total enthalpy *given out* by the bonds forming.

We need to *make* these bonds:

$5 \times$ C—H	5×413 kJ mol^{-1}	$= 2065$ kJ mol^{-1}
$1 \times$ C—C	1×347 kJ mol^{-1}	$= 347$ kJ mol^{-1}
$1 \times$ C—Cl	1×346 kJ mol^{-1}	$= 346$ kJ mol^{-1}
$1 \times$ Cl—H	1×432 kJ mol^{-1}	$= 432$ kJ mol^{-1}
		$= 3190$ kJ mol^{-1}

Table 13.1 *Tabulated bond enthalpies*

Bond	Bond enthalpy/kJ mol^{-1}
C—H	413
C—C	347
Cl—Cl	243
C—Cl	346
Cl—H	432
Br—Br	193
Br—H	366
C—Br	285

So 3190 kJ mol^{-1} is *given out* when we convert the separate hydrogen, chlorine and carbon atoms to chloroethane and hydrogen chloride.

- The difference between the energy put in to break the bonds and the energy given out to form bonds is the approximate enthalpy change of the reaction.

The difference, $3190 - 3068 = 122$ kJ mol^{-1}

- Work out the sign of the enthalpy change. If more energy was put in than was given out, the enthalpy change is positive (the reaction is endothermic). If more energy was given out than was put in the enthalpy change is negative (the reaction is endothermic).

In this case more enthalpy is given out than put in, so the reaction is exothermic and $\Delta H^{\ominus} = -122$ kJ mol^{-1}.

Note that in practice it would be impossible for the reaction to happen like this. However, Hess's law tells us that we will get the same answer whatever route we take – real or theoretical.

13.9.2 A shortcut

We can often shorten bond enthalpy calculations:

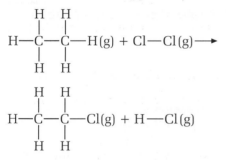

Only the bonds drawn in red actually make or break during the reaction.

So we only need to break:

$$1 \times C{-}H = 413 \text{ kJ mol}^{-1}$$
$$1 \times Cl{-}Cl = 243 \text{ kJ mol}^{-1}$$
$$\text{Total energy put in} = 656 \text{ kJ mol}^{-1}$$

We only need to make:

$$1 \times C{-}Cl = 346 \text{ kJ mol}^{-1}$$
$$1 \times H{-}Cl = 432 \text{ kJ mol}^{-1}$$
$$\text{Total energy given out} = 778 \text{ kJ mol}^{-1}$$
$$\text{The difference is } 778 - 656 = 122 \text{ kJ mol}^{-1}$$

More energy is given out than taken in so:

$$\Delta H^{\ominus} = -122 \text{ kJ mol}^{-1}$$

(as before).

13.9.3 Comparing the result with that from a thermochemical cycle

This is only an approximate value because the bond enthalpies are averages whereas in a compound any bond has a specific value for its enthalpy. We can find an accurate value for $\Delta H^{\ominus}$ by using a thermochemical cycle, see below.

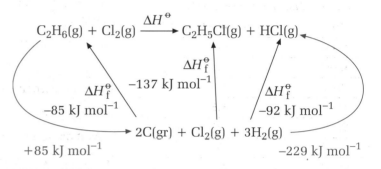

Remember $Cl_2(g)$ is an element so its $\Delta H_f^{\ominus}$ is zero.

$\Delta H^{\ominus} = 85{-}229$ kJ mol^{-1}

$\Delta H^{\ominus} = -144$ kJ mol^{-1} (compared with -122 kJ mol^{-1} calculated from bond enthalpies.) This difference is typical of what may be expected using bond enthalpies. The answer obtained from the thermochemical cycle is the 'right' one as all the $\Delta H_f^{\ominus}$ values have been obtained from the actual compounds involved.

---

14 Reaction rates

14.1 Collision theory

Reaction rates, sometimes called kinetics, is the study of the factors that affect rates of chemical reactions. There is a large variation in reaction rates – 'popping' a test tube full of hydrogen is over in a fraction of a second while the complete rusting away of an iron nail could take several years. Reactions can be speeded up or slowed down under different conditions.

14.1.1 What makes a chemical reaction happen?

For a reaction to take place between two particles, they must collide, and do so with enough energy to break bonds. To get a lot of collisions we need a lot of particles in a small volume. For the particles to have enough energy to break bonds they need to be moving fast. So, for a fast reaction rate we need plenty of rapidly moving particles in a small volume.

14.1.2 Factors that affect the rate of chemical reactions

The following factors will increase the rate of a reaction:

- **Increasing the temperature.** This increases the speed of the molecules, which in turn increases both the number and energy of collisions. A rough rule for many chemical reactions is that, if the temperature goes up by 10 K (10°C), the rate of reaction approximately doubles.
- **Increasing the concentration of a solution.** If there are more particles present in a given volume, collisions are more likely.
- **Increasing the pressure of a gas reaction.** This has the same effect as increasing the concentration of a solution – there are more molecules or atoms in a given volume so collisions are more likely.
- **Increasing the surface area of solid reactants**. The greater the *total* surface area of a solid, the more of its particles are available to react. So, breaking a solid lump into smaller pieces increases the rate of its reaction.
- **Using a catalyst.** A catalyst is a substance that can change the rate of a chemical reaction without being chemically changed itself.

14.1.3 Collision theory

When the temperature increases, molecules move faster, so there will be more collisions per second and the molecules will also hit each other harder (with more energy).

The number of collisions per second between particles depends on:

- the temperature (and therefore the speeds) of the reacting particles;
- the concentrations of the reacting particles.

14.1.4 Activation energy

Only a very small proportion of collisions actually result in a reaction. For a collision to result in a reaction, the molecules must have a certain minimum energy – enough to start breaking bonds. This energy is called the **activation energy** and has the abbreviation E_A.

We can include the idea of activation energy on an enthalpy diagram that shows the course of a reaction.

Exothermic reactions

Figure 14.1 shows an exothermic reaction with a large activation energy.

This reaction will take place extremely slowly at room temperature because very few collisions will have sufficient energy to bring about a reaction.

Figure 14.2 shows the reaction profile for an exothermic reaction with a small activation energy.

This reaction will take place rapidly at room temperature, because many collisions will have enough energy to bring about reaction.

The situation is a little like a ball on a hill, Figure 14.3. A small amount of energy is needed in A, to set the ball rolling, while a large amount of energy is needed in B.

The chemical species that exists at the top of the curve of an enthalpy diagram is called a **transition state** or **activated complex**. Some bonds are in the process of being made and some bonds are in the process of being broken. Like the ball at the very top of the hill, it has extra energy and is unstable.

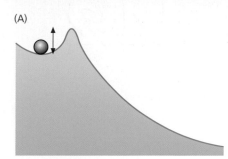
(A)

With low 'activation energy'

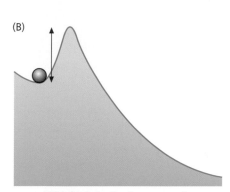
(B)

With high 'activation energy'

Fig 14.3 Ball on a mountainside models

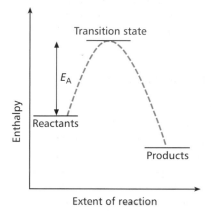

Fig 14.1 An exothermic reaction with a large activation energy, E_A

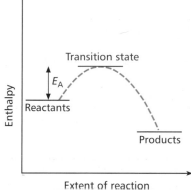

Fig 14.2 An exothermic reaction with a small activation energy, E_A

Endothermic reactions

Endothermic reactions are those in which the products have more energy than the reactants. An endothermic reaction, with activation energy E_A, is shown in Figure 14.4. The transition state has been labelled.

Notice that the activation energy is measured from the reactants to the top of the curve.

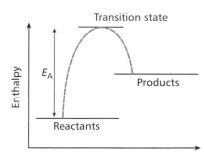

Fig 14.4 An endothermic reaction with activation energy, E_A

QUICK QUESTIONS

1 List five factors that affect the speed of a chemical reaction.

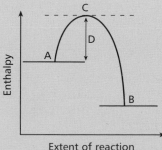

Use the figure to answer questions **2** and **3**:

2 a What is A?

b What is B?

c What is C?

d What is D?

3 a Does the enthalpy profile represent an endothermic or an exothermic reaction?

b Explain your answer to **a**.

14.2.1 **The speeds of particles**

The particles in any gas (or solution) are all moving at different speeds – a few are moving slowly, a few very fast and most somewhere in the middle. The energy of a particle depends on its speed, so the particles also have a range of energies. If we plot a graph of 'energy' against the 'fraction of particles that have that energy', we end up with the curve shown in Figure 14.5. This particular shape is called the **Maxwell–Boltzmann distribution** – it tells us about the distribution of energy amongst the particles.

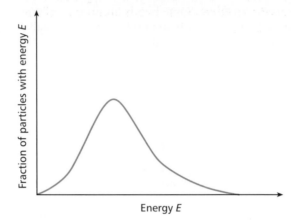

Fig 14.5 *The distribution of the energies of particles. The area under the graph represents the total number of particles*

14.2.2 **Activation energy, E_A**

For a reaction to take place, a collision between particles must have enough energy to start breaking bonds, see Topic 14.1. We call this amount of energy the activation energy, E_A. If we mark E_A on the Maxwell–Boltzmann distribution graph, Figure 14.6, then the area under the graph to the right of the activation energy line represents the number of particles with enough energy to react.

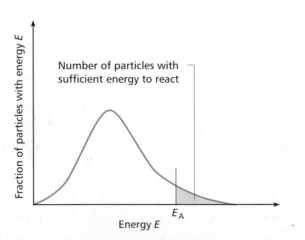

Fig 14.6 *Only particles with energy greater than E_A can react*

14.2.3 The effect of temperature on reaction rate

The shape of the Maxwell–Boltzmann graph changes with temperature, see Figure 14.7.

- At higher temperatures the peak of the curve moves to the right and so does the number of particles with very high energies.
- The shaded areas to the right of the E_A line represent the number of molecules that have greater energy than E_A at each temperature.
- The graphs show that at higher temperatures more of the molecules have energy greater than E_A. So, a higher percentage of collisions will result in reaction, and this is why reaction rates increase with temperature.
- At higher temperatures the peak of the curve is lower, so that the total area under the curve (the total number of particles) remains the same.

The total *number* of collisions also increases as the particles move faster, but this is not as important to the rate of reaction as the increase in the number of *effective* collisions (those with energy greater than E_A).

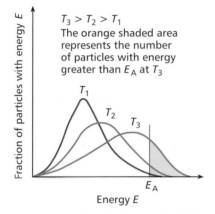

Fig 14.7 *The Maxwell–Boltzmann distribution of the energies of the same number of particles at three temperatures. The total area under the curve is the same for each temperature because it represents the total number of particles*

QUICK QUESTIONS

Use the figure to answer the following:

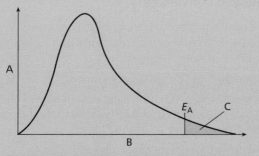

The Maxwell–Boltzmann distribution of energies of particles at a particular temperature, with the activation energy, E_A marked

1 What is the axis labelled A?

2 What is the axis labelled B?

3 What does area C represent?

4 If the temperature is increased, what happens to the peak of the curve? (moves left, moves right, no change)

5 If the temperature is increased, what happens to E_A? (moves left, moves right, no change)

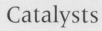

14.3 Catalysts

Catalysts are substances that affect the rate of a chemical reaction without being chemically changed themselves. Catalysts are usually used to speed up reactions so they are important in industry. It is cheaper to speed up a reaction by using a catalyst than by using high temperatures and pressures. This is true even if the catalyst is expensive, because it is not used up.

14.3.1 How catalysts work

Catalysts work because they reduce the activation energy of the reaction (the minimum amount of energy that is needed to start the reaction). They do this by providing a different pathway for the reaction – one with a lower activation energy. We can see this on the enthalpy diagrams in Figure 14.8.

For example, for the decomposition of hydrogen iodide:

$$2HI(g) \rightarrow H_2(g) + I_2(g)$$

$E_A = 183 \, \text{kJ mol}^{-1}$ (without a catalyst)
$E_A = 105 \, \text{kJ mol}^{-1}$ (with a gold catalyst)
$E_A = 58 \, \text{kJ mol}^{-1}$ (with a platinum catalyst)

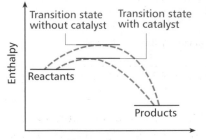

Fig 14.8 *Enthalpy diagrams for a catalysed and an uncatalysed reaction*

We can see what happens when we lower the activation energy if we look at the Maxwell–Boltzmann distribution curve, Figure 14.9. The area shaded pink represents the number of collisions that can result without a catalyst. The area shaded blue, plus the area shaded pink, represents the number of collisions that can result with a catalyst.

Different catalysts work in different ways – many were discovered by trial and error.

We divide them into:

- **heterogeneous** catalysts (where the catalyst is in a different phase to the reactants – usually solid catalyst and liquid or gaseous reactants) and

- **homogeneous** catalysts (where catalyst and reactants are in the same phase).

Different phases are separated by a distinct boundary, for example oil and water form two separate liquid phases.

Some examples are given in Table 14.1.

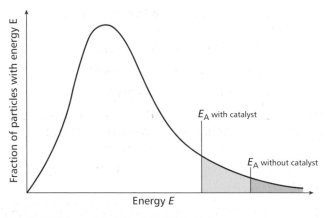

Fig 14.9 *With a catalyst the extra number of particles in the blue shaded area can react*

14.3.2 Catalytic converters

Most cars are now equipped with catalytic converters in their exhaust systems. The combustion reactions in a car engine produce a number of polluting gases:

- carbon monoxide, CO, which is poisonous;

- nitrogen oxides, (NO, NO_2 and N_2O_4) often abbreviated to NO_x, which cause acid rain and help to destroy the ozone layer in the stratosphere;

- unburnt hydrocarbons may cause cancer;

- unburnt hydrocarbons react with nitrogen oxides in sunlight to form smogs (containing ozone) at low levels in the atmosphere.

A catalytic converter

Table 14.1 *Examples of catalysts*

Reaction	Catalyst	Type	Reference	Use
$N_2 + 3H_2 \rightarrow 2NH_3$ The Haber Process	Iron	Heterogeneous	Section 15.3.2	Making fertilisers
$4NH_3 + 5O_2 \rightarrow 4NO + 6H_2O$ Ostwald Process for making nitric acid	Platinum and rhodium	Heterogeneous	Section 15.3.3	Making fertilisers
$CH_2{=}CH_2 + H_2 \rightarrow CH_3CH_3$ Hardening of fats with hydrogen	Nickel	Heterogeneous	Section 14.3.3	Making margarine
Cracking hydrocarbon chains from crude oil	Aluminium oxide and silicon dioxide	Heterogeneous	Topic 9.2	Making petrol
Catalytic converter reactions in car exhausts	Platinum and rhodium	Heterogeneous	Section 14.3.2	Removing polluting gases
$CH_3CO_2H + CH_3OH \rightarrow$ $CH_3CO_2CH_3 + H_2O$ Esterification	H^+ or OH^-	Homogeneous	Section 11.2.5	Solvents
$O_3 + O \rightarrow 2O_2$ Destruction of ozone in the atmosphere	Cl atoms derived from CFCs or NO derived from burning fuels	Homogeneous	Section 14.3.4	Not applicable

The catalytic converter is a honeycomb, made of a ceramic material coated with platinum and rhodium metals – the catalysts. The honeycomb shape provides an enormous surface area, so a little of these expensive metals goes a long way.

As they pass over the catalyst, the polluting gases react with each other to form less harmful products by the following reactions:

carbon monoxide + nitrogen oxide → nitrogen + carbon dioxide
hydrocarbons + nitrogen oxide → nitrogen + carbon dioxide + water

The reactions take place on the surface of the catalyst in two steps:

- The gases first form weak bonds with the metal atoms of the catalyst – this is called adsorption. This holds the gases in just the right position for them to react together. The gases then react on the surface.
- The products then break away from the metal atoms – called desorption. This frees up room on the catalyst surface for more gases to take their place and react.

The strength of the weak bonds holding the gases onto the metal surface is critical. They must be strong enough to hold the gases for long enough to react, but weak enough to release the products easily.

14.3.3 Hardening fats

Unsaturated fats are made more solid or 'hardened' when hydrogen is added across some of the double bonds. This is done by bubbling hydrogen into the liquid fat which has a nickel catalyst mixed with it. The nickel is filtered off after the reaction.

14.3.4 Catalysts and the ozone layer

Until recently, some very unreactive compounds called chlorofluorocarbons (CFCs) were used for a number of applications such as solvents, aerosol propellants and in expanded polystyrene foams. They escaped high into the atmosphere where they remain, because they are so unreactive. This is partly due to the strength of the

carbon–halogen bonds. CFCs do eventually decompose to produce separate chlorine atoms, called free radicals. These act as catalysts in reactions that bring about the destruction of ozone, O_3. Ozone is important because it forms a layer that acts as a shield that prevents too much ultraviolet radiation from reaching the Earth's surface.

The reaction goes via a route involving chlorate free radicals, $ClO\cdot$:

$$O_3(g) + Cl\cdot(g) \rightarrow ClO\cdot(g) + O_2(g)$$
$$ClO\cdot(g) + O(g) \rightarrow Cl\cdot(g) + O_2(g)$$

The overall effect is: $O_3(g) + O(g) \rightarrow 2O_2(g)$

The chlorine free radical is not used up at all – it acts as a catalyst. This is an example of homogeneous catalysis because all the reactions are between gases.

Nitrogen monoxide acts as a catalyst in a similar way to chlorine atoms.

QUICK QUESTIONS

The following questions refer to the figure below which shows a profile for a reaction with and without a catalyst.

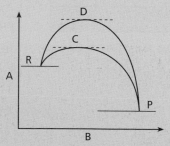

1 What is label   **a** A,   **b** B,   **c** C,   **d** D?

2 What do the distances from D to R and from C to R represent?

3 Is the reaction exothermic or endothermic?

4 What is the difference between a heterogeneous catalyst and a homogeneous catalyst?

Chemical equilibrium

The idea of equilibrium

We usually think of a reaction as starting with the reactants and ending with the products:

$$\text{reactants} \rightarrow \text{products}$$

Some reactions are reversible. For example when we heat blue hydrated copper sulphate it becomes white anhydrous copper sulphate as the water of crystallisation is driven off. The white copper sulphate returns to blue if we add water:

$$CuSO_4.5H_2O \rightleftharpoons CuSO_4 + 5H_2O$$

blue hydrated copper sulphate   white anhydrous copper sulphate

However, something different would happen if we could safely do this reaction in a closed container. As soon as the products are formed they react together and form the reactants again, so that instead of reactants *or* products we get a mixture of both. This mixture is called an **equilibrium** mixture.

15.1.1 Setting up an equilibrium

We can understand how an equilibrium mixture is set up by thinking about what happens with a physical process, like the evaporation of water – easier to picture than a chemical change.

First imagine a puddle of water out in the open. Some of the water molecules at the surface will move fast enough to escape the liquid and evaporate. Evaporation will continue until all the water is gone.

But think about putting some water into a *closed* container. At first the water will begin to evaporate as before. The volume of the liquid will get smaller and the number of vapour molecules will go up. But as more molecules enter the vapour, some vapour molecules will start to re-enter the liquid, see Figure 15.1.

After a time, the rate of evaporation and the rate of condensation will become equal. The level of the liquid water will then stay exactly the same, and so will the number of molecules in the vapour and in the liquid, but the evaporation and condensation are still going on *at the same rate*. This situation is called a **dynamic equilibrium** and is one of the key ideas of this topic.

In fact, we could have started by filling the empty container with the same mass of water vapour as we originally had liquid water. The vapour would begin to condense and in time we would reach exactly the same equilibrium position.

15.1.2 The conditions for equilibrium

Although the system we have used is very simple, we can pick out four conditions that apply to *all* equilibria:

- Equilibrium is reached in a closed system (one where the reactants and products cannot escape). The system does not have to be sealed. For example, an open beaker could be a closed system for a reaction that takes place in a solvent, as long as the reactants, products and solvent did not evaporate.
- Equilibrium can be approached from either direction (in the above example, from liquid or from vapour) and the final equilibrium position will be the same (as long as conditions, such as temperature and pressure stay the same).

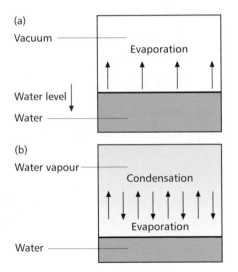

(a)
Vacuum
Evaporation
Water level
Water

(b)
Water vapour
Condensation
Evaporation
Water

Fig 15.1 *(a) Water will evaporate into an empty container. Eventually the rates of evaporation and condensation will be the same. (b) Equilibrium is set up*

- Equilibrium is a **dynamic** process – it is reached when the rates of two opposing processes, which are going on all the time (in this case evaporation and condensation), are the same.
- We know when equilibrium has been reached when the **macroscopic properties** of the system do not change with time. These are properties like density, concentration, colour and pressure – ones that do not depend on the total *quantity* of matter.

A reversible reaction which can reach equilibrium is denoted by the symbol $\rightleftharpoons$ for example:

$$\text{liquid water} \rightleftharpoons \text{water vapour}$$

or:

$$H_2O(l) \rightleftharpoons H_2O(g)$$

15.1.3 Chemical equilibria

The same principles that we found for a physical change also apply to chemical equilibria such as:

$$\underset{\text{reactants}}{A + B} \quad \rightleftharpoons \quad \underset{\text{products}}{C + D}$$

At the start of the reaction the forward rate is fast, because A and B are plentiful and there is no C or D. Then as the concentrations of C and D build up, the reverse reaction speeds up. We reach a point where exactly the same number of particles are changing from A + B to C + D as are changing from C + D to A + B. We have reached equilibrium.

One important point to remember is that an equilibrium mixture can have any proportions of reactants and products. It is not necessarily half reactants and half products, though it could be. The proportions may be changed depending on the conditions of the reaction, such as temperature, pressure and concentration.

QUICK QUESTIONS

1 For each of the following statements about all equilibria, say whether it is true or false.

   a Once equilibrium is reached the concentrations of the reactants and the products do not change.

   b At equilibrium the forward and the back reactions come to a halt.

   c Equilibrium is only reached in a closed system.

   d An equilibrium mixture always contains half reactants and half products.

2 What can be said about the rates of the forward and the back reactions when equilibrium is reached?

Some industrial processes, like the production of ammonia or sulphuric acid, have, as a key step, reversible reactions that in closed systems would produce equilibrium mixtures containing both products and reactants. Other things being equal, we would like to increase the proportion of products. For this reason it is important to understand how to control equilibrium reactions.

15.2.1 The equilibrium mixture

It is possible to change the proportion of reactants to products in an equilibrium mixture. In this way we are able to obtain a greater yield of the products. We call this changing the *position* of equilibrium.

- If the proportion of products in the equilibrium mixture is increased, we say that the equilibrium is moved to the right.
- If the proportion of reactants in the equilibrium mixture is increased, we say that we the equilibrium is moved to the left.

We can often move the equilibrium position to the left or right by varying conditions like temperature, the concentration of species involved and the pressure (in the case of reactions involving gases).

15.2.2 Le Châtelier's principle

This is useful because it gives us a rule to tell us whether the equilibrium moves to the right or to the left when the conditions of an equilibrium mixture are changed.

It says:

> **If a system at equilibrium is disturbed, the equilibrium moves in the direction that tends to reduce the disturbance.**

Le Châtelier's principle does not tell us *how far* the equilibrium moves, so we cannot predict the *quantities* involved.

Changing concentrations

If we *increase* the concentration of one of the reactants, Le Châtelier's principle says that the equilibrium will shift in the direction that tends to *reduce* the concentration of this reactant. Look at the reaction:

$$A(aq) + B(aq) \rightleftharpoons C(aq) + D(aq)$$

Suppose we add some extra A. This would increase the concentration of A. The only way that this system can reduce the concentration of A, is by A reacting with B (thus forming more C and D). So adding more A uses up more B and moves the equilibrium to the right. We end up with a greater proportion of products in the reaction mixture than before we added A. The same thing would happen if we added more B.

We could also remove C as it was formed. The equilibrium would move right to produce more C (and D). The same thing would happen if we removed D as soon as it was formed.

Changing pressure

This only applies to reactions involving gases. An example of a gas reaction that reaches equilibrium is:

$$N_2O_4(g) \rightleftharpoons 2NO_2(g)$$

dinitrogen tetraoxide	nitrogen dioxide
1 mole	2 moles
colourless	brown

Increasing the pressure of a gas means that there are more molecules of it in a given volume – it is equivalent to increasing the concentration of a solution.

If we increase the pressure on this system, Le Châtelier's principle tells us that the position of equilibrium will move to decrease the pressure. This means that it will move left because fewer molecules exert less pressure. In the same way if we decrease the pressure the equilibrium will move to the right.

Dinitrogen tetraoxide is a colourless gas and nitrogen dioxide is brown. If we decrease the pressure we can watch as the equilibrium moves to the right because the colour of the mixture gets browner, see Figure 15.2.

However, if there are the same number of moles of gas on both sides of the equation, then pressure has no effect on the equilibrium position. For example:

$$H_2(g) + I_2(g) \rightleftharpoons 2HI(g)$$

2 moles	2 moles

The equilibrium position will not change in this reaction when the pressure is changed, so the proportions of the three gases will stay the same.

Changing temperature
Reversible reactions that are exothermic (give out heat) in one direction are endothermic (take in heat) in the other direction.

Suppose we increase the temperature of an equilibrium mixture that is exothermic in the forward direction. An example is:

$$2SO_2(g) + O_2(g) \rightleftharpoons 2SO_3(g) \qquad \Delta H^{\ominus} = -197\,kJ\,mol^{-1}$$

The negative sign of $\Delta H^{\ominus}$ means that heat is given out when sulphur dioxide and oxygen react to form sulphur trioxide.

Le Châtelier's principle tells us that if we increase the temperature, the equilibrium moves in the direction that cools the system down. To do this it will move in the direction which absorbs heat (is endothermic) i.e. to the left. The equilibrium mixture will contain a greater proportion of sulphur dioxide and oxygen than before. In the same way, if we cool the mixture the equilibrium will move to the right and increase the proportion of sulphur trioxide.

Catalysts
Catalysts have no effect on the position of equilibrium. They work in such a way that they affect both the forward and reverse reactions equally. Therefore they speed up the rate at which equilibrium is set up but do not alter the composition of the equilibrium mixture.

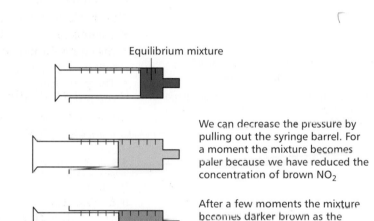

Equilibrium mixture

We can decrease the pressure by pulling out the syringe barrel. For a moment the mixture becomes paler because we have reduced the concentration of brown NO_2

After a few moments the mixture becomes darker brown as the equilibrium moves to the right and more brown NO_2 is formed

Fig 15.2 $N_2O_4(g) \rightleftharpoons 2NO_2(g)$. The equilibrium moves to the right as we decrease the pressure

QUICK QUESTIONS

1 In which of the following reactions will the position of equilibrium be affected by changing the pressure? Explain your answers.

   a $2SO_2(g) + O_2(g) \rightleftharpoons 2SO_3(g)$

   b $CH_3CO_2H(aq) \rightleftharpoons CH_3CO_2^-(aq) + H^+(aq)$

   c $H_2(g) + CO_2(g) \rightleftharpoons H_2O(g) + CO(g)$

2 $N_2(g) + 3H_2(g) \rightleftharpoons 2NH_3(g) \quad \Delta H = -92\,kJ\,mol^{-1}$

   a What would be the effect on the equilibrium position of heating the reaction above (move right, move left, no change)?

   b What would be the effect on the equilibrium of adding an iron catalyst (move right, move left, no change)?

Ammonia is an important chemical in industry. World production is over 140 million tonnes each year. Around 80% is used to make fertilisers like ammonium nitrate, ammonium sulphate and urea. The rest is used to make synthetic fibres (including Nylon), dyes, explosives and plastics like polyurethane.

15.3.1 Making ammonia

Nitrogen and hydrogen react together by a reversible reaction, which at equilibrium, forms a mixture of nitrogen, hydrogen and ammonia:

$$N_2(g) + 3H_2(g) \rightleftharpoons 2NH_3(g) \qquad \Delta H^{\ominus} = -92 \text{ kJ mol}^{-1}$$

The percentage of ammonia obtained *at equilibrium* depends on temperature and pressure as shown in Figure 15.3. The graph shows that high pressure and low temperature would give close to 100% conversion, while low pressure and high temperature would give almost no ammonia.

Le Châtelier's principle

This would be predicted by Le Châtelier's principle because:

- The reaction is exothermic from left to right. So, cooling the mixture will drive the equilibrium to the right (in the direction where heat is given out). There will be a greater percentage of ammonia in the equilibrium mixture.
- There are four molecules of gas on the left and two on the right. So, increasing the pressure will drive the equilibrium to the right (in the direction where the pressure is lower). There will be a greater percentage of ammonia in the reaction mixture.

15.3.2 The Haber process

In industry, ammonia is made by the Haber process, in which the reaction above is the key step.

The raw materials

The raw materials are air (which provides the nitrogen), water and natural gas (methane, CH$_4$). These provide the hydrogen by the following reaction:

$$CH_4(g) + H_2O(g) \rightarrow CO(g) + 3H_2(g)$$

The nitrogen and hydrogen are fed into a converter in the ratio of 1 : 3 and passed over an iron catalyst.

Most plants run at a pressure of around 20 000 kPa (about 200 times atmospheric pressure) and a temperature of about 670 K. This is a lower pressure and a higher temperature than would give the maximum conversion. These compromise conditions are used because:

- a high-pressure plant is expensive, both to build and to maintain;
- a lower temperature would slow down the *rate* of reaction;
- at lower temperatures the catalyst lasts longer.

Nitrogen and hydrogen flow continuously over the catalyst so the gases do not spend long enough in contact with the catalyst to reach equilibrium – there is about 15% conversion to ammonia. The ammonia is cooled so that it becomes liquid and is piped off. Any nitrogen and hydrogen that is not converted into ammonia is fed back into the reactor.

The catalyst is iron in pea-sized lumps (to increase the surface area). It lasts about five years before it becomes 'poisoned' by impurities in the gas stream and has to be replaced. Figure 15.4 shows a flow chart of the Haber process.

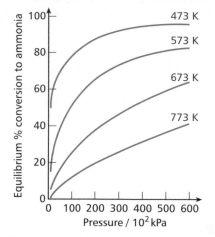

Fig 15.3 *Equilibrium % conversion of nitrogen and hydrogen to ammonia under different conditions*

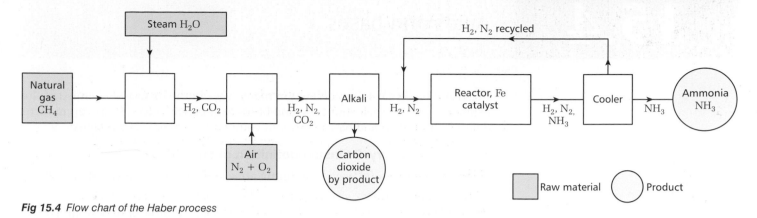

Fig 15.4 *Flow chart of the Haber process*

15.3.3 Uses of ammonia

Making nitric acid, HNO$_3$

Most of the ammonia that is made is converted into nitric acid (often on the same site) as the next step in making other products.

Nitric acid is made from ammonia in two stages:

1. The ammonia is first reacted with oxygen from the air to form nitrogen monoxide, NO.

   Ammonia and oxygen are passed over a hot platinum catalyst:

   $$4NH_3(g) + 5O_2(g) \xrightarrow{\text{platinum catalyst}} 4NO(g) + 6H_2O(l)$$

   About 95% of the ammonia is converted to nitrogen monoxide.

2. The gases are cooled and mixed with more air. Then, under pressure, they are passed up a tower that has water trickling down it. Nitric acid is produced by the reaction between nitrogen monoxide, oxygen and water:

   $$4NO(g) + 3O_2(g) + 2H_2O(l) \rightarrow 4HNO_3(aq)$$

   The overall reaction is:

   $$NH_3(g) + 2O_2(g) \rightarrow HNO_3(aq) + H_2O(l)$$

Nitric acid is used to make fertilisers, explosives and one of the monomers from which Nylon (a polyamide) is made.

Making fertilisers

Ammonium salts are used as fertilisers because they contain nitrogen in a form that plants can use. The fertiliser Nitram is ammonium nitrate and is made from a solution of ammonia in water and nitric acid in an acid–base reaction:

$$NH_3(aq) + HNO_3(aq) \rightarrow NH_4NO_3(aq)$$
$$\text{ammonium nitrate}$$

Similar neutralisation reactions with phosphoric and sulphuric acids produce the fertilisers ammonium phosphate and ammonium sulphate:

$$2NH_3(aq) + H_2SO_4(aq) \rightarrow (NH_4)_2SO_4(aq)$$
$$\text{ammonium sulphate}$$

QUICK QUESTIONS

1 What are the three raw materials used in the Haber process?

2 Use the graph in Figure 15.3 to find the equilibrium percentage conversion to ammonia at 40 000 kPa and 673 K.

3 The platinum catalyst for the oxidation of ammonia is used in the form of a fine gauze. Suggest why it is used in this form.

4 List three uses of **a** ammonia, **b** nitric acid.

Acids and bases

Acids and bases have been defined in many ways in the history of chemistry – for example, acids by their sour taste and bases by their slimy feel. However, modern definitions of acids and bases are about competition for protons, H^+ ions.

15.4.1 The Lowry–Brönsted definition of an acid

One of the most useful ways of defining an acid is called the Lowry–Brönsted definition.

This defines an acid as a substance that can donate a proton (a H^+ ion) and a base as a substance that can accept a proton. Acids and bases can only react in pairs – one acid and one base.

Example 1

Ammonia acts as a base in water by accepting a proton from a molecule of water, using its lone pair to form the bond. In this case the water is acting as an acid.

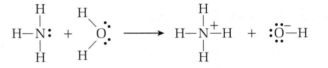

Example 2

Hydrogen chloride is a covalently bonded gas, but when it dissolves in water, the water acts as a base and hydrogen chloride donates a proton to a molecule of water, acting as an acid.

$$HCl + H_2O \rightarrow H_3O^+ + Cl^-$$

A proton has no electrons at all, so to form a covalent bond with another species, that species must have a lone pair of electrons. This is the case with water:

The H_3O^+ ion

When a hydrogen atom loses its one electron all that remains is the proton (the hydrogen nucleus, H^+). This is about 10^{-15} m in diameter, compared to 10^{-10} m or more for any other chemical entity. So, it is over 10 000 times smaller than anything else. This gives it unusual properties compared with other positive ions. It has a very strong electric field and because of this it is never found on its own. In aqueous solutions it is always bonded to at least one water molecule to form the ion H_3O^+. But, for simplicity, we represent a proton in an aqueous solution by $H^+(aq)$ rather than $H_3O^+(aq)$.

Here are some of the typical reactions of acids.

15.4.2 The reactions of acids

All acids react to form salts and the reactions may be written as balanced symbol or ionic equations, see also Section 2.5.2.

- Reactive metal + acid → salt + hydrogen

    For example:

$$\underset{\text{magnesium}}{Mg(s)} + \underset{\text{hydrochloric acid}}{2HCl(aq)} \rightarrow \underset{\text{magnesium chloride}}{MgCl_2(aq)} + \underset{\text{water}}{H_2(l)}$$

    Ionic equation (leaving out the spectator ions – the ones that appear on both sides of the equation):

$$Mg(s) + 2H^+(aq) \rightarrow Mg^{2+}(aq) + H_2(g)$$

- Metal oxide or metal hydroxide + acid → salt + water

  For example:

  $$MgO(s) \ + \ 2HCl(aq) \ \rightarrow \ MgCl_2(aq) \ + \ H_2O(l)$$

  magnesium oxide   hydrochloric acid   magnesium chloride   water

  Ionic equation:

  $$(Mg^{2+} + O^{2-})(s) + 2H^+(aq) \rightarrow Mg^{2+}(aq) + H_2O(l)$$

- Metal hydroxide + acid → salt + water

  For example:

  $$NaOH(aq) \ + \ HCl(aq) \ \rightarrow \ NaCl(aq) \ + \ H_2O(l)$$

  sodium hydroxide   hydrochloric acid   sodium chloride   water

  Ionic equation:

  $$OH^-(aq) + H^+(aq) \rightarrow H_2O(l)$$

HINT

Bases that are soluble in water, like sodium hydroxide, are called alkalis and produce OH⁻ ions in aqueous solution.

- Metal carbonate + acid → salt + water + carbon dioxide

  For example:

  $$MgCO_3(s) + 2HCl(aq) \rightarrow MgCl_2(aq) + H_2O(l) + CO_2(g)$$

  magnesium carbonate   hydrochloric acid   magnesium chloride   water   carbon dioxide

  Ionic equation:

  $$(Mg^{2+} + CO_3^{2-})(s) + 2H^+(aq) \rightarrow Mg^{2+}(aq) + H_2O(l) + CO_2(g)$$

15.4.3 Strong and weak acids and bases

The acidity of a solution depends on the concentration of $H^+(aq)$. (This is what the pH scale measures).

Strong acids

When they dissolve in water, acids such as hydrochloric and nitric break up completely into ions. This is called complete **dissociation**.

For example:

$$HCl(g) \rightarrow H^+(aq) + Cl^-(aq)$$

$$HNO_3(aq) \rightarrow H^+(aq) + NO_3^-(aq)$$

Acids that completely dissociate into ions in aqueous solutions are called **strong** acids. The word strong refers *only* to how much the acid dissociates and *not in any way* to how concentrated it is.

NOTE

The gas hydrogen chloride, HCl, is a covalent molecule. When it dissolves in water it dissociates completely into H^+ and Cl^- ions. There are no covalently bonded HCl molecules remaining.

Weak acids

Weak acids are not fully dissociated when dissolved in water. Ethanoic acid (the acid in vinegar, also called acetic acid) is a good example. In a 1 mol dm⁻³ solution of ethanoic acid, only about 4 in every thousand ethanoic acid molecules are dissociated into ions (we say the **degree of dissociation** is 4/1000); the rest remain dissolved as covalently bonded molecules. In fact an equilibrium is set up:

$$CH_3CO_2 H(aq) \rightleftharpoons H^+(aq) + CH_3CO_2^-(aq)$$

	ethanoic acid	hydrogen ions	ethanoate ions
before dissociation	1000	0	0
at equilibrium	996	4	4

Acids like this are called **weak acids** – weak refers *only* to the degree of dissociation.

We can have a very dilute solution of a strong acid, or a very concentrated solution of a weak acid. Strength and concentration are independent.

Bases

In aqueous solutions, bases dissociate to produce the OH^- ion (which can react with a H^+ ion by forming a bond through the electrons of one of its lone pairs).

Bases can also be classified as weak or strong. Strong bases are completely dissociated into ions in aqueous solutions, while weak bases are only partially dissociated. For example sodium hydroxide, NaOH, is a strong base:

$$NaOH(aq) \rightarrow Na^+(aq) + OH^-(aq)$$

A solution of ammonia in water $(NH_3)aq$, also called ammonium hydroxide, NH_4OH, is a weak base:

$$NH_3(aq) + H_2O(l) \rightleftharpoons NH_4^+(aq) + OH^-(aq)$$

or $\quad NH_4OH(aq) \rightleftharpoons NH_4^+(aq) + OH^-(aq)$

QUICK QUESTIONS

1 Complete the following equations of acids:

  a $Ca(s) + 2HCl(aq) \rightarrow ? + H_2(g)$
  b $Na_2O(s) + H_2SO_4(aq) \rightarrow Na_2SO_4(aq) + ?$
  c $K_2O(s) + ? \rightarrow 2KCl + H_2O(l)$
  d $Mg(OH)_2(aq) + 2HCl \rightarrow ? + 2H_2O(l)$

2 Draw a dot-and-cross diagram of the H_3O^+ ion.

1 Ammonia, NH_3, is made industrially from its elements by the Haber process. This is an exothermic equilibrium reaction.

$$N_2(g) + 3H_2(g) \rightleftharpoons 2NH_3(g) \quad \Delta H = -92\,\text{kJ mol}^{-1}$$

a State **three** reaction conditions that are used in the Haber process. [3]

b Describe and explain the effect of increasing the pressure on the **rate** of this reaction. [2]

c Describe and explain how the **equilibrium position** of this reaction is affected by

(i) increasing the temperature [2]
(ii) increasing the pressure. [2]

d Why is the temperature used described as a compromise? [2]

e Some of the ammonia from the Haber process reacts with carbon dioxide to make the fertiliser urea.

$$\_\_NH_3(g) + \_\_CO_2(g) \rightarrow \_\_NH_2CONH_2(s) + \_\_H_2O(l)$$
urea

(i) Balance the above equation. [1]
(ii) Calculate the maximum mass of urea that could be obtained from 1.00 kg of ammonia. [2]

[Total: 14]

OCR, 24 Jan 2001

2 a Both methane and octane undergo incomplete combustion in a car engine. As a result of this, unburned hydrocarbons and carbon monoxide, CO, occur in the exhaust gases. Nitrogen monoxide, NO, is also formed inside the engine. All three pollutants can be removed by fitting a catalytic converter to the exhaust system.

(i) State **one** environmental consequence of **each** of the following emissions.
unburned hydrocarbons, CO, NO. [3]
(ii) How is the NO formed in a car engine? [1]
(iii) NO and CO react together on the surface of the catalyst. Write an equation for this reaction. [1]
(iv) What is the catalyst made of? [1]
(v) The catalyst is a heterogeneous catalyst. What is the meaning of *heterogeneous*? [1]
(vi) The catalytic converter is positioned as close to the engine as possible, so that it heats up quickly. Why does the converter work best when it is hot? [1]

[Total: 8]

OCR, 29 May 2002

3 Reactions can be speeded up either by increasing the concentration of reagents or by increasing the temperature.

a Explain why an increase in concentration increases the rate of a reaction. [2]

b The diagram in the figure shows the energy distribution of reactant molecules at a temperature T_1. E_a represents the activation energy of the reaction.

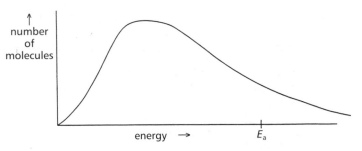

(i) Draw a second curve on the figure to represent the energy distribution of the same number of molecules at a higher temperature. Label your curve T_2. [2]
(ii) Use your curve to explain how an increase in temperature can cause an increase in the rate of a reaction. [2]

[Total: 6]

OCR, 17 Jan 2003

4 Methanol is an important industrial organic chemical. It is used as a solvent and a feedstock for the manufacture of several other comounds such as ethanoic acid. A two-stage process to make methanol from natural gas, methane, is summarised in the following equations.

reaction 1

Ni at 700°C

$$CH_4(g) + H_2O(g) \rightleftharpoons CO(g) + 3H_2(g) \quad \Delta H = +207\,\text{kJ mol}^{-1}$$

reaction 2

Cr at 300°C and 30 MPa

$$CO(g) + 2H_2(g) \rightleftharpoons CH_3OH(g) \qquad \Delta H = -129\,\text{kJ mol}^{-1}$$

a Describe and explain the effect of increasing the pressure on the **rate** of reaction **1**. [2]

b Describe and explain how the **equilibrium position** of reaction **1** is affected by

(i) increasing the temperature [2]
(ii) increasing the pressure. [2]

c Reaction **2** uses the products from reaction **1**. Suggest a reason why these two reactions cannot proceed one after the other in the same reaction vessel. [1]

[Total: 7]

OCR, 29 May 2002

5 Benzene, C_6H_6, can be manufactured by passing the gaseous hydrocarbon ethyne, C_2H_2, over finely divided nickel.

The equation is shown below.

$$3C_2H_2(g) \xrightarrow{\text{nickel}} C_6H_6(l) \qquad \textbf{reaction 1}$$

a Write a chemical equation, including state symbols, to represent the standard enthalpy change of combustion of benzene, $C_6H_6(l)$. [2]

b Use the following standard enthalpy changes of combustion to calculate the standard enthalpy change for reaction **1**.

Compound	$\Delta H_c^\ominus$/kJ mol^{-1}
C_2H_2	−1301
C_6H_6	−3267

[3]

c Suggest, with explanations, how the **rate** of reaction **1** might be affected by

  (i) an increase in temperature [3]
  (ii) an increase in pressure. [2]

d Describe and explain the purpose of the nickel in reaction **1**. [2]

[Total: 12]

OCR, 4 Jun 2001

6 The chlorination of methane in the gas phase involves the following two steps:

$$CH_4 + Cl \rightarrow CH_3 + HCl \qquad \textbf{reaction 1}$$
$$CH_3 + Cl_2 \rightarrow CH_3Cl + Cl \qquad \textbf{reaction 2}$$

The table lists some relevant average bond enthalpies.

Bond	Bond enthalpy/kJ mol^{-1}
C—H	+413
C—Cl	+327
H—Cl	+432
Cl—Cl	+243

a (i) Use these bond enthalpies to calculate the enthalpy changes of reactions **1** and **2**. [2]
  (ii) Suggest which might be the faster of these two reactions. Give a reason for your answer. [1]

b An alternative reaction route has been suggested for this reaction, which involves the following two steps:

$$CH_4 + Cl \rightarrow CH_3Cl + H \qquad \textbf{reaction 3}$$
$$H + Cl_2 \rightarrow HCl + Cl \qquad \textbf{reaction 4}$$

Use the table to suggest why this reaction route is unlikely to take place. [2]

[Total: 5]

OCR, 29 May 2002

7 The enthalpy change for the reaction between hydrochloric acid, HCl(aq), and sodium hydroxide, NaOH(aq), can be determined in the following way.

- 50.0 cm^3 of 2.00 mol dm^{-3} HCl(aq) is placed in a plastic cup, and its temperature recorded.
- 50.0 cm^3 of 2.00 mol dm^{-3} NaOH(aq) is placed in another plastic cup, and its temperature recorded.
- The two solutions are mixed with stirring, and the final temperature recorded.

The following results were obtained from one such experiment:

initial temperature of both HCl(aq) and NaOH(aq) = 18.0°C
final temperature after mixing = 31.9°C

(Take the specific heat capacity of all solutions to be 4.18 J g^{-1} K^{-1}, and the densities of all solutions to be 1.00 g cm^{-1}.)

a Calculate the heat evolved in the above experiment. Include units in your answer. [3]

b Calculate how many moles of HCl were used [1]

c Hence calculate the enthalpy change, in kJ, for the reaction of 1 mol of HCl with 1 mol of NaOH [1]

[Total: 5]

OCR, 29 May 2002

8 It has been sugested that using methane, CH_4, as a fuel for cars rather than petrol would decrease the amount of carbon dioxide produced per mile. This question looks at how much this reduction in CO_2 emission might be. You may assume that petrol is pure octane, C_8H_{18}.

The combustion of methane can be represented by the following equation:

$$CH_4 + 2O_2 \rightarrow CO_2 + 2H_2O \qquad \Delta H_c^\ominus = -890 \text{ kJ mol}^{-1}$$

a Balance the following equation for the combustion of octane:

$$C_8H_{18} + \ldots\ldots\, O_2 \rightarrow \ldots\ldots\, CO_2 + \ldots\ldots\, H_2O \qquad [1]$$

b The enthalpy change of combustion, $\Delta H_c^\ominus$, of octane is -5472 kJ per mole of octane.

Use your balanced equation and the given $\Delta H_c^\ominus$ data to calculate for each fuel:

(i) the enthalpy change **per mole of CO_2 produced**, and hence

(ii) the number of moles of CO_2 produced per kJ of heat energy given out.

Write your answers in the table below.

Fuel	$\Delta H_c^\ominus$ per mole of alkane burned/kJ	$\Delta H_c^\ominus$ per mole of CO_2 produced/kJ	Moles of CO_2 produced per kJ of heat given out
methane	-890		
octane	-5472		

[4]

(ii) Hence calculate a value for the ratio:

$$\frac{\text{moles of } CO_2 \text{ produced per kJ from methane}}{\text{moles of } CO_2 \text{ produced per kJ from octane}}$$

[1]

[Total: 6]

OCR, 29 May 2002

9 *Arcton 133* is a CFC with the molecular formula $C_2H_2ClF_3$.

a When *Arcton 133* is released into the atmosphere, its molecules can absorb energy. The C—Cl bond breaks forming free radicals.

$$C_2H_2ClF_3 \rightarrow C_2H_2F_3\cdot + Cl\cdot$$

(i) What source of energy is required for this reaction to take place? [1]

(ii) Chlorine free radicals catalyse the breakdown of ozone, O_3. Write **two** equations to show how this happens. [2]

(iii) Write an equation for the overall reaction in **a**(ii). [1]

(iv) What **type** of catalysis is shown here? Explain your answer. [2]

b In some applications, CFCs are being replaced by hydrocarbons such as alkanes.

(i) What is the M_r of *Arcton 133*, $C_2H_2ClF_3$? [1]

(ii) The formula of some alkanes are shown below:

C_5H_{12} C_6H_{14} C_7H_{16} C_8H_{18} C_9H_{20}

Draw a circle around the molecular formula of the alkane whose M_r is most similar to that of *Arcton 133*. [1]

(iii) Suggest why hydrocarbons are replacing CFCs. [1]

(iv) Apart from cost, suggest **one** possible **disadvantage** of using a hydrocarbon instead of a CFC. [1]

[Total: 10]

OCR, 24 Jan 2001

10 When the indicator bromothymol blue (which can be repesented by the formula HIn) dissolves in water the following dynamic equilibrium is set up:

$$HIn(aq) \rightleftharpoons In^-(aq) + H^+(aq)$$
yellow   blue

The indicator appears green because it contains both the yellow HIn and the blue In^- forms.

a State **two** features of a *dynamic equilibrium*. [2]

b State le Chatelier's principle. [2]

c Hydrochloric acid is added to the indicator solution above until no further colour change takes place.

Using le Chatelier's principle, suggest and explain what colour change you might see. [2]

d Aqueous sodium hydroxide is gradually added to the resulting solution in **c** until no further colour changes take place.

Suggest all the colour changes you might see.

Explain your answer. [4]

[Total: 10]

OCR, 4 Jun 2001

11 Ethene is an important industrial chemical, used to make plastics, solvents and antifreeze. It is usually made by cracking larger alkanes. The equation for a cracking reaction is shown below:

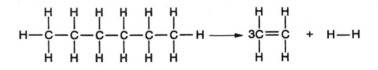

a (i) Define the term *average bond enthalpy*

(ii) Use the average bond enthalpies in the table to calculate the standard enthalpy change, $\Delta H_r^\ominus$, for the reaction. [2]

Bond	Average bond enthalpy/kJ mol^{-1}
H—H	436
C—H	410
C—C	350
C=C	610

[3]

b Complete the enthalpy profile diagram for the reaction.

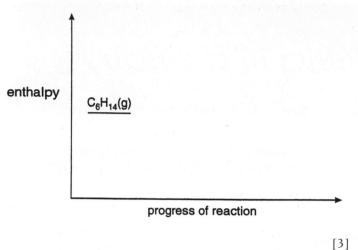

[3]

[Total: 8]

OCR, 17 Jan 2003

In the following question, 1 mark is available for the quality of written communication.

12 Describe, with the aid of a diagram, how the Boltzmann distribution can help to explain the effect of temperature rises and the presence of catalysts on the rates of chemical reactions.

[Total: 7]

OCR, 24 Jan 2001

Mathematics

16

Mathematics in chemistry

NOTE

In this section, work through the quick questions as you read through the text. The answers follow the questions.

Examiners expect you to use the right units in your written work and to quote numbers to an appropriate degree of precision. Both these skills are well worth mastering.

16.1 Units

Ways of representing units

In everyday life we describe the speed of a car in miles per hour. The units 'miles per hour' could be written miles/hour or miles hour^{-1} where $^{-1}$ is just a way of expressing 'per' something. In science we nearly always use the metric system of units and speed has the units metres per second, written m s^{-1}. In each (and every) case you can think of 'per' or '/' or '$^{-}$' as having the meaning 'divided by'.

Units can be surprisingly useful

A mile is a unit of distance and an hour is a unit of time, so the unit 'miles *per* hour' gives you a way or remembering that speed is distance divided by time.

In the same way if you know that the units for density are 'grams *per* cubic centimetre', or g cm^{-3}, where cm^{-3} means 'per cubic centimetre', you can remember that density is mass divided by volume.

16.2 Using numbers in chemistry

Standard form

This is a way of writing very large and very small numbers in a consistent way. It makes comparison and calculations easier.

The number is written as a number multiplied by ten raised to a power. It is usual to put the decimal point to the right of the first digit of the number.

For example, 22 000.0 is written 2.2×10^4. 0.000 002 2 is written 2.2×10^{-6}.

You can work out the power to which ten must be raised by counting the number of places you must move the decimal point:

$$0.00051 \ = \ 5.1 \times 10^{-4}$$

$$51000.0 \ = \ 5.1 \times 10^{4}$$

Moving the decimal point to the right gives a negative index and moving it to the left gives a positive index.

Prefixes

Often in calculations in chemistry, either very small or very large numbers are used. We often use prefixes as a shorthand way of expressing them. The most common prefixes, which multiply the number by a factor of 10^n are:

Prefix	nano	micro	milli	centi	deci	kilo	mega
Factor	10^{-9}	10^{-6}	10^{-3}	10^{-2}	10^{-1}	10^3	10^6
Symbol	n	μ	m	c	d	k	M

If you have a very small or a very large number (and have to handle several zeros), the easiest way is first to convert the number to standard form, see *Standard form* above.

For example convert **a** 2 cm, **b** 100 000 000 mm to metres (m).

a $2 \, \text{cm} = 2 \times 10^{-2} \, \text{m} = 0.02 \, \text{m}$

b $100\,000\,000 \, \text{mm} = \underbrace{1 \times 10^8 \, \text{mm}}_{\text{standard form}} = 1 \times 10^8 \times \underbrace{10^{-3} \, \text{m}}_{\substack{\text{multiply by} \\ \text{conversion factor}}} = 1 \times 10^5 \, \text{m}$

QUICK QUESTION

Convert to metres

a 2 000 000 nm,

b 1 500 000 μm.

Answers

a 2×10^{-3} m,

b 1.5 m.

If you want to convert a number that is expressed in the base units to one with a prefix then divide it by the conversion factor. For example, represent 0.00001 m in **a** nanometres, **b** kilometres.

a $1 \, \text{nm} = 10^{-9} \, \text{m}$ so the conversion factor is 10^{-9}

$$0.00001 \, \text{m} = \underbrace{1.0 \times 10^{-5} \, \text{m}}_{\text{standard form}} = \frac{1.0 \times 10^{-5}}{\underbrace{10^{-9}}_{\substack{\text{divide by} \\ \text{conversion factor}}}} \, \text{nm}$$

So, $0.00001 \, \text{m} = 1.0 \times 10^4 \, \text{nm}$.

Dividing by 10^{-9} is the same as multiplying by 10^9. (*Dividing* by a number expressed as 10 raised to a *negative* power, it is the same as *multiplying* by the number raised to the *positive* power.)

b $1 \, \text{km} = 1000 \, \text{m} = 10^3 \, \text{m}$ so the conversion factor is 10^3

$$0.00001 \, \text{m} = 1.0 \times 10^{-5} \, \text{m} = \frac{1.0 \times 10^{-5}}{10^3} \, \text{km}$$

Dividing by 10^3 is the same as multiplying by 10^{-3}.

So $0.00001 \, \text{m} = 1.0 \times 10^{-8} \, \text{km}$.

QUICK QUESTION

Represent:

a 1000 m in micrometres (μm)

b 0.001 m² in square millimetres (mm²)

Answers

a 1×10^9 μm

b 1.0×10^3 mm² Remember that squared units are divided twice

i.e. $\dfrac{1.0 \times 10^{-3}}{10^{-3} \times 10^{-3}}$

A handy hint for non-mathematicians

We have found that non-mathematicians sometimes lose confidence when using small numbers, such as 0.0002. If you are not sure whether to multiply or divide then use numbers that you are happy with *because the rule will be the same*.

Here is an example:

How many moles of water in 0.0001 g? A mole of water has a mass of 18 g.

Do you divide 18 by 0.0001 or 0.0001 by 18?

If you have any doubts about how to do this then in your head change 0.0001 g to a different number – say 100 g.

How many moles of water in 100 g? A mole of water has a mass of 18 g.

Now you can see that you must divide 100 by 18. You now know that in just the same way, you must divide 0.0001 by 18.

The answer is $\dfrac{0.0001}{18} = 5.6 \times 10^{-6}$

This idea works in any situation when you are handling small numbers.

16.3 Units to learn

It is a good idea to learn the units of some basic quantities by heart.

Volume: dm^3 (1 dm^3 is 1 litre, L which is 1000 cm^3)
Pressure: Pascals, Pa = N m^{-2}
Concentration: mol dm^{-3}, always convert cm^3 to dm^{-3}
Enthalpy: kJ mol^{-1}, occasionally J mol^{-1}

But remember there are no units for relative molecular mass, relative atomic mass or pH. However, we sometimes talk about the 'molar mass', i.e. the mass of one mole of substance. This *does* have units – g mol^{-1} or kg mol^{-1}.

Don't confuse the prefix k meaning kilo- (which uses a lower case letter k) with the symbol K for kelvin (which, like all units that are derived from surnames, uses an upper case lettter).

16.4 Multiplying and dividing units

When you are doing calculations, units cancel and multiply just like numbers and sometimes this can be a guide to whether you have used the right method.

For example: the density of a liquid is 0.8 g cm^{-3}. What is the volume of a mass of 1.6 g of it?

$$density = \frac{mass}{volume}$$

so
$$volume = \frac{mass}{density}$$

Putting in the values and the units:

$$volume = \frac{1.6\,g}{0.8\,g\,cm^{-3}}$$

$$volume = 2.0\,cm^3$$

If you had started with the wrong equation, such as $volume = \dfrac{density}{mass}$ or

volume = mass $\times$ density, you would not have obtained the correct units for volume.

QUICK QUESTION

What volume of a solution of concentration 0.2 mol dm^{-3} contains 0.5 mol of solute?

Answer
2500 cm^3

16.5 Significant figures

Many of the numbers we use in chemistry are measurements – the volume of a liquid, the mass of a solid, the temperature of a reaction vessel, for example – and no measurement can be exact. When we make a measurement, we can indicate how precise it is by the way we write it. For example, a length of 5.0 cm means that we have used a measuring device capable of reading to 0.1 cm, a value of 5.00 cm means that we have measured to the nearest 0.01 cm and so on. So the numbers 5, 5.0 and 5.00 are *different*, we say they have different numbers of **significant figures**.

What exactly is a significant figure?

In a number that has been found or worked out from measurements, the significant figures are all the digits known for certain, *plus the first uncertain one* (which may be a zero). The last figure is the uncertain one and is at the limit of the accuracy of the apparatus used for measuring it.

For example, if we say a substance has a mass of 4.56 grams it means that we are certain about the 4 and the 5 but not the 6 as we are approaching the limit of accuracy of our measuring device – you will have seen the last figure on a top pan balance fluctuate. 4.56 has three significant figures.

When a number contains zeros, the rules for working out the number of significant figures are given below

- Zeros between numbers are significant.

- Zeros to the left of the first non-zero number are not significant (even when there is a decimal point in the number).

- When a number with a decimal point ends in zeros to the right of the decimal point these zeros are significant.

- When a number with no decimal point ends in several zeros, these zeros may or may not be significant. The number of significant figures (sf) should then be stated. For example: 20 000 (to 3 sf) means that the number has been measured to the nearest 100. 20 000 (to 4 sf) means that the number has been measured to the nearest 10.

The following examples of the number of significant figures should help you work out the number of significant figures in your data.

a 11.23

Answer 4 – all non-zero digits are significant.

b 1100

Answer 2 – but we cannot really tell. The number has no decimal point so the zeros may or may not be significant. With numbers with zeros at the end it is best to state the number of significant figures.

c 1100.0

Answer 5 – the decimal point implies a different accuracy of measurement.

d 1.045

Answer 4 – zeros between digits are significant.

e 0.025

Answer 2 – zeros to the left of the decimal point only fix the position of the decimal point. They are not significant.

Most significant figure — First uncertain figure

32.34

Fig 16.1 *A number with 4 significant figures*

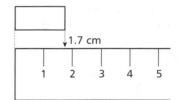
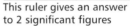

↓1.7 cm

| 1 | 2 | 3 | 4 | 5 |

This ruler gives an answer to 2 significant figures

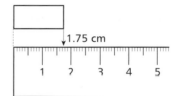

↓1.75 cm

1   2   3   4   5

This ruler gives an answer to 3 significant figures

Fig 16.2 *Rulers with different precisions*

Using significant figures in your answers

When completing a calculation, it is important that you do not just copy down the display of your calculator as this may have far more significant figures than the data in the question justifies. Your answer cannot be more certain than the least certain of the information you used. So your answer should contain the same number of significant figures as the measurement that has the *smallest* number of them.

For example: 81.0 g (3 significant figures) of iron has a volume of 10.16 cm^3 (4 significant figures). What is its density?

$$\text{Density} = \frac{\text{mass}}{\text{volume}} = \frac{81.0}{10.16} = 7.972\,440\,94 \text{ g cm}^{-3} \text{ to 9 significant figures.}$$

Since our least certain measurement was to three significant figures, our answer should not be given beyond this and we should give the density to three significant figures:

$$= 7.97 \text{ g cm}^{-3}$$

If our answer had been 7.976 440 94, we would have rounded it up to 7.98 as the fourth significant figure is five or greater.

The other point to be careful about is *when* to round up. This is best left to the very end of the calculation. Do not round up as you go along because it could make a difference to your final answer.

Decimal places and significant figures

The apparatus we use usually reads to a given number of decimal places (or hundredths or thousandths of a gram). The top pan balance in most schools, for example, weighs to a hundredth of a gram, 0.01 g, which is to two decimal places.

The number of significant figures of a measurement obtained by using the apparatus depends on the mass we are finding. A mass of 10.38 g has four significant figures, but a mass of 0.08 g has only one significant figure.

Glossary

Activation energy. The minimum energy that a particle needs in order to react; the energy (enthalpy) difference between the reactants and the transition state.

Aldehyde. An organic compound with the general formula RCHO in which there is a C=O double bond.

Allotropes. Pure elements which can exist in different physical forms in which their atoms are arranged differently. For example diamond, graphite and buckminsterfullerene are allotropes of carbon.

Anions. Negatively charged ions.

Atomic number (proton number). The number of protons in the nucleus of an atom. Also the order of an element in the Periodic Table.

Average bond enthalpy. The amount of enthalpy (energy) that has to be put in to break a specified chemical bond. It is an average value for the specified bond in a number of different compounds.

Biodegradeable. A substance is biodegradable if it breaks down naturally in the environment under the action of microorganisms, enzymes etc.

Calorimeter. An instrument for measuring the heat changes that accompany chemical reactions.

Carbanion. An organic ion in which one of the carbon atoms has a negative charge.

Carbocation. An organic ion in which one of the carbon atoms has a positive charge.

Carboxylic acids. Organic compounds with the general formula RCOOH in which there is a C=O double bond and an —OH group on the same carbon atom.

Catalytic cracking. The breaking, with the aid of a catalyst, of long-chain alkane molecules (obtained from crude oil) into shorter chain hydrocarbons, some of which are alkenes.

Cations. Positively charged ions.

Chain reaction. A reaction with several steps involving free radicals.

Complex ions. Ions with more than one atom covalently bonded together, for example SO_4^{2-}, CO_3^{2-}.

Coordinate bonding. Covalent bonding in which both the electrons in the bond come from one of the atoms in the bond (also called dative covalent bonding).

Cracking. The breaking of long-chain alkane molecules (obtained from crude oil) into shorter chain hydrocarbons, some of which are alkenes.

Covalent bonding. A type of bonding between non-metal atoms that is the result of electrons being shared between the atoms.

Dative covalent bonding. Covalent bonding in which both the electrons in the bond come from one of the atoms in the bond (also called coordinate bonding).

Disproportionation. Describes a redox reaction in which the oxidation number of some atoms of a particular element increases and that of other atoms of the same element decreases.

Electron. A negatively charged sub-atomic particle that is found at some distance from the nucleus of an atom.

Electron pair repulsion theory. A theory which explains the shapes of simple molecules by assuming that groups of electrons around a central atom repel each other and thus take up positions as far away as possible from each other in space.

Electronegativity. The ability of an atom to attract the electrons in covalent bonds towards itself.

Electrophile. A reagent that attacks electron-rich areas in an organic molecule (such as a carbon–carbon double bond).

Electrostatic forces. The forces of attraction and repulsion between electrically charged particles.

Elimination reaction. A reaction in which a small molecule such as water or hydrogen chloride is ejected from the reactants.

Empirical formula. The simplest whole number ratio in which the atoms in a compound combine together.

Endothermic. Describes a reaction in which heat is taken in as the reactants change to products – the temperature thus drops.

Energy density. Describes the amount of energy stored per kilogram by a fuel. This energy can be released by burning the fuel.

Enthalpy diagrams. Diagrams in which the enthalpies (energies) of the reactants and products of a chemical reaction are plotted on a vertical scale to show their relative levels.

Entity. The simplest formula unit of a compound.

Exothermic. Describes a reaction in which heat is given out as the reactants change to products – the temperature thus rises.

Free radical. A reagent that has an unpaired electron.

General formula. The formula of a family of organic compounds expressed by using n to represent the number of carbon atoms. For example the general formula of the alcohol family is $C_nH_{(2n+1)}OH$.

Giant molecular structure. An arrangement of atoms covalently bonded together in such a way that the structure extends indefinitely in three dimensions.

Giant structure. An arrangement of atoms or ions bonded together in such a way that the structure extends indefinitely in three dimensions.

Group. A vertical column of elements in the Periodic Table. The elements have similar properties because they have the same outer electron arrangement.

Heterolysis. Describes the breaking of a covalent bond such that both the electrons in the bond go to one of the atoms and none to the other. The process results in the formation of a positive ion and a negative ion.

Homologous series. A set of organic compounds with the same functional group. The compounds differ in the length of their hydrocarbon chains.

Homolysis. Describes the breaking of a covalent bond such that one of the electrons in the bond goes to one of the atoms and one to the other. The process results in the formation of a pair of free radicals.

Initiation. The first step of a chain reactions in which a pair of free radicals is formed by bond homolysis.

Intermolecular forces. Forces that act between molecules and atoms that are not covalently bonded together (van der Waals forces, dipole–dipole forces and hydrogen bonding).

Ionic bonding. A type of bonding between metals and non-metals that is the result of the attraction between the positive metal ions and negative non-metal ions, formed from the transfer of electrons.

Ionisation energy. The energy required to remove a mole of electrons from a mole of isolated gaseous atoms.

Ions. Atoms or molecules that have an overall electrical charge.

Isotopes. Atoms of the same element (i.e. having the same number of protons) but having different numbers of neutrons.

Ketone. An organic compound with the general formula R_2CO in which there is a $C=O$ double bond.

Leaving group. In an organic substitution reaction, the leaving group is an atom or group of atoms that is ejected from the starting material, normally taking with it an electron pair and forming a negative ion.

Lone pair. A pair of electrons that is not involved in bonding, in the outer shell of an atom. Also called an unshared pair.

Mass number (or nucleon number). The total number of neutrons and protons (nucleons) in the nucleus of an atom.

Maxwell–Boltzmann distribution. The distribution of energies (and therefore speeds) of the molecules in a gas or liquid.

Metallic bonding. A type of bonding found in metals in which positively charged metal ions are held together by their attraction to their pooled sea of outer electrons.

Molecular formula. A formula that tells us the numbers of atoms of different elements that make up a molecule of a compound.

Molecular orbitals. Volumes of space in which electrons may be found. They spread over two (or more) atoms.

Molecular structure. A compound that consists of small molecules.

Molecule. A small group of atoms held together by covalent bonds.

Monomer. A small molecule that combines with many other monomers to form a polymer.

Neutron. An uncharged sub-atomic particle found in the nuclei of atoms.

Nucleons. Protons and neutrons – the sub-atomic particles found in the nuclei of atoms.

Nucleophile. A reagent that attacks the $C^{\delta+}$ of an organic molecule.

Nucleophilic substitution. An organic reaction in which a molecule with a partially positively charged carbon atom is attacked by a reagent with a negative charge (a nucleophile). It results in the replacement of one of the groups or atoms on the original molecule by the nucleophile.

Nucleus. The tiny, positively charged centre of at atom composed of protons and neutrons.

Orbital. A volume of space in which an electron or pair of electrons may be found.

Oxidation. A reaction in which an atom or group of atoms loses electrons.

Oxidation number. The number of electrons lost or gained by an atom in a compound compared to the uncombined atom. It forms the basis of a way of keeping track of redox (electron transfer) reactions.

Oxidation state. An alternative term for oxidation number.

Oxidising agent. A reagent that oxidises (removes electron from) another species.

Oxidising power. The ability of a reagent to oxidise (remove electron from) another species.

Periodicity. The regular recurrence of the properties of elements when they are arranged in atomic number order as in the Periodic Table.

Period. A horizontal row of elements in the Periodic Table. There are trends in the properties of the elements as we cross a period.

Propagation. One of the steps of a chain reaction in which a free radical converts reactant into product and another free radical is formed which can take part in another propagation step.

Proton. A positively charged sub-atomic particle found in the nuclei of atoms.

Redox. Short for reduction–oxidation, it describes reactions in which electrons are transferred from one species to another.

Reducing agent. A reagent that reduces (adds electron to) another species.

Reduction. A reaction in which an atom or group of atoms gains electrons.

Relative atomic mass, A_r.

$$A_r = \frac{\text{Average mass of an atom (in g)}}{\frac{1}{12}\text{th mass of 1 atom of } {}^{12}C \text{ (in g)}}$$

Relative formula mass, M_r.

$$M_r = \frac{\text{Average mass of an entity (in g)}}{\frac{1}{12}\text{th mass of 1 atom of } {}^{12}C \text{ (in g)}}$$

Relative molecular mass, M_r

$$M_r = \frac{\text{Average mass of a molecule (in g)}}{\frac{1}{12}\text{th mass of 1 atom of } {}^{12}C \text{ (in g)}}$$

Shielded nuclear charge. (Also called effective nuclear charge.) The positive charge from the nucleus that is felt by the outer electrons of an atom – it is the total number of positive charges on the nucleus of an atom minus the total number of inner electrons.

Specific heat capacity, c. The amount of heat needed to raise the temperature of 1 g of substance by 1 K.

Spectator ions. Ions that are unchanged during a chemical reaction, i.e. they take no part in the reaction.

Standard molar enthalpy change of combustion, $\Delta H_c^{\ominus}$. The amount of heat energy given out when 1 mole of a substance is completely burned in oxygen at standard conditions (298 K and 100 kPa).

Standard molar enthalpy change of formation, $\Delta H_f^{\ominus}$. The heat change when 1 mole of substance is formed from its elements at standard conditions (298 K and 100 kPa).

Stoichiometric. Describes the simple whole number ratios in which chemical species react.

Strong nuclear force. The force that holds protons and neutrons together within the nucleus of an atom.

Termination. The stage of a chain reaction in which two free radicals combine together to give a species that is not a free radical.

Thermal decomposition. The breakdown of a compound by heat.

Thermochemical cycle. A sequence of chemical reactions (with their enthalpy changes) that convert a reactant into a product. The total enthalpy change of the sequence of reactions will be the same as that for the conversion of the reactant to the product directly (or by any other route).

Data sheet

Characteristic infra-red absorptions in organic molecules

bond	location	wavenumber
C—O	alcohols, esters	1000–1300 cm^{-1}
C=O	aldehydes, ketones, carboxylic acids, esters	1680–1750 cm^{-1}
O—H	hydrogen bonded in carboxylic acids	2500–3300 cm^{-1} (broad)
N—H	primary amines	3100–3500 cm^{-1}
O—H	hydrogen bonded iin alcohols, phenols	3230–3550 cm^{-1}
O—H	free	3580–3670 cm^{-1}

Chemical shifts for some types of protons in n.m.r. spectra

- Chemical shifts are for hydrogen relative to TMS (tetramethylsilane)
- Chemical shifts are typical values and can vary slightly depending on the solvent, concentration and substituents.

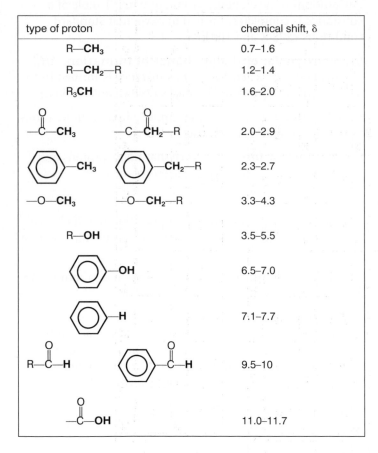

type of proton	chemical shift, δ
R—CH$_3$	0.7–1.6
R—CH$_2$—R	1.2–1.4
R$_3$CH	1.6–2.0
	2.0–2.9
	2.3–2.7
	3.3–4.3
R—OH	3.5–5.5
	6.5–7.0
	7.1–7.7
	9.5–10
	11.0–11.7

The Periodic Table of the Elements

Key

| relative atomic mass |
| atomic symbol |
| name |
| atomic number |

1.0
H
hydrogen
1

Group

Group 1	2											3	4	5	6	7	0
																	4.0 He helium 2
6.9 Li lithium 3	9.0 Be beryllium 4											10.8 B boron 5	12.0 C carbon 6	14.0 N nitrogen 7	16.0 O oxygen 8	19.0 F fluorine 9	20.2 Ne neon 10
23.0 Na sodium 11	24.3 Mg magnesium 12											27.0 Al aluminium 13	28.1 Si silicon 14	31.0 P phosphorus 15	32.1 S sulphur 16	35.5 Cl chlorine 17	39.9 Ar argon 18
39.1 K potassium 19	40.1 Ca calcium 20	45.0 Sc scandium 21	47.9 Ti titanium 22	50.9 V vanadium 23	52.0 Cr chromium 24	54.9 Mn manganese 25	55.8 Fe iron 26	58.9 Co cobalt 27	58.7 Ni nickel 28	63.5 Cu copper 29	65.4 Zn zinc 30	69.7 Ga gallium 31	72.6 Ge germanium 32	74.9 As arsenic 33	79.0 Se selenium 34	79.9 Br bromine 35	83.8 Kr krypton 36
85.5 Rb rubidium 37	87.6 Sr strontium 38	88.9 Y yttrium 39	91.2 Zr zirconium 40	92.9 Nb niobium 41	95.9 Mo molybdenum 42	– Tc technetium 43	101 Ru ruthenium 44	103 Rh rhodium 45	106 Pd palladium 46	108 Ag silver 47	112 Cd cadmium 48	115 In indium 49	119 Sn tin 50	122 Sb antimony 51	128 Te tellurium 52	127 I iodine 53	131 Xe xenon 54
133 Cs caesium 55	137 Ba barium 56	139 La lanthanum 57	178 Hf hafnium 72	181 Ta tantalum 73	184 W tungsten 74	186 Re rhenium 75	190 Os osmium 76	192 Ir iridium 77	195 Pt platinum 78	197 Au gold 79	201 Hg mercury 80	204 Tl thallium 81	207 Pb lead 82	209 Bi bismuth 83	– Po polonium 84	– At astatine 85	– Rn radon 86
– Fr francium 87	– Ra radium 88	– Ac actinium 89	– Rf rutherfordium 104	– Db dubnium 105	– Sg seaborgium 106	– Bh bohrium 107	– Hs hassium 108	– Mt meitnerium 109	– Uun ununnilium 110	– Uuu unununium 111	– Uub ununbium 112		– Uuq ununquadium 114		– Uuh ununhexium 116		– Uuo ununoctium 118

* lanthanides

140 Ce cerium 58	141 Pr praseodymium 59	144 Nd neodymium 60	– Pm promethium 61	150 Sm samarium 62	152 Eu europium 63	157 Gd gadolinium 64	159 Tb terbium 65	163 Dy dysprosium 66	165 Ho holmium 67	167 Er erbium 68	169 Tm thulium 69	173 Yb ytterbium 70	175 Lu lutetium 71

* actinides

– Th thorium 90	– Pa protactinium 91	– U uranium 92	– Np neptunium 93	– Pu plutonium 94	– Am americium 95	– Cm curium 96	– Bk berkelium 97	– Cf californium 98	– Es einsteinium 99	– Fm fermium 100	– Md mendelevium 101	– No nobelium 102	– Lr lawrencium 103

© OCR 2002

(Oxford, Cambridge and RSA Examinations)

Answers to quick questions

Chapter 1

1.1
1 a 4p, 4e, 5n   b 15p, 15e, 16n
   c 7p, 7e, 7n   d 19p, 19e, 20n
2 19p, 18e, 20n   3 7p, 10e, 7n
4 a 20   b 40   c 40
5 The electrons have almost no mass.

1.2
1 20.2   2 $^{14}_{7}X$, $^{15}_{7}Z$ 3 98.1   4 142.1
5 Sulphuric acid is a covalent molecule whereas sodium sulphate exists as ions.

1.3
1 The electron gun removes electrons leaving positive ions.
2 Positive ions are attracted towards negatively charged plates.
3 The ions pass through a slit.
4 A magnetic field at right angles to the beam
5 63.6

1.4
1

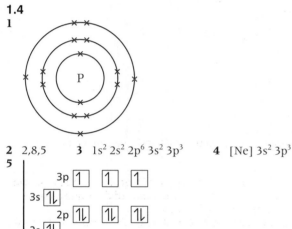

2 2,8,5   3 $1s^2 2s^2 2p^6 3s^2 3p^3$ 4 [Ne] $3s^2 3p^3$
5

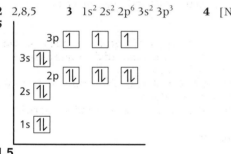

1.5
1 The first ionisation removes an electron from a neutral atom whereas the second ionisation energy is the energy needed to remove an electron from a 1+ ion.

2

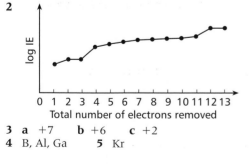

3 a +7   b +6   c +2
4 B, Al, Ga   5 Kr

Chapter 2

2.1
1 a Se   b Be   c Sc
2 a 16.0   b 106.0   c 58.3   d 132.1

3 a 2   b 0.05   c 0.05
4 4 g of oxygen   5 11 g carbon dioxide

2.2
1 a H_2SO_4 sulphuric acid,
   b BeO_2H_2 which is $Be(OH)_2$ beryllium hydroxide,
   c $MgCl_2$ magnesium chloride
2 a 0.16 moles of each   b MgO
3 a CH_2 b CHCl   c CH
4 $C_2H_6O_2$

2.3
1 a 1 mol dm^{-3} b 0.125 mol dm^{-3} c 10 mol dm^{-3}
2 a 0.002   b 0.025   c 0.05
3 0.016 mol dm^{-3}
4 a 0.02   b 0.005   c 1.5

2.4
1 and 2
   a $2Mg + O_2 \rightarrow 2MgO$
          2   1   2
   b $Ca(OH)_2 + 2HCl \rightarrow CaCl_2 + 2H_2O$
          1   2   1   2
   c $Na_2O + 2HNO_3 \rightarrow 2NaNO_3 + H_2O$
          1   2   2   1
3 0.25 mol dm^{-3}
4 a Magnesium,   b yes, it is in excess.

2.5
1 $Cu(s) + 2AgNO_3(aq) \rightarrow Cu(NO_3)_2(aq) + 2Ag(s)$
   $Cu(s) + 2Ag^+(aq) \rightarrow Cu^{2+}(aq) + 2Ag(s)$
2 $2Mg(s) + H_2SO_4(aq) \rightarrow Mg_2SO_4(aq) + H_2(g)$
   $2Mg(s) + 2H^+(aq) \rightarrow 2Mg^{2+}(aq) + H_2(g)$
3 $CaCO_3(s) + 2HCl(aq) \rightarrow CaCl_2(aq) + CO_2(g) + H_2O(l)$
   $CaCO_3(s) + 2H^+(aq) \rightarrow Ca^{2+}(aq) + CO_2(g) + H_2O(l)$
4 $NaOH(aq) + HCl(aq) \rightarrow NaCl(aq) + H_2O(l)$
   $OH^-(aq) + H^+(aq) \rightarrow H_2O(l)$

Chapter 3

3.1
1 b KF and
   c CaO because they are compounds of metal and non-metal.
2 Ionic compounds have giant structures so the bonds extend throughout the compound.
3 They conduct when molten or when dissolved in water.
4 a

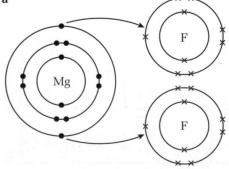

b

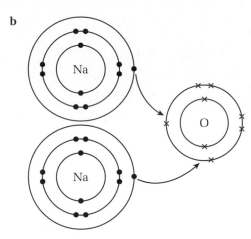

5 a MgF$_2$ **b** Na$_2$O

3.2
1 A pair of electrons shared between two atoms
2 **b** SO$_2$
  d C$_2$H$_4$. They are compounds of non-metals only.
3 There is very little attraction between the molecules.

4   5   **b** H

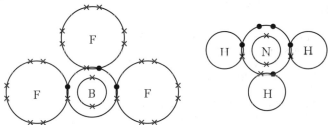

3.3
1

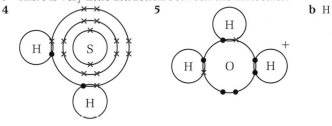

2 Boron trifluoride is trigonal planar, based on a boron atom with just three groups of electrons around it. In ammonia the nitrogen atom has a lone pair plus three other electron groups, so its shape is based on a tetrahedron with one arm missing.

3 **a**   **b** tetrahedral

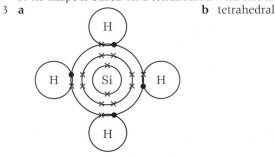

4 109.5°
5 There are four groups of electrons around the oxygen atom so the shape is based on a tetrahedron with two arms missing.

3.4
1 The outer shell in fluorine is closer to the nucleus than the outer shell in chlorine.

2
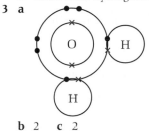

3 **a** H—H   **b** F—F
4 The atoms are the same so they have the same electronegativity.
5 MgS, because
  a magnesium is more highly charged than sodium and can pull electrons towards it, and
  b S^{2-} is larger and more highly charged than F$^-$, so its electron cloud will be easier to distort.

3.5
1 He, Ne, Ar, Kr – the more electrons, the greater the van der Waals forces.
2 H$_2$
3 The van der Waals forces are stronger in hexane because it has more electrons.
4 H$^{\delta+}$ – Cl$^{\delta-}$ H$^{\delta+}$ – Cl$^{\delta-}$

3.6
1 HBr
2 **a** There is no electronegative atom.
  b There is no hydrogen atom.
3 **a**

  b 2   **c** 2
  d There are two hydrogen atoms and two lone pairs.

3.7
1 Allotropes are forms of the same element where the atoms are arranged differently. Isotopes are atoms of the same element with different numbers of neutrons.
2 The layers of carbon atoms can slide easily because of the weak van der Waals forces between them.
3 It conducts along the plane of carbon atoms and not at right angles to them.
4 They both have giant structures.

3.8
1 Metals are shiny, are malleable, are good conductors of heat and electricity.
  Non-metals are dull, brittle, poor conductors of heat and electricity.
2 2,8,8,2   **3** 2   **4** 2

3.9
1 A, C, D   **2** B   **3** A   **4** B, D   **5** C

Chapter 4

4.1
1 **a** (i) Br and K or Fe and K, (ii) Br and Cl, (iii) Br and Cl
  b (i) Sb, (ii) Cs
2 **a** Xe   **b** Ge

4.2
1 **a** Decrease   **b** no trend   **c** decrease
2 **a** Left   **b** middle   **c** right

171

4.3

1 Decrease   2 Increase   3 +3   4 Increase
5 The outer electrons feel the greatest shielded nuclear charge (+8).

4.4

1 **a** $1s^2 2s^2$ **b** $1s^2 2s^2 2p^1$
2 **a** 2s   **b** 2p
3 The 2p electron is further from the nucleus than the 2s electron and thus easier to remove.
4 **a** Group 4,
   b There is a large jump in ionisation energy after four electrons so the four elecrons must be in the outer shell.

Chapter 5

5.1

a Bromine   **b** Calcium   **c** Calcium   **d** Bromine   **e** +II
2 **a** +I   **b** +III   **c** +II   **d** 0

5.2

1 **a** Lead(II)chloride   **b** lead(IV) chloride
   c sodium nitrate(V)   **d** sodium nitrate (III)
2 –II before and after
3 +II before, +III after
4 **a** +VI   **b** +V   **c** –III

5.3

1 +II
2 The electrons in the outer shell are at an increasing distance from the nucleus.
3 **a** More reactive   **b** less reactive
4 The elements are more reactive as we go down the group so strontium is more reactive than calcium. Rubidium is in Group 1 and therefore needs to lose only one electron compared with strontium (in the same Period) which must lose two.
5 Calcium is losing electrons (is oxidised) and chlorine is gaining electrons (is reduced).

5.4

1 **a** Calcium nitrate   **b** strontium chloride
2 Calcium oxide, made by heating calcium carbonate
3 $CO_2(g) + Ca(OH)_2(aq) \rightarrow \underline{CaCO_3(s)} + H_2O(l)$
4 It neutralises the hydrochloric acid in the stomach:
$MgCO_3(s) + 2HCl(aq) \rightarrow MgCl_2(aq) + CO_2(g) + H_2O(l)$

Chapter 6

6.1

1 Electrons in a covalent bond are closer to the nucleus in chlorine than in bromine, but feel the same shielded nuclear charge in both cases.
2 The van der Waals forces between the molecules are smaller.
3 **a** $\overset{0}{2Na} + \overset{0}{Cl_2} \rightarrow \overset{+I\ -I}{2NaCl}$ **b** chlorine
   c It brings about an increase in oxidation number of the sodium.
4 They all have one space in their outer electron shells.

6.2

1 **a** $\overset{0}{2NaOH} + \overset{+I}{Br_2(aq)} \rightarrow \overset{-I}{NaOBr(aq)} + NaBr(l) + H_2O(l)$
   b Above   **c** Disproportionation
   d The oxidation number of one bromine atom increases, while that of the other decreases.
2 **a** Mixture (ii)
   b Chlorine is more reactive than iodine.
   c $Cl_2(aq) + 2NaI(aq) \rightarrow 2NaCl(aq) + I_2(aq)$
3 **a** Pale cream precipitate
   b $NaBr(aq) + AgNO_3(aq) \rightarrow NaNO_3(aq) + AgBr(s)$
   c The precipitate dissolves.

Chapter 7

7.1

1 0.4   2 1   3 C_2H_5 4 C_4H_{10}
5

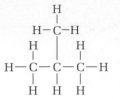

7.2

1 $CH_2CHCH_2CH_2CH_3$ 2 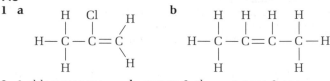   3 C_5H_{10} 4 CH_2

7.3

1 **a**

| H | Cl | H |

$$H-\overset{\overset{\displaystyle H}{|}}{\underset{\underset{\displaystyle H}{|}}{C}}-\overset{\overset{\displaystyle Cl}{|}}{C}=C\begin{smallmatrix}H\\ \\H\end{smallmatrix}$$

b

$$H-\overset{\overset{\displaystyle H}{|}}{\underset{\underset{\displaystyle H}{|}}{C}}-\overset{\overset{\displaystyle H}{|}}{C}=\overset{\overset{\displaystyle H}{|}}{C}-\overset{\overset{\displaystyle H}{|}}{\underset{\underset{\displaystyle H}{|}}{C}}-H$$

2 1-chloropropane,   **b** propan-2-ol,   **c** pent-2-ene

7.4

1 **a** B,   **b** A,   **c** C   2 *cis–trans* isomerism
3 *trans*–pent-2-ene and *cis*–pent-2-ene
4 A double bond is needed for geometrical isomerism.

7.5

1

$$H-\overset{\overset{\displaystyle H}{|}}{\underset{\underset{\displaystyle H}{|}}{C}}-\overset{\overset{\displaystyle H}{|}}{\underset{\underset{\displaystyle H}{|}}{C}}-\overset{\overset{\displaystyle H}{|}}{\underset{}{C}}\overset{\delta+\ \delta-}{-Br}$$

2 At the $C^{\delta+}$

3

$$H\underset{413}{\overset{413}{-\!\!-}}\overset{\overset{\displaystyle H}{413|}}{\underset{\underset{\displaystyle H}{413|}}{C}}\underset{347}{\overset{2.5}{-\!\!-}}\overset{\overset{\displaystyle H}{413|}}{\underset{\underset{\displaystyle H}{413|}}{C}}\underset{347}{\overset{413}{-\!\!-}}\overset{\overset{\displaystyle H}{413|}}{\underset{\underset{\displaystyle H}{413|}}{C}}\underset{290}{-\!\!-}Br$$

(all in $kJ\ mol^{-1}$)

4 **a** C—H   **b** C—Br

7.6

1 A   2 B   3 C   4 D   5 C

7.7

1 81.5%   2 76%   3 75%   4 Burn the methane in oxygen.

7.8

1 **c** σ 2 **b** π
3 It is composed of a σ and a π, not two σs, and π orbitals do not concentrate electron density between the nuclei.
4 **c** σ

Chapter 8

8.1

1 Methylbutane
2

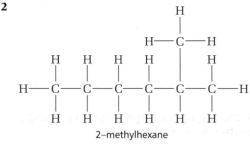

2–methylhexane

3 Heptane   **4** Heptane
5 The molecules will pack more closely together.

8.2
1 $C_4H_{10} + 6\frac{1}{2}O_2 \rightarrow 4CO_2 + 5H_2O$
2 a Termination **b** propagation **c** propagation **d** initiation

Chapter 9

9.1
1 C_7H_{16} **2** Petrol fraction   **3** $S + O_2 \rightarrow SO_2$

9.2
1 Decane → octane + ethene
2 They are gases.
3 It is used for petrol.
4 A catalyst reduces the temperature required.
5 Cracking produces **a** fuels and
  b alkenes (the starting materials for many other chemicals).

9.3
1 A fossil fuel is one derived from plants and animals that died millions of years ago.
2 A fossil fuel takes over a million years to form.
3 a $2H_2 + O_2 \rightarrow 2H_2O$
  b $C_2H_5OH + 3O_2 \rightarrow 2CO_2 + 3H_2O$
4 Ethanol is a renewable fuel.
5 Ethanol has a lower energy density than petrol. Engines need to be modified to use ethanol.

Chapter 10

10.1
1 Hex-2-ene   **2**

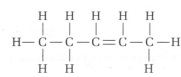

3 a Electrophiles   **4 d** Electron-rich
5 The four electrons in a double bond repel more than the pair of electrons in a single bond.

10.2
1 $C_3H_6 + 4\frac{1}{2}O_2 \rightarrow 3CO_2 + 3H_2O$ **2** 1,2-dibromopropane
3 c Electrophilic additions
4 c Bromine solution is decolourised.

10.3
1 b Chloroethane   **2 b** Alkanes
3 Porous materials have a high surface area.

10.4
1 1000
2 a monomer $CHRH_2$ repeat unit $CHRH_2$
  b monomer $CHRCHR$ repeat unit CHR

Chapter 11

11.1
1

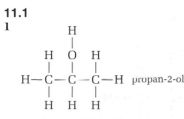

propan-2-ol

2 The lone pairs on the oxygen atom repel more than bonding pairs and squeeze the bonds together.

3 There is hydrogen bonding between alcohol molecules and water molecules.

11.2
1 $CH_3OH + 2O_2 \rightarrow CO_2 + 2H_2O$
2 Sodium + hydrochloric acid → sodium chloride + hydrogen. Alcohols also react with sodium to produce hydrogen.
3 $C_2H_5OH + HCl \rightarrow C_2H_5Cl + H_2O$
4 Nucleophilic substitution
5 $C_2H_5OH \rightarrow C_2H_4 + H_2O$, ethene

11.3
1 a A carboxylic acid is formed.
  b A ketone is formed.
2 C—C bonds are too difficult to break.
3 Distilling removes the vapours produced by boiling, cools them and collects them in a different flask, refluxing cools them and returns them to the reaction flask.

11.4
1 a propanone or
  b ethanoic acid
2 This IR peak represents C=O. Both propanone and ethanoic acid have a C=O
3 c Ethanol or **b** ethanoic acid
4 This IR peak represents O—H. Both ethanol and ethanoic acid have an O—H
5 Ethanoic acid

Chapter 12

12.1
1 a a

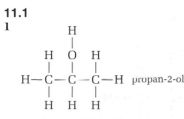

b A 1-iodobutane   C 1-chlorobutane
  B 2-bromopropane   D 2-bromobutane
c A primary   C primary
  B secondary   D secondary
2 A reagent with a lone pair of electrons and either a full or partial negative charge.
3 Because they have a carbon atom that has a $\delta+$ charge.
4 The C—halogen bond becomes stronger.

12.2
1 Because halogenoalkanes will not mix with the water in an aqueous solution of sodium hydroxide.
2 OH^-

3 Because OH replaces X.
4 X^-
5 R—I

12.3

1 a A base   **2 c** CF_3CH_2Cl
3

H Cl H Cl H Cl
| | | | | |
—C—C—C—C—C—C—
| | | | | |
H H H H H H

4 a Propan-2-ol and propene
5 It would decolourise a solution of bromine.

Chapter 13

13.1

1 445 kJ
2 Endothermic
3 It is the reverse of the reaction at the beginning of the question in which heat is given out (exothermic).
4 1.6 g

13.2

1 An enthalpy *change*
2 Enthalpy
3 That the enthalpy change is measured at 298 K.
4 That enthalpy is given out as the reaction proceeds.
5 Exothermic

13.3

1 a The enthalpy change of the reaction
  b The mass of the material (usually water) in the calorimeter
  c The specific heat capacity of the material (usually water) in the calorimeter
  d The temperature change
2 $-1008 \, kJ \, mol^{-1}$
3 It has a lid, insulation at the sides and a screen to prevent draughts.

13.4

1 $-1615 \, kJ \, mol^{-1}$
2 a $-46.2 \, kJ \, mol^{-1}$
  b It will be smaller (less negative) than the accepted value.
  c There will be heat losses from the polystyrene beaker.

13.8

(a) **1** $-70 \, kJ \, mol^{-1}$ **2** $-217 \, kJ \, mol^{-1}$
    3 $-97 \, kJ \, mol^{-1}$ **4** $-195 \, kJ \, mol^{-1}$
    5 $+301 \, kJ \, mol^{-1}$
(b) **1** $-70 \, kJ \, mol^{-1}$ **2** $-217 \, kJ \, mol^{-1}$
    3 $-97 \, kJ \, mol^{-1}$ **4** $-195 \, kJ \, mol^{-1}$
    5 $+301 \, kJ \, mol^{-1}$

13.9

1

H H   H H
| | | |
H—C—C—H + Br—Br → H—C—C—Br + H—Br
| | | |
H H   H H

2 a $1 \times$ C—C; $6 \times$ C—H; $1 \times$ Br—Br   **b** $3018 \, kJ \, mol^{-1}$
3 a $1 \times$ C—C; $5 \times$ C—H; $1 \times$ C—Br; $1 \times$ H—Br
  b $3061 \, kJ \, mol^{-1}$
4 $43 \, kJ \, mol^{-1}$
5 a $-43 \, kJ \, mol^{-1}$ **b** exothermic

Chapter 14

14.1

1 Temperature, concentration of reactants, pressure (in gas reactions), catalysts, surface area of solid reactants.
2 a Enthalpy of the reactants   **b** Enthalpy of the products
  c Enthalpy of the transition state   **d** Activation energy
3 a Exothermic
  b The enthalpy of the products is less than that of the reactants.

14.2

1 Fraction of particles with energy, E **2** Energy, E
3 The number of particles with enough energy to react
4 Moves right.   **5** No change

14.3

1 a Enthalpy (or energy)
  b Extent of reaction
  c Transition state with the catalyst
  d Transition state without the catalyst
2 D to R: Activation energy without the catalyst; C to R: Activation energy with the catalyst.
3 Exothermic
4 Heterogeneous catalysts are in a different phase from the reactants and products. Homogeneous catalysts are in the same phase as the reactants and products.

Chapter 15

15.1

1 a True   **b** False   **c** True   **d** False
2 They are the same.

15.2

1 a Equilibrium position will be affected – there are different numbers of gas molecules on each side of the arrow.
  b Equilibrium position will not be affected – this is not a gas reaction.
  c Equilibrium position will not be affected – there are the same numbers of gas molecules on each side of the arrow.
2 a Move left.
  b no change.

15.3

1 Methane (natural gas), nitrogen (from air) and water.
2 Approximately 50%
3 To increase its surface area.
4 a Three from: making fertilisers, explosives, dyes, drugs, polymers (e.g. Nylon).
  b Three from: making fertilisers, explosives, dyes, drugs, polymers (e.g. Nylon).
NB the two answers are the same because a great deal of ammonia is converted into nitric acid.

15.4

1 a $Ca(s) + 2HCl(aq) \rightarrow CaCl_2(aq) + H_2(g)$
  b $Na_2O(s) + H_2SO_4(aq) \rightarrow Na_2SO_4(aq) + H_2O(l)$
  c $K_2O(s) + 2HCl(aq) \rightarrow 2KCl(aq) + H_2O(l)$
  d $Mg(OH)_2(aq) + 2HCl \rightarrow MgCl_2(aq) + 2H_2O(l)$

2

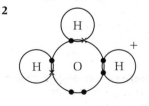

Index